The
Most Splendid Failure

Faulkner's *The Sound and the Fury*

THE
SOUND AND THE FURY

BY WILLIAM FAULKNER

NEW YORK
JONATHAN CAPE AND HARRISON SMITH

ANDRÉ BLEIKASTEN

The
Most Splendid Failure

Faulkner's *The Sound and the Fury*

Indiana University Press

BLOOMINGTON / LONDON

Published in Canada by Fitzhenry & Whiteside Limited, Don Mills, Ontario
Manufactured in the United States of America

Library of Congress Cataloging in Publication Data

Bleikasten, André.
  The most splendid failure.

  Bibliography.
  Includes index.
  1. Faulkner, William, 1897-1962. The sound and the
fury. I. Title.
PS3511.A86S78 1976 813'.5'2 75-22638
ISBN 0-253-33877-8 1 2 3 4 5 80 79 78 77 76

Contents

PREFACE

WHEN *The Sound and the Fury* was published in October 1929, most reviewers greeted it with puzzled respect. Few of them were prepared to accept it on its own terms and to meet the challenge of its newness. Whether this challenge has been eventually met is an open question, but at least there is now general agreement that *The Sound and the Fury* is one of the classics of modern fiction. Which is to say that it has already outlived its modernity, that its newness, if not fully understood and accepted, has been partly neutralized, and that its assimilation by official culture is in process of completion. The critics have probably been the busiest agents of this assimilation. None of Faulkner's novels has provoked as much critical response. Indeed, there is so much of it that one may wonder if there is not too much of it, and that one hesitates to join the host of the novel's exegetes. The more so as anyone attempting a new study of the book has to make himself familiar with the huge body of appreciation and interpretation that has grown around it over the past decades. Working through this mass of commentary is no unmitigated pleasure, for it goes without saying that a good deal of what has been written on the novel is badly dated, and that half of it is trivial or inept. The amount of unnecessary repetition is enormous, critical commonplaces abound, and like so much Faulkner criticism, many discussions of *The Sound and the Fury* are founded on disabling misconceptions about literature in general and modern literature in particular.

This does not mean, of course, that there have been no relevant inquiries into the novel. The perceptive general studies of Olga Vickery, Michael Millgate, Cleanth Brooks, John W. Hunt, and Edmond L. Volpe have undeniably added to our understanding of the book; there is no shortage either of valid essays on specific points such as theme or structure, characterization or symbolism, and in the present study my considerable debt to previous critics, whether in agreement or disagreement, will easily be seen. To write about *The Sound and the Fury* as though nobody had ever written about it before would have been both dishonest and utterly naïve. Spontaneous, "natural" responses to literature are as a rule the most banal, and criticism is not a "natural" activity anyway. I have, then, done my homework as conscientiously as I could, and attempted to integrate (what I consider) the best of Faulkner criticism and scholarship, while trying at the same time to distance myself from it so as to maintain a perspective of my own.

My reading of *The Sound and the Fury* makes no claim to objectivity nor has it been intended to offer a "definitive" interpretation of the book. Whether he admits it or not, each critic operates within a given cultural environment and proceeds from a given set of presuppositions and prejudices. To interpret a text is to do it violence. No criticism is innocent of distortion; no interpreter leaves a text as he found it, and the kind of transparency which critical discourse manages to achieve is always obtained through reductive procedures. In other words: no critic can totally master the object of his investigations. The interpretive codes which he needs to produce meaning are at once sources of insight and of blindness, and whatever the range of his competence and the sharpness of his discriminations, there will always be residues, zones of opacity left for future inquirers to explore. And the greater a work of art, the more stubborn its resistance to our exegetical purposes. What distinguishes works like *The Sound and the Fury* is their closedness to final, canonical exegeses, that is, their openness to ever-new interpretations. This very inexhaustibility is what makes them classics.

Given these limitations and these constraints, how should one read *The Sound and the Fury?* The first requirement is certainly to read it as a *novel*, to approach it as an autonomous literary creation rather than as a "reflection" of the outer world or as an "expression" of the author's inner experience. In writing this study my constant concern has been to attend to the book itself, to its structure and texture, to the dense network of its intratextual relationships and to the various ways in which these relationships combine with one another and function in the overall pattern of the novel. *The Sound and the Fury* must be read both vertically (or paradigmatically) and horizontally (or syntagmatically), as one would read an orchestral score. I have therefore tried to model my reading upon the internal development of the novel itself, following its four sections in sequential order, so as to recapture something of the movement and momentum of its own unfolding. Concomitantly, however, I have sought to see the novel as an organized whole and to trace out the many homological correlations developing between its parts. One of the underlying assumptions of my study is that the latter occupy the same space of utterance, that they should be read in superimposition as well as in juxtaposition, each section being a different articulation of the same question, a different metaphor (or trans-lation) of the same creative endeavor. On the other hand, I have carefully (but perhaps not quite successfully) avoided arresting the fluidity of the novel's complex circuits of meaning, and resisted the impulse to enclose them within a rigidly unified scheme of interpretation.

Priority has been accorded throughout to Faulkner's text, yet my approach to it is not exclusively and consistently textual. To recognize *The Sound and the Fury* as a literary artifact, to treat it as a self-contained system of internal relations is not to deny that its mode of being and meaning is also determined by its various environments. Indeed, if the critic's most immediate task is to attend to the text in its singularity, his chances to seize that singularity are certainly better if instead of viewing the object of his inquiry in aseptic isolation, he examines it differentially, against its cultural and historical background and in the context of the writer's life and work. Hence my introductory chapter, where I have attempted to chart out Faulkner's development up to *The Sound and the Fury;* hence, in the course of my study, the frequent references to intertextual relationships and the novel's psychobiographical implications.

I willingly confess to the "impurity" of the method adopted for my analysis. While doing my best to remain in touch with the unique quality of the book, I have felt free to draw on "extrinsic" disciplines whenever they could be used to further my purposes. Conceived of as an inviolable absolute (as it was by the New Critics), the autonomy of literature is clearly a myth, and the critical theory which it implies proves ultimately sterilizing in its effects. I can see no valid reason why a literary critic should virtuously abstain from all traffic with the "sciences of man," nor is it obvious to me that recourse to them leads necessarily to an impoverishment of aesthetic appreciation. To accommodate the teeming complexities of Faulkner's work, no approach can be inclusive enough, and consequently none of the available critical languages should be dismissed beforehand as irrelevant. In the present study one can find a number of references to Freud and Lacan, to Jakobson and Barthes, and to other leading figures of the contemporary intellectual scene. I have borrowed concepts and ideas from various fields, and acknowledge a general debt to the *nouvelle critique* and to what has come to be known as structuralism. My method, however, is no more structuralist than it is psychoanalytic. I am aware that in avoiding commitment to any fixed set of critical tenets I expose myself to the charge of eclecticism, yet for a full discussion of a single work such a strategy seems defensible, and one might even argue that in the present case an undogmatic and pluralistic approach, flexible enough to be modulated according to the difficulties encountered on one's way, is perhaps the most appropriate and the most effective.

Not that it possesses more truth value than others. My assumptions about the novel are only working hypotheses, and the results of my investigation are partial and provisional. Criticism has always been a dubious business: the critic names, orders, classifies, attempts to "make sense" of a text, and in so doing he is apt to forget how problematic all his procedures are. Yet an awareness of their questionable character is precisely what differentiates, or should differentiate, critical reading from common reading. A novel like *The Sound and the Fury* is ideally suited to promote such an awareness, for through its emphasis on the distorting activity of individual minds and its presentation of conflicting points of view, it is itself calling attention to the inescapable limits and hazards of interpretation. Like all great novels, *The Sound and the Fury* is a fiction arrayed against fictions, including those of literary criticism. If read with proper humility, it will even teach us how to read it.

Strasbourg, August 1975

ACKNOWLEDGMENTS

In my research on Faulkner's novels, I have profited from the assistance of various people and institutions. I wish to renew my thanks to the Fulbright and Smith-Mundt Foundations for financing my first research visit to the United States in 1967, and to the American Council of Learned Societies for granting me the fellowship which enabled me to spend a year at the University of Virginia in 1969–70. My thanks are also due to the Alderman Library of the University of Virginia and the William Faulkner Foundation, for giving me access to the Faulkner materials in their possession, and to Mrs. Jill Faulkner Summers, for her kind permission to quote from the manuscript of *The Sound and the Fury* and to reproduce pages thereof. Finally, I wish to acknowledge my debt to my friends and colleagues Jean Deurbergue, Michael Issacharoff, Guy Lambrechts, Jean Paira, and Simone Vauthier, who gave my manuscript careful reading and made many valuable suggestions; and especially to Roger Little, who translated the early, fairly shorter versions, in French, of chapters 3–7.

The
Most Splendid Failure

Faulkner's *The Sound and the Fury*

Q. *Mr. Faulkner, what do you consider your best book?*

A. *The one that failed the most tragically and the most splendidly. That was* The Sound and the Fury—*the one that I worked at the longest, the hardest, that was to me the most passionate and moving idea, and made the most splendid failure....*

FAULKNER IN THE UNIVERSITY

The most accurate text of *The Sound and the Fury* yet published is the first printing, first edition text (New York: Jonathan Cape and Harrison Smith, 1929). It has been reproduced by photo-offset in the 1966 Random House edition, the 1967 Modern Library edition, and the Vintage paperback edition. All page references in my study refer to these reissues as well as to the 1929 Cape and Smith text.

The quotations from the "Compson Appendix" refer to the 1967 Modern Library edition and to the Vintage edition.

1

Faulkner before Faulkner: Masks and Mirrors

L'origine de l'oeuvre, ce n'est pas la première influence, c'est la première posture.

ROLAND BARTHES

ASSUMING THAT A WRITER'S PROGRESS is similar to a natural process, and that the sum of his work is given unity and meaning through some sustaining organic principle, most critics describe literary achievements in terms of growth and development. These assumptions are so common that their legitimacy has seldom been questioned. Yet, widely held as they are, they should perhaps not be left unexamined, and one would do well at least to realize their dubious origins in metaphor. To a large extent, they are of course fostered by the very nature of the critic's relation to his object: critical inspection is inevitably retrospection; it deals with works forever completed so that the temptation is almost irresistible to read them as the necessary fulfillments of a preestablished design.

3

And the temptation is all the greater because such readings satisfy our hunger for consistency, order, and significance: if everything was already virtually there at the outset, in the "germ," then the beginning becomes inseparable from the end, every aspect of the work assumes by necessity a teleological character, and every phase in the writer's career must be viewed in relation to the triumphant overall purpose of his *oeuvre*. In this respect critics are like dishonest novelists: they fabricate shapely fictions, neat patterns from which any trace of randomness has been carefully removed.

The notion that a writer's work forms a pregnant totality, that it has come into being through a purposive and orderly process (generally described in organicistic terms), and that it may be accounted for in its entirety, is now beginning to arouse suspicion. Yet to recognize the doubtful nature of these postulates does not imply that there are others to hand. Perhaps they are little more than time-honored fallacies, but at the present stage of literary theory no coherent alternative is available. "How can one grasp an organized totality except by starting with its end?" Jacques Derrida asks,[1] and as he rightly points out, even structuralist criticism proceeds from the premise of some ultima ratio through which structures can be apprehended and made intelligible. Whatever its ideological or methodological bias, critical inquiry has always been founded on the belief that a literary work is informed by a more or less hidden rationale, and on the hope that the latter can be brought to light. To renounce this belief, to give up this hope altogether would be to deny the very possibility of critical elucidation.

These preliminary observations, then, are only intended as a caveat, and I realize that in making them I am giving the reader a stick to beat me with. It is possible that whenever we establish consistency and purpose we succumb to an illusion, but it is possible too that this illusion is vital to the critic.

Faulkner is in this connection a particularly complex and challenging case. Among the major literary achievements of the twentieth century, there is probably none that conveys a stronger sense of direction and purpose than his. And the more closely one examines his work, the more obvious it becomes how much Faulkner was aware of his strategies. Contrary to what has long been current opinion, he belongs with the most sophisticated artists in modern fiction, and few novelists have been able to master their materials and medium with the sustained effectiveness that was his. Yet it is important to remember that Faulkner was a writer of many births (this is my first lapse into genetic metaphor; there will be many others), and that there was also something essentially wayward in the actual unfolding of his creation: rather than a smooth unbroken "natural" growth, its development suggests a series of discrete creative moments, each of which was a fresh start and a new risk. For in contrast to Hemingway and most of his contemporaries, Faulkner was a restless experimentalist, an indefatigable rebeginner. That there are many constants and continuities in his work is evident enough, and some of them we shall attempt to trace in the following pages; one should always keep in mind, however, that there are just as many discontinuities, and that the movement of Faulkner's writing was above all a movement of invention. If not a chartless voyage, it was an unpredictable adventure.

The Sound and the Fury provides an apt illustration of this unpredictability. It was a sudden leap, unforeseen and unforeseeable. Hints may be found in Faulkner's early work of what he was to achieve in *The Sound and the Fury* and in his other major novels. Yet they are promises only for having been kept. Faulkner's early poetry and prose are evidence of immature talent and nothing more. Between them and his first masterpiece there is all the inexplicable distance from talent to genius.

Faulkner's early writings would have little interest for us were it not for their being Faulkner's. They allow us into a writer's workshop at the uncertain time of his beginnings, when his vocation was still open to doubt, and when the very tools of his trade were still to be forged; they testify to the delicate and devious processes of absorption, assimilation, and transformation Faulkner had to go through before he could rid himself of "the anxiety of influence" and shape an idiom of his own. Moreover his early writings may be read as documents on the artist as a young man, since this was as well a time when the quest for literary identity was still closely entangled with the hazardous pursuit of identity *tout court*. Faulkner, at this point of his life, had not yet outgrown the adolescent stage of role-playing, nor was he then capable of the detachment that would later allow him to use his emotions and experiences as mere material for his fiction. Instead, like most young men with vague literary ambitions, he used literature as a vehicle for thinly disguised self-expression and self-dramatization.

It is hardly surprising that private emotion should show most plainly and innocently in his earliest attempts, that is, in his poetry, most of which was written between 1914 and 1925.[2] And as might be expected, this is also where his writing is least personal. Faulkner's early poems are indeed little more than slender imitations of the late romantic, decadent verse of the eighties and nineties. As Phil Stone, his friend and mentor, put it in his preface to *The Marble Faun:* "They are the poems of youth. . . . They belong inevitably to that period of uncertainty and illusion. . . . They also have the defects of youth—youth's impatience, unsophistication and immaturity."[3] Little has been written on Faulkner's poetry, and most of the rare studies devoted to the subject are understandably concerned with the question of sources.[4] The discernible influences are many: they range from Elizabethan lyric and pastoral verse through the Romantics (Shelley, Keats) and the poets of the eighties (especially Swinburne) and nineties (notably A. E. Housman) to more recent writers like Yeats, Conrad Aiken or T. S. Eliot. To these must be added the French Symbolists; namely, Mallarmé (from whom Faulkner borrowed the title of his first published poem, "L'Après-Midi d'un Faune") and Verlaine (four adaptations of whose poems he published in *The Mississippian* in 1920). The trouble with Faulkner's poetry is not so much its derivative character—there is no spontaneous generation in literature and, after all, T. S. Eliot and Ezra Pound were poets of many voices—as its tame Georgian conventionality. When Eliot published his first volume of poems in 1917, he had already discarded the literary conventions of the nineteenth century, and managed to achieve a manner distinctively his own; the poems of *The Marble Faun* (1924), on the other hand, still conform in the main to the pallid poetic code of the late Victorians—a code already obsolete at the time of their composition.[5] Had Faulkner persevered as a poet, he might have evolved eventually a personal style (in some of the poems he was later to publish in *A Green Bough* there are hints of what it would have been like), but *The Marble Faun* reads too much like the self-conscious exercises of a belated disciple of *fin-de-siècle* writers to appeal to the modern reader. At best, the poems collected in this volume have the wistful charm of elegant mood pieces; at worst, they are absurdly high-flown; for the most part, their precious diction, contorted syntax, and stereotyped pastoral imagery strike one as remorselessly "poetic." Yet, for all its weaknesses, *The Marble Faun* cannot be dismissed as the work of a callow dilettante. It not only evinces a keen awareness of literary traditions; it also bears witness to Faulkner's meticulous craftsmanship and—most important with regard to future developments—to his incipient concern for form and structure. As George P. Garrett has noted, *The Marble Faun* is indeed already "a highly complex literary exercise," and one which "would scarcely have been attempted by an unlettered, accidental poet."[6]

While faintly foreshadowing in its formal organization the far bolder and much more intricate patterns of Faulkner's fiction, *The Marble Faun* also points ahead to a number of later themes and motifs. Its nature imagery and seasonal framework, for example, were to be reused in the complex symbolic configurations of the novels, and the pastoral mode was likewise to reemerge in wholly different guises: *As I Lay Dying* has been termed "a pastoral elegy."[7] *Light in August* might be defined as a pastoral tragedy, and the pastoral element is even more prominent in the

Snopes trilogy. But more than as a seminal work, *The Marble Faun* engages our interest as a psycho-biographical document. This book of early verse is at once Faulkner's most shallow and most ingenuous work. As literature, it has no doubt little of substance to offer; yet insofar as it is naïvely poeticized self-projection, it has a great deal to tell about Faulkner as a young man. The major clue in this connection is to be found in the mythological figure whose voice the writer assumed in the poems and to which the book owes its oxymoronic title: the marble faun, as the poet's elegiac persona, aptly symbolizes the sense of frustration and paralysis which Faulkner must have experienced at this juncture, suspended as he then was between the extravagant dreams of his youth and the yet remote accomplishments of his adulthood. The immobile figure at the center of the poetic scene is an emblem of blocked potentials and unresolved tensions; while the *faun* serves as an ironic and nostalgic reminder of the uninhibited vitality and freely flowing energies of a lost Arcadia, the cold *marble* suggests the deathlike inertia of a petrified self. A "sad, bound prisoner" of impotent awareness and barren knowledge (". . . things I know, yet cannot know"), watching the spectacle of life from which he is forever estranged, the marble faun reflects the young poet's own impasse: both thirsting for the experience of reality and tempted by the timeless vision of art, and too self-involved to achieve a working relationship with either. The faun's predicament embodies polarities and oppositions to be found again in all of Faulkner's later writings: stasis vs. motion, consciousness vs. experience, dream vs. reality, self vs. world. And in his tortured impotence he may be seen as well as the prototype of the series of Faulkner's increasingly complex and increasingly distanced "sick heroes": Donald Mahon, Horace Benbow, Bayard Sartoris, Quentin Compson, Joe Christmas, Gail Hightower, and others. One might regard him, too, as an early metaphor of what was to become Faulkner's central concept of art: like a figure on an urn or a frieze, the marble faun evokes the Keatsian paradox of arrested motion so often referred to in his fiction. Yet the main significance of the faun in this "cold

pastoral" is assuredly that of a self-image; he is above all a poetic
double of the young writer himself—a writer in solipsistic isolation, whose creative powers are still waiting for release, and for
whom art is then little more than a consoling fiction—a drowsy
dreamland for solitary souls.

What Yeats wrote of late nineteenth century poets fairly applies to the young Faulkner: "At once the fault and the beauty of
the nature-description of most modern poets is that for them the
stars, and streams, the leaves, and the animals, are only masks
behind which go on the sad soliloquies of nineteenth century egoism."[8] *The Marble Faun* was both mask and mirror to a melancholy young Narcissus. It did not take Faulkner very long,
however, to realize that his first poetic impulse had mostly sprung
from juvenile egotism. As early as 1925, in describing the "pilgrimage" which had taken him from Swinburne to the "moderns,"
he willingly admitted that his love of poetry had begun as a pose,
and that his first poems had been merely an outlet for adolescent
emotion:

> I was not interested in verse for verse's sake then. I read and em-
> ployed verse, firstly for the purpose of furthering various philander-
> ings in which I was engaged, secondly, to complete a youthful
> gesture I was then making, of being "different" in a small town.
> Later, my concupiscence waning, I turned inevitably to verse, find-
> ing therein an emotional counterpart far more satisfactory. . . .[9]

It is significant too that Faulkner's early pieces of literary
criticism read so often like oblique comments and speculations on
his own poetic endeavors. In the writers whom he reviewed, he
perceived echoes of his own moods and perplexities, and he seldom
failed to detect in them those blind spots and shortcomings which
he probably knew to be also his. Thus, in his review of William
Alexander Percy's *In April Once*,[10] he compared the author to "a
little boy closing his eyes against the dark of modernity which
threatens the bright simplicity and the colorful romantic pageantry
of the middle ages with which his eyes are full."[11] And in noting

that Percy "—like alas! how many of us—suffered the misfortune of having been born out of his time,"[12] he no doubt also expressed his own sense of temporal dislocation. Faulkner's early critical pieces reveal much more about the preoccupations of their author than about the writers they are supposed to deal with. One recurrent concern to be found in them is the relationship between art and the artist or more precisely the psychological roots of literary creation. "Writing people," he remarks in one of his reviews,[13] "are all so pathetically torn between a desire to make a figure in the world and a morbid interest in their personal egos."[14] His own experience had probably taught Faulkner that narcissism is the mainspring of literature, but he also soon came to realize that unless it is in some way transcended, it becomes an alibi for self-indulgence and emotionalism. Hence his reservations about Joseph Hergesheimer, whose *Linda Condon* he reviewed in his final *Mississippian* piece; Faulkner charged him with "a deliberate pandering to the emotions,"[15] and argued that his book, however brilliant, was too self-complacent to be considered a novel:

> It is more like a lovely Byzantine frieze: a few unforgettable figures in silent arrested motion, forever beyond the reach of time and troubling the heart like music. His people are never actuated from within; they do not create life about them; they are like puppets assuming graceful but meaningless postures in answer to the author's compulsions, and holding these attitudes until he arranges their limbs again in other gestures as graceful and meaningless.[16]

What strikes us in this evocation of Hergesheimer's world is that it anticipates peculiarities of Faulkner's own (the still scenes, the puppet imagery). But at the same time it also evinces his growing concern for an art that would infuse form with life and meaning. His comments on Hergesheimer announce what he was later to state as the artist's first ambition: "to arrest motion, which is life, by artificial means and hold it fixed so that a hundred years later, when a stranger looks at it, it moves again, since it is life."[17]

Noteworthy too in these short critical essays, especially the later ones on American drama, is the assumption that "art is preeminently provincial: i.e., it comes directly from a certain age and a certain locality."[18] The same idea was to be restated emphatically in Phil Stone's preface to *The Marble Faun:*

> The author of these poems is a man steeped in the soil of his native land, a Southerner by every instinct, and, more than that, a Mississippian. George Moore said that all universal art became great by first being provincial, and the sunlight and mocking-birds and blue hills of North Mississippi are a part of this young man's very being.[19]

With regard to *The Marble Faun,* Stone's claim for Faulkner's rootedness in his native soil was unsubstantiated, for there is no trace of the blue hills in the highly stylized Arcadian landscapes of the poems. Yet it was presumably under the influence of his mentor that the young writer gradually came to acknowledge the literary potential of his Southern environment, and to explore the possibilities of "regional realism." Not that Faulkner ever was to become a regional writer: his literary ambitions, even at this tentative stage, by far exceeded those of a local colorist, and he probably never totally shared Stone's naïve romantic assumptions about literature. But the crucial discovery he then began to make was that his knowledge and experience of the South would provide him with all the material he needed to build a world of his own: "a man with real ability finds sufficient what he has to hand."[20]

This dawning awareness is likely to have accelerated his turning from poetry to prose. There was no sudden shift, however: although the young Faulkner had thought of himself primarily as a poet, his passion for poetry had at no time precluded experiments in other modes. He had been writing stories and prose sketches since his boyhood;[21] he continued to do so during the early twenties, and even tried his hand at drama in *Marionettes,* the extremely formal play which he wrote in 1920.[22] His first published piece of fiction, "Landing in Luck," appeared in *The Mississippian* on November 26, 1919: it was a mildly entertaining short story, obviously inspired by Faulkner's recent experience as a cadet pilot in Canada. More than two years later, the same newspaper published "The Hill" (March 10, 1922): this very remarkable prose sketch is far more relevant to a study of the writer's development insofar as it may be considered the embryo of the work to come.[23] Closely related in tone and manner to *The Marble Faun,* "The Hill" is a prose poem rather than a story, yet although it may be easily identified as early Faulkner, it looks forward to his fiction, and does so much more clearly than any of his previous writings. The pastoral landscape recedes, and the specific contours of Faulkner country begin to emerge with startling distinctness: the description of the hamlet in the valley, seen from the hilltop by a "tieless casual," is undeniably the first adumbration of what was to become Faulkner's mythical Jefferson. Moreover, the hill-and-valley pattern of the sketch foreshadows in many ways his later use of space symbolism: high and low, verticality and horizontality, ascent and descent are revealingly contrasted, and while the valley and its somnolent hamlet evoke the "joys and sorrows, hopes and despairs"[24] of an earthbound humanity, the hill—as so often in Faulkner's fiction—suggests the remote possibility of a transcendental mode of being, high above the muddy flux of time and life. That the experience recorded in the sketch occurs at sunset is equally worth noting: twilight, as Michel Gresset remarks, is to Faulkner as to many other writers of the Symbolist tradition, "the moment of all possible revelations,"[25] and in "The Hill" it functions as "the medium and agent of what happens to the tieless casual."[26] But what exactly happens to him? Nothing much. The text refers to "the terrific groping of his mind";[27] very little is gained in the process, however: ". . . for a moment he had almost grasped something alien to him, but it eluded him; and being unaware that there was anything which had tried to break down the barriers of his mind and communicate with him, he was unaware that he had been eluded."[28] Twilight holds out the promise of revelation; the stage seems set for a Joycean epiphany, yet no spiritual insight is achieved except, perhaps, the character's sudden realization of "the devastating unimportance of his destiny."[29] "The Hill" is the description of a negative epiphany. Like the marble-bound faun of Faulkner's poems and like some of his later heroes, its protagonist appears as a passive watcher to whom true vision is denied. Like the faun, too, he might be taken for a fictional double of that other would-be seer: the artist, confronted with the impossible task of transmuting the cluttered and chaotic everyday world of common experience into a timeless and meaningful vision of order and beauty. "The Hill," then, could be read as an ironic parable on the ever-frustrated ambitions and ever-delusive achievements of art at large. For, as Jorge Luis Borges suggests in *Labyrinths:* "This imminence of a revelation which does not occur is, perhaps, the aesthetic phenomenon." [30]

Yet to Faulkner himself "The Hill" must have been a decisive discovery: something that had so far eluded him was coming into focus; a world was taking shape, however hesitantly. As Gresset rightly emphasizes, "The Hill" is a double threshold: "to Faulkner's world and to Faulkner's universe, the physical setting of the Yoknapatawpha novels and the inner theater of literary creation." [31] True, it was only a short sketch, with little more than discreet hints of future developments. That the seeds were indeed there, however, is fully confirmed by "Nympholepsy," the expanded version of the sketch which Faulkner wrote three years later.[32] In "Nympholepsy" a nameless farm laborer again climbs a hill at sunset, but there is much more of a story than in the earlier sketch. Dramatic tension is created through the introduction of an elusive feminine figure, first glimpsed as "a golden light among the dark pines,"[33] then frantically and vainly pursued by the protagonist of the story. Faulkner here reverts to the motif of the amorous chase, which he had already used in some of his poems (notably in "L'Après-Midi d'un Faune," the first to be published), and returns once again to the mythological scene of the pastoral: while the girl turns out to be a tantalizing nymph, the "tieless casual" is cast for the traditional role of the lusting faun. Contrary to "The Hill," the second sketch is suffused with heady sensuality; the still confrontation of self and world becomes a sexual encounter, and the evanescent object of the vision sought after by the hero is shown to be a woman. The erotic quality particular to "Nympholepsy" is reinforced through the image patterns of the sketch: Faulkner uses religious imagery (references to cathedrals and naves, priests and orisons he may have borrowed from Joyce or Sherwood Anderson) to bestow solemnity upon the scene, but more revealing is his symbolic use of the natural setting. The sexual implications of the hill/valley contrast are far more perceptible than in "The Hill." At the bottom of the valley there is this time "a small stream,"[34] and the first occurrence of the phrase is significantly preceded by a reference to the protagonist's "desire for a woman's body."[35] It is even more remarkable that when he falls into the stream, "the water [takes] him,"[36] hugs him in its perilous embrace like the body of a mistress, and that he eventually sees "death like a woman shining and drowned and waiting"[37] Water is thus equated with woman, and the symbolic equation connotes both desire and death—a highly pregnant complex of associations recurring in many of Faulkner's novels, and at the very core of the Quentin section in *The Sound and the Fury*. Equally important in the symbolism of the sketch are the many references to the earth. Dust is repeatedly alluded to in the opening and closing paragraphs, and with the same suggestions that it will have in the final page of *Soldiers' Pay*. But like the valley and like water, the earth is first and foremost a feminine symbol, and in "Nympholepsy" both elements unite, forming the archetypal stage where male meets female—a conjunction again paralleled in Faulkner's fiction by the setting given to many of his love scenes.[38]

"Nympholepsy" lacks the fine economy of "The Hill," but in the dense suggestiveness of its symbolic pattern it is perhaps even more fascinating to Faulkner students than the earlier sketch. Faulkner presumably wrote it within the first month or two of his second visit to New Orleans in the spring of 1925. He was then moving into a new phase of his literary apprenticeship, a phase predominantly marked by his close and fecund association with

Sherwood Anderson, whose example, advice, and encouragement were decisive in his conversion from poetry to prose. During his stay in New Orleans, Faulkner was still writing poems and he was to write more in the following years; 1925, however, was the year when fiction came to supplant poetry as his major medium. It certainly also was a landmark in his intellectual development: in the course of the six months spent in New Orleans, Faulkner became immersed in the sophisticated cosmopolitan atmosphere of the city's artistic and literary bohemia, discovering, through conversations and readings, the more fashionable trends of the midtwenties, and growing aware of such influential figures as Freud,[39] Frazer,[40] and Joyce.[41] Faulkner never showed much interest in ideas for their own sake, and in all likelihood these influences were absorbed through spontaneous osmosis rather than through serious study, but there is no doubt that they were instrumental in shaping his later work.

As to his literary output during that period, it offers conclusive evidence of his broadening interests. In 1925, Faulkner published two groups of prose pieces: one consisted of eleven short sketches in the New Orleans literary magazine, *The Double Dealer* (January-February); the other was a series of sixteen stories and sketches in the Sunday feature section of the *Times-Picayune* (February-September).[42] In these vignettes Faulkner explored new material and experimented with new modes and new techniques. True, to some extent they are still prose poems, and the many connections with his earlier writings are readily discernible. Yet here are Faulkner's first deliberate attempts at character creation and story telling, with an unmistakable move in the direction of realistic prose. Anderson's pervasive influence is felt in the choice of familiar subjects, mostly borrowed from the street life of New Orleans. The characters presented in the sketches are common people—cops, cobblers, sailors, longshoremen—or belong to the outer fringes of society: beggars, tramps, hoodlums, whores. In some ways they are reminiscent of Anderson's "grotesques"; more

generally, they indicate Faulkner's transient and partial adhesion
to some of the conventions of naturalistic fiction, and evince the
latter's emphasis on low life, its penchant for melodramatic incident, and its partiality to outsiders and misfits. Joyce's influence
is perceptible too, notably in the handling of narrative point of
view: in the impressionistic sketches of the *Double Dealer* series,
Faulkner uses throughout first-person narrators, and in some of
the longer stories like "Home" or "Out of Nazareth" are found
stretches of interior monologue anticipating *The Sound and the
Fury* and *As I Lay Dying*. And lastly there are occasional echoes
of Conrad, nowhere more audible than in "Yo Ho and Two Bot-
tles of Rum," which reads like a crude pastiche of Conrad's sea-
tales.

Faulkner's New Orleans sketches may be seen as a testing-
plant: new procedures and techniques are being tried out; characters, themes and motifs begin to emerge, which will reappear
in the novels.[43] Thus "The Kingdom of God" portrays an idiot
with cornflower blue eyes—a clear prefiguration of Benjy Compson, the dim-witted brother in *The Sound and the Fury*. Similarly,
Ek, the taleteller in "The Liar," Faulkner's first published story
with a rural setting, anticipates V. K. Ratliff, the narrator-character
of the Snopes trilogy. Further hints of later developments could be
easily traced in almost any of the sketches, but perhaps even more
striking than all these anticipations is the extreme facility displayed
by the author. Faulkner was a fast learner, and the all but magical
promptness and deftness with which he picked up the tricks of his
new trade and assimilated the lessons of his many masters are
indeed amazing. Not that the sketches possess much intrinsic
merit: Faulkner's attempts at fusing the rhythms and imagery of
late romantic poetry with realistic narrative are seldom successful;
his stories often betray hasty writing, and in some of them there is
even a touch of the slickly commercial, reminding one that they
were also written for money. In literary terms, the sketches represented no advance over "The Hill," and Anderson's warning to the
budding virtuoso was quite to the point: "You've got too much

talent. You can do it too easy, in too many different ways. If you're not careful, you'll never write anything." [44]

In all fairness it should not be forgotten, however, that the sketches were little more than by-products, since during the first months of 1925 Faulkner's creative energies were mostly absorbed by the writing of his first novel: *Soldiers' Pay*. Written at the urging of Anderson and published in 1926 thanks to his recommendation, this book marks the beginning of Faulkner's career as a novelist. Not surprisingly, it is a novel about World War I and its aftermath, a novel about the war Faulkner had been deprived of, and which fascinated him all the more as he had not fought in it. That his motivations in choosing his subject were deeply personal is beyond doubt, and in this connection it is worth recalling that Faulkner felt so frustrated about not having been able to take an active (and possibly heroic) part in the fight that during the postwar years one of his favorite roles—besides those of the literary bohemian and the aristocratic foreigner—was the role of the wounded pilot returning from France. [45] As can be seen from his war stories and from *A Fable*, the "Great Crusade" of 1914–18 was to haunt Faulkner's imagination throughout his career. His non-experience of the war may indeed be said to have proved as much of a shock to him as actual participation in it had to other Americans of his generation. The wound was there, even though, unlike Hemingway's, it was an imaginary one.

Still, the depth of his emotional involvement with the war was not enough to produce a great novel. *Soldiers' Pay* reflects the feeling of bitterness and disillusionment that characterized so much of American postwar fiction. [46] Like *Three Soldiers, The Enormous Room*, or the early stories and novels of Hemingway, it is in many ways a typical "lost generation" novel, expressing the sense of futility and frustration which then afflicted those whom the war had suddenly made aware of the irretrievable loss of American innocence. But its very typicality is what dates the novel. By 1926 this mood of world-weariness had become something of a pose, and figures like the sad young man, the discharged soldier or the Fitzgeraldian flapper were already literary stereotypes. Faulkner's first novel is an illustration of the fashionable clichés and attitudes of the early twenties rather than a truly personal creation; it is derivative in tone, outlook, and manner, and here again, as in *The Marble Faun,* source hunting is apt to become an exhausting game. The book is full of literary echoes and borrowings, reminding one all too often of the more popular writers of the day: there are suggestions of James Branch Cabell's urbane eroticism as well as of Joseph Hergesheimer's languid elegancies, of Aldous Huxley's clever juggling with ideas as well as of T. S. Eliot's "Waste Land" mood. Another strongly felt influence is that of Aubrey Beardsley, whom Faulkner had imitated in his drawings for the University of Mississippi's yearbook and humor magazine, and whose perversely artificial graphic style is at times reflected in the novel's characters and setting. Throughout one also senses Faulkner's persistent fidelity to the mannerisms of *fin-de-siècle* literature,[47] and the proximity of his poetic past.[48]

Faulkner's shortcomings in *Soldiers' Pay* are those one would expect in a first novel: extreme self-consciousness; too many echoes and reminiscences; too many directions taken at once. The attempt to graft poetry on prose is hardly more convincing here than it was in the New Orleans sketches. Yet to this attempt the book owes its distinctive quality as an experiment in fiction. In abandoning verse for prose, Faulkner did not settle for a lesser medium, or if he did, it was with the hope that its possibilities could be enlarged in such ways as to make it an art form of equal dignity. And to Faulkner as to Joyce before him, one of the chief means to achieve this purpose was by subjecting prose to the formal discipline and structural demands of poetic discourse. In Faulkner's first novel the experiment no doubt miscarried; yet, as Michael Millgate judiciously notes, "what gives *Soldiers' Pay* its special character is its origin as a novel about the realities of war and its aftermath written by a young writer self-consciously pursuing the abstract formalism of late romantic prose."[49] Indeed, the most remarkable feature of the book is perhaps that from the outset of his career as a novelist Faulkner made so clean a break with the standards and conventions of realistic fiction. What unity the novel possesses it derives in fact from pattern rather than plot. There is no orderly chronological progression underlying the narrative; nor is there a stable dramatic focus: characters flit in and out, brief scenes follow each other in kaleidoscopic succession. The time sequence is repeatedly broken up, unrelated actions are linked through montage-like juxtaposition, and discrepant moods are telescoped for ironic effect—techniques reminiscent of Joyce and foreshadowing the contrapuntal methods evolved by Faulkner in his later fiction. But what is thus lost in narrative coherence and continuity is in some measure regained through compositional tightness. To harmonize his disparate materials, Faulkner resorts again to structural procedures he had used in *The Marble Faun*: emphasis on the progress of the seasons; incorporation of mythical references; reliance on reverberant repetition of imagery and symbol; elaborate modulation of theme and motif.

The overall effect of *Soldiers' Pay* is therefore one of deliberate disconnectedness as well as of intricate patterning. Not that it is quite convincing: the novel's structure suffers from overelaboration, just as its stylistic texture does from overwriting. Faulkner manages to be aggressively modernistic; he fails to be truly modern. It should be urged, however, that in writing his first novel, he was already fully aware of the potentialities of his medium, and determined to exploit them to their utmost limit.

Soldiers' Pay also deserves close attention as a nexus between Faulkner's early poetry and prose and the novels to come. Insofar as the book has a dramatic focus, it is centered upon the mute motionless figure of Donald Mahon, a maimed, disfigured, and nearly blind soldier back from the war, and the novel's action may be said to develop as a kind of last vigil around his long dying, as it will around Addie Bundren's in the very different context of *As I Lay Dying*. A general pattern is thus established, to be reused in a number of later works: some fading figure—a shadowy presence or a haunting absence rather than a fully realized character in the usual sense—becomes the static center which sets everything in motion, and around which all the other characters revolve in concentric circles, each of them responding to it in his own personal way. In this respect, Donald Mahon, Caddy Compson, Addie Bundren, Laverne Shumann, Thomas Sutpen, and Flem Snopes occupy similar positions and fulfill similar functions, however much they differ as characters. At the same time Donald Mahon is also related to a significant series of male figures: in Faulkner's earlier work, he is prefigured by "the marble faun" (severed, like him, from life's motion), and has his direct prototype in the terribly injured airman evoked in "The Lilacs," a poem written in 1920 and later published in *A Green Bough*;[50] on the other hand, he is himself a crude prefiguration of later heroes such as Bayard Sartoris, and in some measure even anticipates Quentin Compson, the death-haunted young man of *The Sound and the Fury*. Moreover, through Donald's drama, Faulkner begins to tackle one of his major themes: time. Donald is only the empty shell of a man, a living corpse with neither past nor present, imprisoned in a timeless limbo from which there is no return to life and no escape into death. Deliverance is denied to him as long as he has not recovered his memory, that is, consciousness of his identity. Only when the elusive past is eventually recaptured as he remembers the fatal encounter with the enemy plane does death become a possibility again. Then at last, the past having been reunited for a fleeting moment to the present, Donald again has a future, even though, ironically, it is a future of nothingness. Time and memory, consciousness and identity: all Faulkner readers will recognize here the nucleus of later thematic developments. And in a sense Donald's tragic fate may even be considered the inverted emblem of Faulkner's own quest: to the writer as to his first fictional hero, the struggle for identity passes of necessity through the difficult rediscovery of a submerged past. Donald must retrieve it to be able to die; Faulkner will reconquer it in the process of his writing and find his *raison d'être* through the agency of his work.

A symbol of death among the living, Donald also serves as a constant reminder of the realities of war amidst the preposterous bustle of a small Southern town. In this dual function, he is set over against Januarius Jones, the fat satyr whose frantic amorous pursuits form a grotesque counterpoint to the silent suffering of the dying soldier. Donald and Januarius are the novel's polar extremes: while the former represents the war veterans and their traumatic experiences of violence and death, the latter is made to embody the futility of the postwar civilian world. The contrast is further emphasized through the opposition of Donald's heroic romanticism and Januarius' cheap hedonism, and given additional significance by the two figures' suggested relatedness, since Januarius appears as a flabby caricature of what Donald was before the war: an ardent young lover, with "the serenity of a wild thing, the passionate serene alertness of a faun."[51] Donald's love affair with Emmy had been an idyll of tender sensuality; all that Januarius is capable of is barren lust.

Soldiers' Pay is as much a novel about sex and love as about war and death, and in associating the funeral wake with the ludicrous erotic ballet presided over by Januarius Jones, it comes to resemble a *danse macabre*. Sex and death are throughout intimately linked, and it is of course no accident that Donald's burial coincides with Emmy's final surrender to the lecherous Jones. Contrived coincidences like the latter no doubt show how heavy-handed Faulkner was then apt to be in his use of life's little ironies, and it is clear that at this point he lacked the maturity which a more satisfactory treatment of these two themes would have required. Still, it should be noted that even at this early stage they were perceived and dramatized in close conjunction. "Sex and death: the front door and the back door of the world. How indissolubly are they associated in us!"[52] In *Soldiers' Pay* Faulkner's attitude toward death is still seen to be largely indebted to the romantic reveries of adolescence, and for all its display of smartness and cynicism, his handling of the sex comedy is likewise immature. Yet death and sex are acknowledged from the first as the controlling powers of man's fate; their twin enigma will never cease to haunt Faulkner's imagination, and nowhere, perhaps, is his obsession with them as pervasive as in his early masterpieces, the most significant in this respect being assuredly *The Sound and the Fury*.

In his first novel Faulkner already describes a fairly wide range of responses to love and death—responses which vary according to whether the characters involved are soldiers or civilians, young or old people, men or women. The sexual or sentimental subplots develop around three feminine figures, two of whom are unmistakable adumbrations of later heroines. One is Cecily Saunders, Donald's former fiancée: shallow, selfish, eager to please yet unable to love, she is portrayed as "the symbol of a delicate bodyless lust,"[53] and satirized as "a papier-mâché Virgin";[54] while recalling the nymphs and naiads of Faulkner's poems (on account of her symbolic association with trees, flowers, and water), Cecily inaugurates the series of "epicene" flappers of his early fiction, and her acid grace and sexy sexlessness are traits we shall find again in Temple Drake, the equally frail but even more disquieting heroine of *Sanctuary*. At the other extreme is Emmy, the constant nymph (she too is associated with water): simple, submissive, tenderhearted—the first of Faulkner's earth mothers. As to the third figure, Margaret Powers, she is a neurotic war widow, guilt-ridden and most anxious to expiate her imagined guilt through a sacrificial gesture. Yet although she is made to act the maternal part of a spiritual nurse to the dying Donald, Faulkner describes her as a Beardsleyan avatar of the *femme fatale*. Like Januarius Jones, she is in fact an outgrowth of his early infatuation with the Decadents, and has no recognizable posterity in his mature fiction. A great deal of Faulkner's characterization in *Soldiers' Pay* is derivative and inconsistent. In creating his characters, he relies too much on currently popular types, or falls back on outdated literary models, and the symbolic significance they are invested with is all too often contradicted by the functions they are asked to assume on the realistic level of the narrative. In spite of its weaknesses, however, his characterization is never divorced from structure, and one cannot fail to be struck by the elaborate care with which the novel's characters are grouped, balanced and contrasted. Remarkable too, as far as the feminine figures are concerned, is the crystallization, in Faulkner's very first novel, of the two complementary mythic images of woman which, however qualified and differentiated, were to underlie all his fiction: Eve and Lilith, the archetypal mother figure and the perennial temptress.

Less obvious, but surely as pertinent to an inquiry into Faulkner's development as a writer, are the various ways in which the characters and situations presented in *Soldiers' Pay* relate to his personal experience. Only recently have the many autobiographical implications of the novel been fully recognized.[55] In 1925, when Faulkner wrote the book, it must have been with the awareness that most of his early expectations had come to nothing. His youthful love affair with Estelle Oldham had been thwarted by the latter's marriage to another man;[56] his heroic dreams, as we have already seen, had been likewise betrayed by reality. As to his prospects as a writer, they were as yet largely problematical. It seems therefore fairly safe to assume that, no matter how shallow and conventional its literary expression, the sense of frustration and failure pervading the novel had its deeper roots in the author's experience. Thus Faulkner's harsh exposure of Cecily Saunders certainly owes something to the bitterness he felt toward Estelle after her betrayal, and Mrs. Faulkner's own testimony bears out one's suspicion that he had taken her as a model.[57] The autobiographical relevance of the novel's masculine figures is even easier to trace. There are a number of physical and biographical details relating Donald Mahon to the young Faulkner, and the mythic figure of the wounded war hero—a figure which also was one of his favorite impersonations in life—may be seen as the fictional projection of the novelist's frustrated fantasies. Donald's funeral becomes in a sense the symbolic burial of Faulkner's juvenile dream of military glory and heroic death. And while Donald stands as the pathetic embodiment of the *dream,* other characters turn out to be ironical portraits of the romantic *dreamer,* especially

Julian Lowe, the callow cadet and hero-worshiper, to whom Donald comes to represent all the glamor of gallant romance. What unites the male characters of the novel is their common experience of frustration. Frustrated heroes, frustrated lovers, all of them. For just as they are defeated in their heroic aspirations, they are thwarted in their erotic yearnings: Donald is forsaken by Cecily; George Farr, the fickle girl's eventual husband, is tormented by morbid jealousy; Gilligan's love for Margaret Powers is a hopeless affair; and even Januarius Jones' frantic woman-chasing is destined to end more often than not in grotesque failure.

Whether shown in comic or pathetic light, all these stories of frustration may be referred back to Faulkner's own experience; whether portrayed with sympathy or satiric detachment, their protagonists are all to a point extensions of his self into the feelings and gestures of possible surrogates. In *The Marble Faun* Faulkner only used one persona; here the writer's self is split into a plurality of fragmentary doubles. And not only does none of them represent him whole; each one redoubles a double, that is, is made to relay a self-*image,* and not at all to represent a unique and *real* self. In *Soldiers' Pay* written fiction starts its devious game with the fiction of life, and irony and humor are already at play, creating distance and preventing self-projection from turning into mere imaginary wish-fulfillment. True, the movement toward objective dramatization has barely begun, the umbilical cord between autobiography and fiction has not yet been severed, and the author's presence behind his various masks is still heavily felt. Yet even though *Soldiers' Pay* still betrays an excessive amount of narcissistic self-involvement, it also marks the beginning of a necessary process of exorcism whose final stage will be reached in *The Sound and the Fury.*

Faulkner's next novel, *Mosquitoes* (1927), is generally considered to be his weakest, and the author dismissed it himself as mere apprentice work: "That one, if I could write it over, I probably wouldn't write it at all. I'm not ashamed of it, because that was the chips, the badly sawn planks that the carpenter produces while he's learning to be a first-rate carpenter, but it's not a—not an important book in my list."[58] As in *Soldiers' Pay* there are many influences to be traced, and by and large they are the same as those of the earlier novel.[59] Particularly conspicuous here are the numerous verbal echoes from the early Eliot,[60] and among novelists, Faulkner's greatest debt is probably to the Huxley of the twenties. The circumstances are those that the English novelist would have liked: a group of miscellaneous people thrown on to their own resources; the characters themselves are of the intellectual type that he favored, and as an isolating device to justify unbroken conversation among them, Faulkner's yacht functions in much the same way as Huxley's country houses. *Mosquitoes* was a venture into the then fashionable "novel of ideas"; it was obviously a faux pas, a misguided attempt at a genre quite alien to Faulkner's own gifts. There are highly entertaining passages in the book, passages in which his native genius for humor and comedy comes to the fore (as for instance the superb tall tale about the sheep farm in the swamp, where flock and farmer undergo a farcical metamorphosis into fish), but the kind of Peacockian conversation in which Huxley excelled was something he could not manage, and in trying to equal the witty sophistication and flippant cynicism of his British model, he could only go astray.

Mosquitoes is the first literary outcome of Faulkner's New Orleans experience. Its characters are borrowed from the artistic bohemia of the Vieux Carré in the midtwenties, and at times the novel reads almost like a *roman à clef*.[61] But few of the people who recognized themselves in the book (among them Sherwood Anderson, the model for Dawson Fairchild) can have felt particularly flattered, for most of the portraits are sharply satirical. Indeed, *Mosquitoes* often resembles a private settling of accounts. Faulkner's sojourn at New Orleans had certainly been a very stimulating experience, and from Anderson he had received all the help and encouragement he could expect. Yet although he was too honest ever to deny his debt, his was in some measure the ingratitude one so often encounters in writers toward their erstwhile patrons and benefactors; it had not taken him very long to perceive the limitations of Anderson's literary talent, and, as with Hemingway, the naughty impulse soon followed to poke fun at the elderly novelist through pastiche of his style,[62] and, eventually, to expose the man himself through caricature. *Mosquitoes* may thus be seen as a gesture of irreverence toward a literary father figure. More generally, with regard to Faulkner's development, it appears as an act of repudiation: by ridiculing the shallow intellectuality of the New Orleans world, he rejected his own recent past and asserted his independence as a writer.

Like *Soldiers' Pay*, *Mosquitoes* is largely satire, and one of Faulkner's favorite targets is again sex, or rather what it came to be in the rootless society of the twenties: a permanent obsession feeding on impotence and barrenness. Sexual desire, as depicted in the novel, is either thwarted or perverted, and even sexual identity becomes problematical. The traditional sex roles are inverted: men are effeminate, women masculinized, and girls will be boys. Echoing the familiar *fin-de-siècle* motif of androgyny, Faulkner here describes a sterile, bisexual world. His characters include a lesbian poetess and a sexless poet, and even those who escape from plain abnormality are at the very least crippled by sexual repression and frustration. The more grotesque characters are to be found among the older people: Mrs. Maurier, the silly patroness of the arts; Dorothy Jameson, the male-chasing painter, and above all the Prufrockian figure of Mr. Talliaferro. As in *Soldiers' Pay*, the old are contrasted with the young.[63] It should be noted, however, that in their own inarticulate and heedless way the young are just as egotistical as their elders, and the couples they form in the novel (Jenny-Pete; Patricia-Theodore) suggest rather equivocal brother-sister relationships. It is significant too that Patricia's escapade with David, the only attempted flight from the closed world of the *Nausikaa*, ends in disaster. Again as in *Soldiers' Pay*, the ballet of desire is little more than the empty flutter of prurient marionettes.

Yet if sexuality looms as large in *Mosquitoes* as in Faulkners'
first novel, the thematic configuration within which it appears is
fairly different. The emphasis is not on sexual perversion and
sterility alone; it is also on the extreme barrenness of verbal intercourse: "Talk, talk, talk: the utter and heartbreaking stupidity of
words. It seemed endless, as though it might go on forever. Ideas,
thoughts, became mere sounds to be bandied about until they were
dead."[64] Words are divorced from living thought, just as they are
from real action: " 'Well, it is a kind of sterility—Words,' Fairchild admitted. 'You begin to substitute words for things and
deeds, like the withered cuckold husband that took the Decameron
to bed with him every night, and pretty soon the thing or the deed
becomes just a kind of shadow of a certain sound you make by
shaping your mouth a certain way.' "[65] As Olga W. Vickery has
shown,[66] this seemingly irreducible antagonism between the reality
of experience and the unreality of words is dramatized in the novel
by the division of the characters into doers and talkers. Those who
evince true vitality and are capable of meaningful action are people
of few words, like Mark Gordon, the only authentic artist in the
group. Mr. Talliaferro, on the other hand, is both an insufferable
chatterbox and a pathetically inept lover. For him and his like,
words become paltry surrogates for the experience of life they are
either unable or unwilling to accept and make their own. Gar-
rulity thus functions as an index to futility and failure, while being
taciturn signals unimpaired powers to live and create.[67] The notion,
both stated in the novel and exemplified by its characters, that
words and deeds are at variance was of course no new idea; it was
so common in fact as to be a commonplace at a time when there
was a widespread revulsion from rhetorical abstractions and
pseudo-intellectual verbiage among writers.[68] Moreover, in *Mosquitoes* the treatment of the theme is the less convincing as the
author indulges in the very sins his novel is supposed to denounce.
Still, the emergence of the theme calls for attention, since the opposition of language and life informs so much of Faulkner's later
fiction, and embodies itself in so many of his later heroes and

antiheroes. Coming after Januarius Jones, the hardly less ludicrous would-be Don Juan of *Soldiers' Pay,* Talliaferro is one in a long series of intemperate talkers, in which we also encounter Horace Benbow ("a man given to much talk and not much else," as Ruby says in *Sanctuary*[69]) and the ghostlike "Reporter" of *Pylon.* As to the masculine Mark Gordon, he belongs unquestionably to the sturdy race of Faulkner's quiet men.

The relationship between life and language was to become one of Faulkner's abiding concerns as a novelist, and its permanence is attested both in and by his fiction. It is not merely a recurring theme in his novels; his whole work may be read as an ever-renewed attempt to bridge the gap between words and things, and to restore language to the energies of life. Which means that to Faulkner the contradiction could be solved after all through the creation of another language: the language of art. What art is or should be, how it relates to the world and to the artist's self—these are precisely the questions he is raising in this early novel, as if, before embarking on his great venture, he had felt the need to clarify his position and outline a poetic of his own.

Mosquitoes has been called Faulkner's "Portrait of the Artist."[70] As far as literary merit is concerned, the comparison with Joyce's first major achievement is hardly to Faulkner's advantage, yet the two novels do resemble each other in that both are early attempts at defining a workable poetic and tentative statements of their authors' ambitions. Further, there is evidence that *A Portrait of the Artist as a Young Man* was in Faulkner's mind when he wrote *Mosquitoes.* Stephen Dedalus and Mark Gordon, the two dominating artist figures, are alike in their proud aloofness, and there are close analogies between Joyce's and Faulkner's definitions of aesthetic experience and creation: Joyce's "enchantment of the heart" is echoed by Faulkner's "Passion Week of the heart,"[71] and Joyce's "silent stasis" is likewise paralleled in Faulkner's "frozen time."[72] Another common trait is the assimilation of art to life: for Stephen, the moment of inspiration is that privileged instant when "in the virgin womb of the imagination the word was made flesh,"[73] and his proclaimed ambition is "to recreate life out of life";[74] in *Mosquitoes* Fairchild likens artistic creation to procreation, and the "Semitic man" reflects that "Dante invented Beatrice, creating himself a maid that life had not had time to create."[75] Yet in both novels art is also envisioned as a negation of life, since life thus recreated is forever preserved from mortality: while Stephen dreams of creating "a living thing, new and soaring and beautiful, impalpable, imperishable,"[76] Gordon's marble torso of a girl is described as "passionate and simple and eternal in the equivocal derisive darkness of the world."[77]

To turn from Joyce's *Portrait* to Faulkner's *Mosquitoes,* however, is to perceive significant differences in formulation and emphasis. Both are indebted in their theorizings to the tradition of romantic idealism, and both borrow part of their aesthetic vocabulary from Christianity. Yet, unlike Joyce's, Faulkner's reflections owe nothing to Scholastic philosophy and Thomist theology, and they are far more sketchy than the highly ambitious speculations attributed to Stephen. In *Mosquitoes* there is no trace whatever of the latter's cold intellectual arrogance and narcissistic elation; what is stressed is not so much the "ecstasy" of artistic creation as its "agony": to Faulkner art is a "passion" in the two senses of the word. Sorrow and suffering are seen to be at the dark core of art as well as of life: "Only an idiot has no grief," Gordon says at the close of the novel, "only a fool would forget it. What else is there in this world sharp enough to stick to your guts?"[78] Stephen's theory of art—not to be mistaken for that of Joyce himself when he wrote the *Portrait*—is still pretty close to pure aestheticism (as can be seen from its contemptuous dismissal of kinesis). Faulkner, on the other hand, is already moving from the shallow idealism of his literary beginnings to the tragicomic realism of his major works. This shift is illustrated in his novel by the converging changes undergone by three of its artist figures—Gordon, Fairchild, and Julius—in the closing *Walpurgisnacht* section,[79] and is most tellingly symbolized by two artifacts: the marble torso and the clay mask. Gordon's first masterpiece is "the virginal breastless torso of a girl, headless, armless, legless, in marble temporarily caught and hushed yet passionate still for escape."[80] The statue no doubt fuses passion and art, motion and stasis; yet its beauty is "marble-bound" (as was the faun of Faulkner's poem), and its perfect form has been obtained through a process of subtraction and abstraction, that is, through a deliberate denial or, at least, diminishment of life and, more specifically, through a willful cancellation of sex— evidence that Gordon himself, at this point, has not yet broken free from the sterile bisexual or asexual world to which most of the other characters belong. His later achievement—the mask of Mrs. Maurier—is something very different:

> It was clay, yet damp, and from out its dull dead grayness Mrs. Maurier looked at them. Her chins, harshly, and her flaccid jaw muscles with savage verisimilitude. Her eyes were caverns thumbed with two motions into the dead familiar astonishment of her face; and yet, behind them, somewhere within those empty sockets, behind all her familiar surprise, there was something else—something that exposed her face for the mask it was, and still more, a mask un-aware.[81]

The very choice of material and model points to the new direction taken by Gordon's art. The grey earthiness of clay is given precedence over the cold purity and hard splendor of marble, and instead of a beautiful young girl the sculptor has chosen this time to portray a silly old woman. While the virginal torso embodied a private dream of sexless beauty and timeless youth, the mask reveals the humble and poignant truth of a human face; the former sprang from the romantic impulse to dissociate art from life, the latter from the wish to relate it back to life. Not that Gordon reverts to a tamely academic imitation of "nature"; in its grim concentration on essentials, the hollow-eyed mask of Mrs. Maurier rather suggests a figure by Giacometti or a portrait by Rouault: it is life surprised, seized and stripped to its tragic core, the startling revelation of a heretofore unsuspected world of "love and life and death and sex and sorrow."[82] The implied aesthetic here is a far cry from Gordon's earlier stance, and it has very little in common with the theory Stephen expounds in the *Portrait*. If one insists on analogies with Joyce, its spirit comes in fact much closer to the definition he has given of "the classical temper" in *Stephen Hero*, the first draft of the *Portrait:*

> The classical temper . . . ever mindful of limitations, chooses rather to bend upon those present things and so to work upon them and fashion them that the quick intelligence may go beyond them to their meaning which is still unuttered.[83]

Joyce defined the classical temper in opposition to the romantic one, "an insecure, unsatisfied, impatient temper which sees no fit abode here for its ideals and chooses therefore to behold them under insensible figures."[84] His own trajectory was from the poses of late romanticism to his own, highly idiosyncratic and utterly unconventional kind of "classicism." But only in *Ulysses* did he achieve the firm grasp on concrete particulars, the mature, impersonal detachment, and the dramatic power which allegiance to the classical temper required. As to Faulkner's development, it may be said to have followed a broadly similar route, and his aesthetic purposes were likewise conceptualized before they began to be put to full creative use. In both cases, theory ran ahead of practice. Gordon's portrait of Mrs. Maurier is assumed to penetrate beyond appearances to the hard kernel of truth; in the novel, as a character, however, she remains a mere cardboard figure of grinning silliness.

At the outset of their literary careers Joyce and Faulkner alike were anxious to reach a fuller understanding of the relation between life and art. What strikes one in both cases is that the quest for a workable aesthetic went along with a search for identity. What mattered to Joyce as well as to Faulkner was probably less the discovery of a consistent poetic than finding out about themselves as writers. Their ruling concern was one of self-definition in terms of life and art, not articulation of a theoretical creed of universal validity. Yet in this respect it is again interesting to see how widely they differed. Joyce's *Portrait* fits squarely into the tradition of the *Künstlerroman:* it is the chronicle of a young artist's sensibility, an education novel focused on the single figure of Stephen Dedalus, and more or less closely patterned on Joyce's own experience. The portrait of Stephen is a self-portrait, even though the intentions of the portraitist have long been an object of ardent controversy among Joyce critics. Whatever the distance assumed between the author and his hero, it is clear that the novel belongs to the category of autobiographical fiction; no matter how much irony may be involved, it is indeed the "portrait of the artist as a young man." With Faulkner, on the contrary, the autobiographical element is at once less central and less opaque. Had he completed "Elmer," the story of a young American painter he had started to write in 1925 after leaving New Orleans,[85] his second novel might have been a comic portrait of the artist; in *Mosquitoes,* however, there is no attempt to trace the development of a focal artist figure. As in *Soldiers' Pay,* the writer's self explodes into a whole constellation of partial selves: in the first novel the stage was crowded with soldier figures; in the second one finds a similar proliferation of artist and pseudo-artist figures. Both series are related in various ways to Faulkner's own experience and fantasies (his role-playing during the postwar years providing the link between fantasy and fiction). *Soldiers' Pay* portrays the writer as a returned soldier; *Mosquitoes* depicts him both as artist *and* aesthete. For while Gordon, the true artist, represents the author's idealized self, the creative writer he would like to become, the dilettantes surrounding him embody the distortion or betrayal of that ideal, and are as many versions of Faulkner, the "failed poet."

Noteworthy too in this connection is the furtive appearance made in the novel by the author under his own name as "the little kind of black man,"[86] and the fact that he has his characters comment disparagingly on three of the poems he would later publish in *A Green Bough.*[87] The dominant note in *Mosquitoes* is one of wry self-mockery, and what it points to is Faulkner's increasing impatience with the posturings of his early aestheticism. Like *Soldiers' Pay,* his second novel is still largely a fiction of the self, but it is also a purging of the ego, a salubrious exercise in distancing, and a sincere attempt at clarification. As for its literary merits, they are no doubt slight if compared to those of his major achievements; yet the book possesses a mischievous charm whose seeming brittleness has resisted the erosion of time: its humor, for all its farcical crudities, survives through sheer exuberance, and Faulkner's style, despite the ostentatious mannerisms and indiscreet borrowings, comes out unabashedly with an alertness all its own. Conrad Aiken, in reviewing the novel, called it "a distinctly unusual and amusing book," and added that "it is good enough to make one wish it were better."[88] In Faulkner's development, *Mosquitoes* is indeed little more than a divertissement of intermittent brilliancy; it probably also was a necessary detour through alien territory—the last detour before he began at last to touch his true ground.

Faulkner's next novel was finished on September 29, 1927, only one year after the completion of *Mosquitoes*. Originally entitled *Flags in the Dust*,[89] it was published in 1929 in a shortened version as *Sartoris*. Faulkner told Jean Stein in his 1955 interview what this novel meant to him:

> With *Soldiers' Pay* I found out writing was fun. But I found out after that not only each book had to have a design but the whole output or sum of an artist's work had to have a design. With *Soldiers' Pay* and *Mosquitoes* I wrote for the sake of writing because it was fun. Beginning with *Sartoris* I discovered that my own little postage stamp of native soil was worth writing about and that I would never live long enough to exhaust it, and by sublimating the actual into apocryphal I would have complete liberty to use whatever talent I might have to its absolute top. It opened up a gold mine of other peoples, so I created a cosmos of my own.[90]

While working alternately on *Flags in the Dust* and on "Father Abraham," his first project on the Snopes saga,[91] Faulkner thus came to realize how right Sherwood Anderson had been in advising him to write about "that little patch up there in Mississippi where

[he] started from."[92] Now he was at last taking possession of his true territory—a territory his imagination would expand and transmute into the vast, teeming world of his books.

As Conrad noted: "In truth every novelist must begin by creating for himself a world, great or little, in which he can honestly believe."[93] This is precisely what Faulkner did in *Sartoris,* the first of his Yoknapatawpha novels. Not only is the setting for the first time Jefferson, Mississippi, but many of the characters that are to return in his later fiction—the Sartorises, the Snopeses, Horace and Narcissa Benbow, Dr. Peabody, the MacCallums, and a host of minor figures—here make their first appearance. In the course of the creative process, Faulkner's approach to his material was to change time and again, but in *Sartoris* the données of his "world" were already fully assembled. Faulkner considered this novel the very "germ of [his] apocrypha";[94] to us, his readers, it appears retrospectively as a fascinating source book, an inexhaustible reservoir of potentialities.

Reading *Sartoris,* one can hardly fail to be struck at once by the almost Balzacian scope of Faulkner's ambition. Never before had he paid such scrupulous attention to the social and regional context; never before had he attempted to evoke the ambience and décor of a particular place in such painstaking detail. In *Flags in the Dust,* Douglas Day notes, "Faulkner clearly wished to make of his novel and anatomy of the entire Yoknapatawpha social structure, excluding only the Indian";[95] in the shortened published version, the emphasis falls on the Sartoris clan, yet the social spectrum is still fairly wide, ranging from town to country, from white to Negro, from the old aristocratic families and the rising new middle class to the yeomen and the sharecroppers. All these classes and categories are carefully differentiated through their respective codes of behavior,[96] and actions, characters, and setting are for the first time closely interrelated. In *Soldiers' Pay* the choice of a Southern locale had little bearing on the novel's pattern and meaning; in *Sartoris* the spirit of the place becomes a presence pervasively felt. Throughout one senses the pressure of an established and fairly intricate system of social values, and the inescapable power of common traditions. *Sartoris* is the portrait of a society as firmly rooted in space and time as Hardy's Wessex or Joyce's Dublin, and therefore it is also one of the most markedly "Southern" of all Faulkner novels.

In writing *Sartoris* Faulkner drew more than ever on his own experience. But whereas in his two previous novels his starting point had been a recent and strictly personal past, he now came to use broader segments and deeper strata of his memory, reaching back to early recollections and reaching out concentrically toward his family, his town, his county, and toward the South, past and present, to which they all belonged. As Faulkner himself stated in a letter to Malcolm Cowley, his prestigious great-grandfather, Colonel William Clark Falkner, "was prototype of John Sartoris,"[97] the towering ancestral figure of the novel; many other characters in the book were likewise modeled on members of his own family and on Oxford citizens he knew or had heard about.[98] What prompted Faulkner to recreate the familiar world of his childhood and youth was, at least at the outset, the desire to make up beforehand for an impending loss, and to conquer time through the ruses of art: "All that I really desired," he wrote in commenting upon the genesis of *Sartoris,* "was a touchstone simply; a simple word or gesture, but having been these 2 years previously under the curse of words, having known twice before the agony of ink, nothing served but that I try by main strength to recreate between the covers of a book the world as I was already preparing to lose and regret, feeling, with the morbidity of the young, that I was not only on the verge of decrepitude, but that growing old was to be an experience peculiar to myself alone out of all the teeming world, and desiring, if not the capture of that world and the feeling of it as you'd preserve a kernel or a leaf to indicate the lost forest, at least to keep the evocative skeleton of the dessicated [sic] leaf."[99]

As so often with Faulkner, the creative impulse sprang from a private sense of frustration and loss. Yet more was certainly involved than nostalgia for a passing world and the desire to rescue

it from sheer oblivion. With *Sartoris* Faulkner began to realize—
as some of his heroes would after him—that his own individual
existence, the fate of his family, and the destiny of the South were
so inextricably interwoven that, as man and writer, he had to come
to grips with all of it. From then on, literature, for him, was to be
less and less a matter of romantic self-concern and self-dramatization, and to become more and more an imaginative exploration of
the familiar strangeness of the world. His novels would still be
autobiography in a sense, yet to the extent only that all great literary
fictions are: not mirrors of the self, nor even self-probings so much
as immersions into the opaqueness of *other* selves.

In *Sartoris,* however, this sense of otherness, which is the mark
of the truly dramatic imagination, is not yet given full play. Bayard
Sartoris and Horace Benbow, the novel's two most significant characters, are still related in many ways to the author's private per-
sonas.

Through Bayard, his hero, Faulkner reverted to the war theme
which he had begun to deal with in *Soldiers' Pay*. Like Donald
Mahon, Bayard is a young man home from the war; Donald's physical injuries are paralleled by Bayard's psychic trauma, and both are
found in a condition that isolates them altogether from their family
and community. In both cases, too, a woman—Margaret Powers for
Donald, Narcissa Benbow for Bayard—comes to represent a transient and illusory promise of recovery and reinsertion in life.
Equally noteworthy is the motif of the *double* linked to both characters: in *Soldiers' Pay* the dying Donald of the present is set off
against the dead Donald of the past; in *Sartoris* the "dying" Bayard
is likewise contrasted with Johnny, his dead twin brother, and it
is significant too that in both novels the dead figures—the faunlike
Donald, the wild but lovable Johnny—are made to suggest a lost
ideal of warm carefree vitality. At this point, however, the similarities end. While Donald was but a rudimentary emblem of the
dying hero, Bayard is an almost fully realized character; while the
former was a passive sufferer, the latter is shown to be both agent
and victim of his tragic fate. Moreover, their plights are different:

Donald must recapture the past to be able to die; Bayard, in court-
ing death, does his utmost to escape from its burden. The most
obvious cause of Bayard's suicidal behavior is beyond doubt his
shattering experience of the war; he is one of those airplane pilots
of World War I of whom Faulkner said that "in a way they were
dead, they had exhausted themselves psychically."[100] Yet his compulsive death-wish is given further significance in terms of family
relationships, notably with reference to his brother John. His intense emotional involvement with the latter is at once narcissistic
and ambivalent: he loves and admires him as his heroic double,
while unconsciously resenting his superiority and feeling dimly
responsible for his death. Hence his headlong plunge into violence
as a release from unbearable tensions; hence the irresistible urgency
of his suicidal drive. For Bayard, as later for Quentin Compson,
death is the only way out, since only through death—a death re-
enacting Johnny's—can he hope to achieve identification with his
brother and expiate his assumed guilt.

Horace Benbow's self-destructiveness operates less dramatically,
yet it should be noted that he too is returning from the war and
that his experience of it prevents him likewise from readjusting
to the routines of civilian life. There is little doubt that Bayard and
Horace were initially meant to be seen and interpreted as anti-
thetical and complementary figures; their coupling was even more
evident in the early version of the novel, where Horace played a
much more important role than the one he was eventually given
in *Sartoris*. As far as their personalities are concerned, the two
characters could be hardly further apart: Bayard is one of Faulkner's harshly masculine heroes; Horace appears throughout as a
garrulous and ineffectual dreamer. Their opposition exemplifies
polarities already adumbrated in Faulkner's earlier fiction and reused in varying patterns in the later works—furious action vs.
passive suffering, aggressive masculinity vs. effeminacy, inarticulate
brooding vs. febrile intellectuality. For all their differences, though,
Bayard and Horace are two "lost generation" figures fundamentally
alike in their disorientation and estrangement from life, and the

former's morbid fascination by his twin brother originates in the same kind of regressive self-absorption as the latter's quasi-incestuous relationship with his sister.

It is clear too, as Cleanth Brooks has pointed out,[101] that both are at heart incorrigible romantics. Presented alternately as a fallen angel and a cold demon, Bayard is in many ways the archetypal romantic hero, and his literary lineage can be traced back to Milton's Satan, to the Gothic villain and, above all, to the Byronic rebel.[102] Horace, on the other hand, represents the carefully cultivated disenchantment and ironical self-awareness of late romanticism, and his "air of fine and delicate futility"[103] relates him to Faulkner's ludicrous Prufrock figures. Yet more to the point perhaps than the all too obvious literary ancestry of the two characters is their significance with regard to their creator. In their complementarity they may be said to epitomize the dual trend of Faulkner's youthful romanticism—a romanticism from which he was not yet totally cured, and which his characters are intended not so much to express as to exorcise. Less schematically than Donald Mahon, Bayard stands for the failure of Faulkner's *heroic* dream: the desire to transcend finiteness through the apotheosis of a violent, self-willed death. And the same desire for transcendence is equally apparent in Horace, the disillusioned dilettante, under the guise of the *aesthetic* temptation. Whereas Bayard rushes into the timeless world of heroic romance, Horace voyages "in lonely regions . . . beyond the moon,"[104] and seeks refuge in the stilled perfection of art. One is the portrait of the young man as the would-be hero; the other, like the protagonist of "Elmer" and the pseudo-artists of *Mosquitoes,* his ironical portrait as a would-be poet.[105]

The contrasting but parallel destinies of Bayard and Horace dramatize a conflict central to nearly all of Faulkner's fiction: the conflict between what might be called the *vertical* impulse, that is, the urge toward absolute freedom and transcendence, and the never to be silenced demands of life. The two characters' inability to meet these demands can perhaps best be seen in their failure to come to terms with sex. Bayard is not saved by his marriage to Narcissa, and he obviously prefers the company of men and horses to that of women; Horace, it is true, feels deeply attracted to the other sex, but his immaturity is shown up both in his incestuous attachment to Narcissa and in his degrading love for a bitchy divorcée. Sex is either denied or perverted. Bayard is in love with death, Horace with his sister; in Quentin Compson, who takes from both, these two loves will be paradoxically one.

Again, as in Faulkner's first novel, the atmosphere is saturated with sex and death. The obsession with death is present in Bayard's suicidal race as it was in Donald Mahon's mute agony, and once again the death motif is counterpointed against a tragicomic *chassé-croisé* of amorous pursuits: love rejected (Bayard-Narcissa), love as bondage (Benbow-Belle Mitchell), incestuous love (Benbow-Narcissa), and sheer lust (Byron Snopes-Narcissa). Yet in *Sartoris* the dual theme of sex and death is given richer resonance through Faulkner's purposeful use of the Southern background. The typically modern rootlessness of Bayard and Horace is set off against the relative order and stability of a settled rural society in which traditional values and standards still prevail. What is more, the present drama is brought into significant perspective by being related to the past. As in *Soldiers' Pay* the novel's action unfolds within the cosmic, cyclic time symbolized by the return of the seasons (the narrative proceeding from one spring to the next), yet it also develops, vertically as it were, out of the perplexing depths of a remote but ever-recurring past. For the first time in Faulkner's fiction, *time* comes to be felt as an active, shaping force, a force whose "palpable presence"[106] is already suggested in the very first pages of the novel through the quasi-ritual incantation of the formidable phantom of John Sartoris, the long-dead founder of the family line. Owing to the repeated recalls of past figures and events (mainly through the reminiscences of old Bayard, old Will Falls and Miss Jenny), narrative time is extended and made to span four generations of Sartorises. The area of speculation and investigation is thus expanded beyond the narrow confines of the contemporary scene, allowing the author to manipulate different time levels and to order them in various perspectives. Past and present are woven into an intricate tapestry of correspondences, so that young Bayard Sartoris, the novel's twentieth-century protagonist, invites comparison not only with his dead twin brother, but also with the patriarchal figure of the Colonel, and with the gallant Carolina Bayard of Miss Jenny's memory who died in the Civil War. Analogies are so close and so many that the past almost appears as a rehearsal of the present, and that the present seems to be a reenactment of the past. The characters are turned into replicas of one another (the confusion being carefully maintained by the use of identical first names); their destinies become as many exemplifications of the Sartoris way of death. Hence the suspicion that Colonel Sartoris has set up a rigid paradigm for all his male descendants to conform to, and that none of them is ever allowed to escape from the family doom. Repetition, though, is not the return of the identical. There are many hints that the stubborn persistence of the same "dream" and the recurrence of the same compulsive action patterns from generation to generation are no safeguard against disorder and decline, as though the repetition scheme were as well an entropic process, and as though the present could be nothing more than an anemic copy of the past. Measured against the past, the present is found wanting: while the Civil War is remembered as a glamorous adventure, World War I is seen as senseless confusion; while the ancestors performed heroic deeds, all young Bayard is capable of is a futile gesture of despair.

This is not to say that Faulkner is content with exalting a glorious past at the expense of a lusterless present. Rather than a celebration of the Southern mythology, *Sartoris* is his first inquiry into mythopoeia.[107] What matters for the novelist and his readers is not so much the "Sartoris myth" in itself as the process of telling and retelling through which it came into being, the subtle alchemy of memory and imagination by means of which facts have been gradually enriched, embellished and transmuted into the finer fabric of fiction. The process of mythmaking is clearly seen at work in Miss Jenny's account of the Carolina Bayard's raid during the Civil War: what had been "a hare-brained prank of two heedless and reckless boys" becomes, in her telling, "a gallant and finely tragical focal point to which the history of the race had been raised from out of the old miasmic swamps of spiritual sloth by two angels valiantly fallen and strayed."[108] What haunts the Sartorises, then, is not at all a "real," objective past, but a legend of their own fabrication—a verbal and imaginary construct, a fantasy abstracted from reality. And the family myth is not unlike the artifacts shaped by the novelist himself: it is a way of ordering and aesthetizing experience, of lending it beauty and significance. Yet its effects in *Sartoris* turn out to be largely destructive. The world it generates is one in which the dead ceaselessly prey on the living. For the mythic past has been formalized into an oppressive pattern: far from making the present meaningful, it reduces it to a paltry pantomime, and encloses life in the nightmarish circles of endless repetition. To men like Bayard, it leaves no other prospect than despair and an absurd death.

There is much in *Sartoris* to suggest and support such a reading, yet in fact we can never know for sure whether we are intended to regard the Sartorises as the blind victims of their own fantasies and fabrications or as the helpless pawns of a cruel cosmic Player. In the last analysis, *Sartoris* is an ambiguous novel or more precisely an equivocal one; it is not ambiguous as is *The Sound and the Fury* or *Absalom, Absalom!*: its uncertainties proceed from a muddled purpose rather than from a deliberate strategy on the author's part. Faulkner's attitude toward the Sartoris myth, as reflected in his rhetoric and in his handling of the narrative point of view, is ambivalent in a way reminiscent of Miss Jenny's in the novel: even though he is able to see it in the light of irony, he as yet cannot free himself completely from its spell, divided as he himself is at this point between sentimental allegiance to the past and the impulse to question it. *Sartoris* stands halfway between the romanticism of his adolescence and the complex critical awareness he was to reach in his mature fiction. In all respects a transitional work, it may be said to represent the end of his apprenticeship; it cannot be counted yet among his great achievements. It suffers from the plethora of many early novels: the author is trying to say too much, to cram too many novels into one. *Sartoris* is like a storehouse or a treasure chest, in which Faulkner accumulates materials for the books to come; everything is there, ready to hand, but not yet fully mastered, not yet fully owned. However intricately patterned, *Sartoris* lacks the economy of means and concentration of effect of the major works.

It is nonetheless an impressive advance over his previous novels and a decisive step in his development. Faulkner has not yet found his voice, but he has discovered his world. Through the shaping of this world, a truth will be invented and enacted in the very process of writing—a truth become fiction, a fiction become truth.

2

Caddy, or The Quest for

Eurydice

Regarder Eurydice, sans souci du chant, dans l'impatience et l'imprudence du désir qui oublie la loi, c'est cela même, l'inspiration.

MAURICE BLANCHOT

A pregnant emptiness. Object-loss, world-loss, is the precondition for all creation. Creation is in or out of the void; ex nihilo.

NORMAN O. BROWN

W$_{\text{ITH}}$ *The Sound and the Fury* something happened to Faulkner that had never happened before and would never happen again. For us, his readers, this novel is the first of his major works; for the writer, however, it was much more than a book: a crucial moment in his career, a unique experience in his life. On what the experience meant to him we are fortunate enough to have his own comment: the introduction he wrote during the summer of 1933 for a new edition of the novel that was to be published by Random House.[1] Of the many statements Faulkner made on *The Sound and the Fury,* none provides a fuller account of the book's genesis, and, what is more, none gives us as sharp a sense of the emotional climate in which it was conceived and written.

> I wrote this book and learned to read. I had learned a little about writing from Soldiers' Pay—how to approach language, words: not with seriousness so much, as an essayist does, but with a kind of alert respect, as you approach dynamite; even with joy, as you approach women: perhaps with the same secretly unscrupulous intentions. But when I finished The Sound and The Fury I discovered that there is actually something to which the shabby term Art not only can, but must be applied. I discovered then that I had gone through all that I had ever read, from Henry James through Henty to newspaper murders, without making any distinction or digesting any of it, as a moth or a goat might. After The Sound and The Fury and without heeding to open another book and in a series of delayed repercussions like summer thunder, I discovered the Flauberts and Dostoievskys and Conrads whose books I had read ten years ago. With The Sound and The Fury I learned to read and quit reading, since I have read nothing since.[2]

It is with these startling reflections that Faulkner's introduction begins. If *The Sound and the Fury* was a revelation, it was first of all the revelation of Literature, through the sudden (re-) discovery of all the major novelists with whom Faulkner had just joined company. True, he had read them before, but if we are to believe his testimony, his first reading had been nothing but blind consumption—consumption without "digestion." His second reading, on the contrary, was a process of assimilation carried to its furthest limits, that is, to the point where reading becomes writing. What Faulkner implicitly acknowledges here is that the relationship between reading and writing is one of reversibility: reading is always a virtual writing, and writing always a way of reading.

In working on his fourth novel, he re-discovers the texts of his predecessors in the production of his own text, and becomes aware of how they interact in the chemistry of his own writing.[3] Which is not to say that his novel simply derives from others: the process at work is a process of radical transformation, a way of displacing and, eventually, replacing the models from which the book proceeds. *The Sound and the Fury,* then, may be considered a rereading of Flaubert, Dostoevski and Conrad—a reading at once attentive and forgetful, fascinated and treacherous, and, by virtue of its very infidelity, creative. The very gesture of appropriation is also a gesture of dismissal. From now on, Faulkner can dispense with reading others. It will be enough for him to be his own reader.

The Sound and the Fury marks Faulkner's decisive encounter with Literature, his final entry into what might be called its infinite text, a space in which novels are endlessly born out of novels. With *Sartoris* he had discovered that his experience as a Southerner could be used for literary purposes; with *The Sound and the Fury* he came to realize that, far from being the mere expression or reflection of prior experience, writing could be in itself an experience in the fullest sense.

What Faulkner then experienced was the pure *adventure* of writing, free of any preestablished design. "When I began it," he notes, "I had no plan at all. I wasn't even writing a book."[4] And he felt free too from any external pressure or constraint; he did not even care about getting published. The commercial failure of his previous books became an encouragement to disregard the demands of the publishers as well as the expectations of his potential public. *The Sound and the Fury* would be a strictly private affair: "One day I seemed to shut a door between me and all publishers' addresses and book lists. I said to myself, Now I can write."[5]

Having thus cleared the ground, Faulkner discovered in himself a power and a freedom heretofore unsuspected: the power and freedom to write. And no sooner were they discovered than they were put at the service of desire: "Now," the text goes on, "I can make myself a vase like that which the old Roman kept at his bedside and wore the rim slowly away with kissing it."[6] *The Sound and the Fury* thus became the occasion for a doubly significant experience: through the reversal from "reading" into writing, Faulkner was at last able to appropriate his literary legacy, and to transcend it into a creation irreducibly his own; yet this breakthrough to mastery was not simply a matter of artistic maturation, and it would not have been possible, perhaps, without the onrush of emotion he experienced during the composition of the novel. What made the writing of *The Sound and the Fury* such an extraordinary experience was probably more than anything else its being quickened by the full energy of desire.

The work of art has been defined in psychoanalytical terms as a *transnarcissistic* object, meant to establish a connection between the narcissism of its producer and that of its consumer.[7] It is interesting to note that in the case of Faulkner's novel, the creative impulse, at least in its earliest phase, was purely self-oriented. The object to be shaped was to serve no other purpose than self-gratification. Giver and receiver were to be identical. As to the object itself, its narcissistic nature and function are emphasized through the image of the vase kept by the old Roman at his bedside and whose rim is slowly worn away by his kisses. Another reminder of the Keatsian urn, the vase is of course a metaphor for the world of art. But the point here is that the aesthetic is made one with the erotic.[8] The kissed vase is clearly a libidinal object or, more precisely, a fetish, that is, an object standing *instead* of something else, the mark and mask of an absence. It functions as a surrogate—an assumption fully confirmed by the sentence following the one quoted above, the very last of Faulkner's text: "So I, who had never had a sister and was fated to lose my daughter in infancy, set out to make myself a beautiful and tragic little girl."[9]

Through the detour of a fiction, Faulkner thus attempted to make up for a lack. And the impatience and impetus of his desire were such that he felt irresistibly carried away, propelled beyond himself by what he was to call an "ecstasy";

> . . . that other quality which The Sound and The Fury had given me . . . : that emotion definite and physical and yet nebulous to describe: that ecstasy, that eager and joyous faith and anticipation of surprise which the yet unmarred sheet beneath my hand held inviolate and unfailing, waiting for release.[10]

According to this account of his creative experience, none of his novels sprang up more spontaneously. It was indeed a unique experience, for this state of grace was never to return again. When he wrote his next book, *Sanctuary,* "there was something missing; something which The Sound and The Fury gave me and Sanctuary did not";[11] when he began *As I Lay Dying,* he knew "that it would be also missing in this case because this would be a deliberate book."[12] And with *Light in August* it had become clear to him that this "something" would elude him forever:

> I believed that I knew then why I had not recaptured that first ecstasy, and that I should never again recapture it; that whatever novels I should write in the future would be written without reluctance, but also without anticipation or joy.[13]

This quasi-trancelike condition was radically different from "the cold satisfaction"[14] he would derive from his later works; nor can it be compared to the lighthearted approach (what he used to call "fun" in his interviews) associated with his earlier novels. Are we to assume, therefore, that this experience was unmitigated creative euphoria, sweet surrender to afflatus, and that to complete his enterprise Faulkner had only to submit to the injunction of his demon? Are we to infer that *The Sound and the Fury* was written under the spell of an irrepressible and infallible inspiration? In his introduction of 1933 Faulkner emphasizes the fact that "this is the only one of the seven novels [he] wrote without any accompanying feeling of drive or effort, or any following feeling of exhaustion or relief or distaste."[15] It should be noted, however, that this assertion is flatly contradicted by some of his later statements on the novel. Thus, in one of the class conferences he held at the University of Virginia in 1957, he declared:

> It was the one that I anguished the most over, that I worked the hardest at, that even when I knew I couldn't bring it off, I still worked at it.[16]

To wonder when Faulkner told the truth is not the right question to ask, for the whole truth lies precisely in the contradiction: *The Sound and the Fury* was the child of care as well as of inspiration, of agony as well as of ecstasy.

Something of the same seeming contradiction may be detected in Faulkner's evaluation of the novel. In October 1928, after typing its final version, he told his friend and literary agent Ben Wasson: "Read this, Bud. It's a real sonofabitch."[17] Yet whenever he was questioned about *The Sound and the Fury,* he referred to it in terms of "failure."[18] True, he considered it "the most gallant, the most magnificent failure,"[19] but a failure it was all the same. There had been others before; with this book, however, Faulkner met failure in a deeper, more inescapable sense—failure as the very destiny of all artistic endeavor. What then became evident to him was the sobering truth that, as Samuel Beckett put it, "to be an artist is to fail, as no other dare fail," and that "failure is his world and the shrink from it desertion."[20] Had Faulkner remained a writer of talent only, he would never have reached that awareness. Less paradoxically than it might seem, it was when the powers of language appeared to be within his grasp as never before that he came to recognize the *necessity* of failure.

Faulkner's own description of the novel's genesis reads like a record of abortive attempts:

> That began as a short story, it was a story without plot, of some children being sent away from the house during the grandmother's funeral. They were too young to be told what was going on and they saw things only incidentally to the childish games they were playing, which was the lugubrious matter of removing the corpse from the house, etc., and then the idea struck me to see how much more I could have got out of the idea of the blind self-centeredness of

innocence typified by children, if one of those children had been truly innocent, that is, an idiot. So the idiot was born and then I became interested in the relationship of the idiot to the world that he was in but would never be able to cope with and just where could he get the tenderness, the help, to shield him in his innocence. I mean 'innocence' in the sense that God had stricken him blind at birth, that is, mindless at birth, there was nothing he could ever do about it. And so the character of his sister began to emerge, then the brother, who, that Jason (who to me represented complete evil. He's the most vicious character in my opinion I ever thought of), then he appeared. Then it needs the protagonist, someone to tell the story, so Quentin appeared. By that time I found out I couldn't possibly tell that in a short story. And so I told the idiot's experience of that day, and that was incomprehensible, even I could not have told what was going on then, so I had to write another chapter. Then I decided to let Quentin tell his version of that same day, or that same occasion, so he told it. Then there had to be the counterpoint, which was the other brother, Jason. By that time it was completely confusing. I knew that it was not anywhere near finished and then I had to write another section from the outside with an outsider, which was the writer, to tell what had happened on that particular day. And that's how that book grew. That is, I wrote that same story four times. None of them were right, but I had anguished so much that I could not throw any of it away and start over, so I printed it in the four sections. That was not a deliberate *tour de force* at all, the book just grew that way. That I was still trying to tell one story which moved me very much and each time I failed, but I had put so much anguish into it that I couldn't throw it away, like the mother that had four bad children, that she would have been better off if they had all been eliminated, but she couldn't relinquish any of them. And that's the reason I have the most tenderness for that book, because it failed four times.[21]

It is interesting to note that like many great modern novels— *Ulysses* and *The Magic Mountain* come at once to mind—*The Sound and the Fury* began by taking the form of a short story in the mind of its creator.[22] The novel form was resorted to as a *pis aller,* and the book may thus be seen as the outgrowth of an initial failure: Faulkner's incapacity to complete the narrative within the limits of the short story, which he considered "the

most demanding form after poetry."[23] What is more, failure informs the very pattern of the novel, since the four sections it consists of represent as many vain attempts at getting the story told.
Most readers will of course protest that the sum of these failures
is a success, and dismiss this confession of impotence as an excess
of modesty. Yet Faulkner's insistence on his failure was no pose.
Experience had already taught him that "being a writer is having
the worst vocation . . . a lonely frustrating work which is never as
good as you want it to be."[24]

The *Sound and the Fury* had first been the sudden opening up
of a boundless field of possibilities, the happy vertigo of a creation
still innocent and unaware of its limitations, whose movement bore
Faulkner along in quick elation, as if he were the entranced beholder of his own inventions. But once the wonder of this privileged first moment was dispelled, and the book was no longer the
bright mirage of desire but a work in progress, doubt and anxiety
took over. And when Faulkner looked back on what he had accomplished, he knew that his work was "still not finished,"[25] that
the story he so wanted to tell, the only one to his eyes that was
really worth the telling, was still to be told.

The *Sound and the Fury* was Faulkner's first great creative adventure. It assured him at once a major place in what has been,
since Hawthorne, Poe, and Melville, the great tradition of failure
in American literature. Like them and like other modern writers,
from Flaubert and Mallarmé through Joyce, Kafka, Musil, and
Beckett, it led him to the experience of the impossible. According
to Faulkner himself, failure was the common fate of all writers of
his generation: "All of us failed to match our dream of perfection."[26] Whether the blame falls on the artist or on his medium,
language, everything happens as though the writing process could
never be completed, as though it could only be the gauging of a
lack. Creation then ceases to be a triumphant gesture of assertion;
it resigns itself to be the record of its errors, trials and defeats, the
chronicle of its successive miscarriages, the inscription of the very
impossibility from which it springs.

Hence an increased self-reflexiveness. Novels tend to turn into extended metaphors for the hazardous game of their writing. Novelists no longer seek to give a semblance of order to the chaos of life by relying on well-rounded characters and well-made plots. Instead of following a logical sequential pattern, events are subordinated to the process of the fictitious discourse itself as it takes shape, or fails to do so—unfolding, infolding, progressing, regressing, turning in on itself, spiraling, endlessly doubling back on itself in a never-completed quest for form and meaning. What is told then is not a story in the traditional sense, but the venture of its telling: the novel becomes the narrative of an impossible narrative. Commenting upon *The Man Without Qualities,* Robert Musil observed that "what the story of this novel amounts to is that the story which it should tell is not told."[27] Faulkner might have said as much of *The Sound and the Fury.* The fragments of his story do not cohere into a unified scheme; they flout our expectations of order and significance. We have to accept them as such, in all their random brokenness and intriguing opaqueness, or rather we must join the author in his effort "to draw his disparate materials together, to compel his fiction into discovery of the unity of its seemingly opposed parts."[28] For *The Sound and the Fury* is as much the locus as the product of its gestation.

It grows out of and refers back to an empty center, a center which one might paradoxically call eccentric, or define—to borrow a phrase from Wallace Stevens—as a "center on the horizon,"[29] insofar as it represents at once the novel's origin and its *telos,* its generating principle and the ever-receding object of its quest. Which is to say again that the novel arises out of the emptiness of desire, in much the same way as dreams do. Like the latter, it aims at a fictive wish-fulfillment, as can be clearly seen from Faulkner's own statements on its conception and genesis. Indeed, the processes at work in the writing of *The Sound and the Fury* in many ways invite comparison with the metonymic and metaphoric procedures of dream-work. Yet it is perhaps even more enlightening to relate them to what Freud termed *Trauerarbeit,* the "work of mourning" whereby the psyche seeks to detach itself from a lost love-object. Writing, as André Green argues, "presupposes a wound, a loss, a bereavement, which the written work will transform to the point of producing its own fictitious positivity. No creation goes without effort, without a painful labor over which it carries a pseudo-victory. It can only be a pseudo-victory because it is short-lived, because it is always contested by the author himself who feels the tireless urge to start again, and hence to negate his previous achievements, or at least to reject the idea that the result, no matter how satisfactory it may have seemed, is his last word. . . . Reading and writing are a ceaseless work of mourning. If there is a pleasure to be found in the text, we always know that this pleasure is a surrogate for a lost gratification, which we are trying to recover through other means."[30]

That literature functions as a substitute is an assumption veri-fied by Faulkner's own testimony: "the beautiful and tragic little girl" whom he set out to create through the power of words was manifestly intended to fill a vacancy. In his introduction to the novel, he refers to absence ("I, who had never had a sister") as well as to mourning (". . . fated to lose my daughter in infancy"), equating in retrospect the imaginary *lack* with an actual *loss.* It is also interesting to note that the seminal image of the novel is fo-cused on the grandmother's death, and that Faulkner's initial con-cern was with the Compson children's reactions to this event:

It struck me that it would be interesting to imagine the thoughts of a group of children who were sent away from the house the day of their grandmother's funeral, their curiosity about the activity in the house, their efforts to find out what was going on, and the notions that would come into their minds.[31]

It is worth recalling, too, that *As I Lay Dying,* whose composition is chronologically close to that of *The Sound and the Fury,* revolves around a mother's death and the behavior of her family during and after the event. Mourning, then, is not only a possible key to the process of Faulkner's creation, but a motif readily traced in the novels themselves, notably those of his early maturity. One would like to know, of course, what its emergence at this point means in psycho-biographical terms; yet, apart from the hints one can find in Faulkner's comments and above all in his fiction, there is unfortunately little to gratify our curiosity. *The Sound and the Fury*, Faulkner told Maurice-Edgar Coindreau, his French translator, was written at a time when he "was beset with personal problems."[32] What these "personal problems" actually were must remain a matter of pure speculation.

What is fairly obvious, however, is that the novels written during those years, especially *The Sound and the Fury* and *As I Lay Dying*, are novels *about* lack and loss, in which desire is always intimately bound up with death. And it is clear too that they have sprung *out of* a deep sense of lack and loss—texts spun around a primal gap.

In *The Sound and the Fury* this gap is reduplicated and represented in the pathetic and intriguing figure of Caddy Compson, the lost sister. Even when the novel was still a vague project in the author's mind, "the beautiful and tragic little girl" was already there, and we find her again in the basic image which was to inform the whole book:

> . . . perhaps the only thing in literature which would ever move me very much: Caddy climbing the pear tree to look in the window at her grandmother's funeral while Quentin and Jason and Benjy and the negroes looked up at the muddy seat of her drawers.[33]

Out of this emotion-packed image the novel grew. In retrospect, one is tempted to read it as the latter's prefiguration, or at least as a foreshadowing of its dominant themes: an image of innocence confronted with what eludes and threatens it; an image of childhood caught on the brink of forbidden knowledge—evil, sex, death. To Faulkner it must have presented itself as an enigma to be questioned, a secret to be deciphered, and in this respect one should note the emphasis given in the little tableau to the act of seeing and watching: the three brothers looking up at Caddy's

muddy drawers; Caddy looking in the window at the funeral preparations. Curiosity about sex and curiosity about death prompt their
common desire to see. Yet it is certainly not fortuitous that while
the boys' curiosity comes close to sexual voyeurism, their reckless
sister is fascinated by the mystery of death. Caddy is the only one
to climb the tree of knowledge; her brothers stay timidly below
and are content with staring at the stain on her drawers. Caddy
occupies in fact an intermediary position, suspended as she is between her brothers and the intriguing scene of death—a symbolic
reminder, perhaps, of the mythic mediating function of woman
through whom, for man, passes all knowledge about the origins, all
knowledge about the twin enigmas of life and death.

One could carry the investigation further and point out the
striking parallels between this matricial scene and the "primal
fantasies" postulated by psychoanalysis. The symbolic significance
of the scene lies first of all in its insistence on perplexed watching:
hinging upon the question of origins, as all *ur*-fantasies do,[34] it
relates a desire to *know* back to the primitive, infantile wish to
see. As to the ultimate objects of the children's curiosity, they are
clearly designated as death and sex, but the point here is that in
the spatial pattern of the scene the brothers are to Caddy as Caddy
is to the window, thus suggesting a virtual equation of sex (the
muddy drawers) with death (Damuddy's funeral).[35] Equally relevant in this connection is the fact that the boys are peering at a
little girl's drawers—that which both conceals and betrays her sexual identity, that is, in psychoanalytic terms, her lack of a penis.
Freud writes in his essay on fetishism that "probably no male
human being is spared the terrifying shock of threatened castration
at the sight of the female genitals."[36] True, there is no such shock
in Faulkner's evocation of the scene; yet, curiously enough, when
in the same essay Freud accounts for the nature of certain fetishes
by "the circumstance that the inquisitive boy used to peer up the
woman's legs towards her genitals."[37] he seems to be describing
the very position of the Compson brothers in relation to Caddy.
Moreover, even though castration is not referred to explicitly, it is

suggested by the symbolic intersection of sex and death. Castration
—according to Freud the equivalent of death in the language of
the unconscious—provides a further link between the two themes.

The whole scene may thus be read as the emblem of a dual
revelation: the simultaneous discovery of the difference between
the sexes and of death. The working out of the episode of Damuddy's death in the first section of the novel definitely bears
out such a reading. Revelation (etymologically the removal of the
velum, i.e., the veil) becomes there quite literally a denudation, a
laying bare: on the day when their grandmother dies, Caddy
undresses at the branch—an act to which Quentin responds with
violence by slapping her (see 20–21), and the scene is strangely
echoed by Caddy's later allusions to the "undressing" of the dead
mare Nancy by the buzzards (see 40), and to the possibility of
an identical fate for Damuddy's corpse (see 42). Once again, sex
and death are brought into resonance through a common motif.

Considered in all its implications, the seminal scene points
unmistakably forward to what is at stake in the novel. It also sheds
light on the author's deeper motivations, for in a sense these
curious children, confronted with the mysteries of sex and death,
are the fictive delegates of that supreme voyeur who is none other
than the novelist. He too wants to see and know. Just as we, his
readers, do.

At the heart of the enigma: Caddy, a turbulent little Eve,
rash and defiant, perched on a pear tree,[38] and already significantly
associated with the Edenic innocence of trees and with mud, symbol of guilt and sin. It is her story—and that of her daughter
Quentin, Caddy's debased copy—that Faulkner wanted to tell in
The Sound and the Fury: "a tragedy of two lost women."[39] And
the privileged place this book held in his affection is inseparable
from his abiding tenderness for Caddy:

> To me she was the beautiful one, she was my heart's darling. That's
> what I wrote the book about and I used the tools which seemed to
> me the proper tools to try to tell, try to draw the picture of Caddy.[40]

It is hardly surprising that Faulkner should speak of Caddy with the accents of love.[41] Wasn't she from the outset a creation of desire? Before becoming the "real" sister of Benjy, Quentin and Jason in the novel, Caddy had been Faulkner's imaginary one, invented to make up for a lack. Yet fiction here does not play the customary game of illusion; it does not work out as a consoling substitute. For Caddy is exposed as a fiction within the fiction, her presence in the novel being rendered in such a way as to make her appear throughout as a pure figure of *absence*. Caddy, "the beautiful one," is no sooner found than she is lost again. *The Sound and the Fury* does not celebrate the (imaginary) triumph of desire, but reduplicates its necessary defeat. This novel is Faulkner's first descent into Hell, and Caddy remains his ever-elusive Eurydice.

This is why Caddy, the novelist's secret Muse and the very soul of the novel, cannot be considered the heroine of the book in any traditional sense. A chimera to the author, she never ceases to be a chimera in the novel. To deplore that she escapes satisfactory definition is a hardly relevant complaint, for she is both more and less than a "character": she is at once the focal and the vanishing point, the bewitching *image* around which everything revolves. From the writer's mind she has slipped into the narrators'; from being Faulkner's private fantasy she becomes the obsessive memory of the Compson brothers, without ever really assuming shape and substance in the space of fiction.

One might even argue that Caddy is little more than a blank counter, an empty signifier, a name in itself void of meaning and thus apt to receive any meaning. Her function within the novel's semantic structure could be compared to that of a joker in a game of cards: the word "Caddy" assumes meaning only in relation to the contextual network within which it occurs, and since, from one section to another, it is drawn into different verbal environments, woven into different textures, it is invested with ever-renewed significances. Caddy is a sign, with all the arbitrariness of the sign, and Faulkner's keen awareness of the chancy and shifting relationships between word and thing, language and meaning, is attested on the very first page of the novel by his deliberate punning on "caddie" and "Caddy."[42] The homophony is confusing to Benjy, who mistakes "caddie" for the name of his beloved sister, and so it is, ironically enough, to the reader who, at this point, realizes that the setting is a golf course, but is not yet in a position to understand what "caddie" evokes in Benjy's mind and why it makes him moan with grief. As most openings in fiction do, the initial golf course scene in *The Sound and the Fury* serves the purpose of establishing the rules of the game to be played by the readers. By exploiting from the outset the polysemy of words, Faulkner disorients the reader, frustrates his expectations, alerts him to the trickeries and duplicities of language, as if to warn him that the world he is about to enter is not *his* world. The words used in Benjy's monologue may be simple, but their familiar surfaces soon turn out to be extremely deceptive. We must learn the alphabet and grammar of his idiolect before we can begin to discover what his fumbling speech is all about.

Words are an inexhaustible source of ambiguities and confusions, so that the communication they permit is always liable to misapprehensions. Words are signs everyone assembles in transitory patterns and fills with private significances that often make sense for him alone. What "caddie" means for the golfers is different from what it means for Benjy; what it means for Benjy is different from what it means for us. Yet in its active emptiness and its extreme plasticity, language possesses formidable powers, and the random utterance of two syllables is enough to arouse Benjy's anguish and grief.

Caddy is just a name, or the deceptive echo of a name. On the day when the novel begins—April 7, 1928—the person to whom it refers has been missing from the Compson family for many years. Benjy's moaning points at once to an absence, an absence which the perception of anything however remotely related to his lost sister instantly quickens and thickens in his vacant mind. To Benjy, Caddy is the nearest of absences. His memory has no memories. He cannot remember; he cannot forget. For him it is

Twilight   April 7, 1928

Through the fence, between the curling flower spaces, I could see them hitting. They came on toward where the flag was and I went along the fence. I passed where T. P. was leaning against the flower tree. There they stopped hitting where the flag was and they went to the table and hit again and went on. Along the I went along beside the fence and T. P. came away from the flower tree.

"Here, Caddy," ~~anoushe~~ one of them said.

They boy came to here and the one took there he hit again and went along the fence. Then the fence stopped and I held to it and watched them go away.

"Hush up that moaning," T. P. said. "They'll be some more coming by in a minute." They went on away, hitting again.

"Hush it up, now," T. P. said. So I hushed, and went back along the fence to where the flag was.

"Come on." T. P. said. "Les go down to the branch, where they playing."

I held to the fence and watched the flag, and the pasture.

"Stop up that moaning," T. P. said. "~~If Benjamin~~ I cant make these come back, just for you to watch them. Come on, les go down to the branch. Maybe we can find one they balls. Here, how they is. Way over yonder. Look." It came to the fence and pointed through it. "See them? They aint coming back here. Come on, now."

We went along the fence and came to the ~~other~~ ~~fence~~ place, where our shadows were. My shadow was higher up the fence than Luster's. ~~The~~ We came to the broken place and went through it.

~~"Wait," Caddy said. "You're caught on a nail." She uncaught me and we crawled through.~~

"Wait a minute," Luster said. "You caught on that nail again. Cant you never crawl through this place without snagging on that nail?"

Caddy uncaught me and we crawled through. "Uncle Maury said to not let anybody see us, so we better stoop over. Stoop over, Benjy. Like this, see?" We stooped over and crossed the garden, where the flowers rasped and rattled against us. The ground was hard. We climbed the fence, where the pigs were grunting and snuffing. The ground was hard, churned and knotted.

"Keep your hands in your pockets," Caddy said. "Or they'll freeze got froze. You dont want your hands froze on Xmas, do you?"

Versh said. "It want to go outdoors."

"Let him go," Uncle Maury said.

"It's too cold," Mother said. "He'd better stay in. Benjamin. You Benjamin. If you ~~You Benjamin,~~ Mother said.

"It wont hurt him," Uncle Maury said.

"You, Benjamin," Mother said. "If you dont be good, you'll have to go to the kitchen."

"Mammy say to keep him out the kitchen today," Versh said. "She say she got all that cooking to do."

"Let him go, Caroline," Uncle Maury said. "You'll worry yourself sick over him."

"I know it," Mother said. "It's a judgment on me. I sometimes wonder ~~why~~"

~~"I know, I know," Uncle Maury said, "Keep him up good, boy, and take him out for a while." Uncle Maury went away, Versh got went away.~~

~~"Mother, Mother said. "You can get out"~~

"Please Mother," Mother said. "We're trying to get you well so fast as we can." ~~ne~~

Versh put my overcoat and cap and ~~ourselves~~ on and we went out. ~~There~~ Uncle Maury put the bottle back ~~~~

"I know, I know," Uncle Maury said. "You must keep your strength up. I'll make you a toddy."

as though Caddy had only departed a few seconds ago: her trace is forever fresh, and the merest sensation—something seen, heard, smelled—recalls her presence with agonizing immediacy. In surprisingly similar ways, Caddy also haunts her brother Quentin, holding him in her spell, leaving him no rest and no escape except in death. And even to Jason, for all his declared indifference and contempt, she will be a festering wound.

Yet at the same time—precisely because she is nothing but a haunting memory—Caddy remains to the end a being out of reach, an elusive figure not unlike Proust's "creatures of flight." She is the presence of what is not there, the imperious call of absence, and it is from her tantalizing remoteness that she holds her uncanny power over those she has left.

All the scenes out of the past which come to beset memory both bring her closer and remove her further away. Of Caddy nothing remains but a series of snapshots, vivid and unreal, in which her fleeting image is forever fixed:

> Only she was running already when I heard it. In the mirror she was running before I knew what it was. That quick, her train caught up over her arm she ran out of the mirror like a cloud, her veil swirling in long glints her heels brittle and fast clutching her dress onto her shoulder with the other hand, running out of the mirror . . . (100).

Barely glimpsed, Caddy the (no longer "unravish'd") bride at once vanishes, and all that a glance could grasp was a silent rush reflected in a mirror. What lingers in the memory is at best the reflection of a reflection.

Or consider this other obsessive image of the lost sister, likewise linked to an event that Quentin cannot forget, the loss of her virginity: Caddy no longer caught running away, but immobilized in the silent suddenness of her appearance: "One minute she was standing by the door" (98).[43] Whether Caddy's silhouette is fleetingly reflected in a mirror or emerges unexpectedly in the doorway, there is each time the same disturbing oscillation between absence and presence, the same paradoxical sense of receding proximity or close remoteness.

It is noteworthy too that Caddy is associated time and again with the immaterial and the impalpable: reflections (79, 95, 100, 186), shadows (100, 192), moonlight (100), a cloud (100), a breath (186), "a long veil like shining wind" (47; see also 48, 100). Caddy's evanescence in space constantly parallels her inaccessibility in time. Not that she is ever etherealized into a conventionally "poetic" creature. But insofar as she must remain the ambiguous and evasive object of desire and memory, she can be approached and apprehended only in oblique ways. Caddy cannot be described; she can only be *circumscribed*, conjured up through the suggestive powers of metaphor and metonymy. A realistic rendering of the character is out of the question. Only the ruses and indirections of poetic discourse can do justice to the burning absence which Caddy "embodies" in the novel.

To the very extent that Caddy is literally nowhere, she is metaphorically everywhere. Her presence/absence becomes diffused all over the world, pointing, like so many feminine figures of Faulkner's earlier and later work, to an elemental complicity between Woman and the immemorial Earth. Her swiftness and lightness relate her to the wind; her vital warmth to "the bright smooth shapes" of fire;[44] her muddy drawers and treelike odor[45] to the fecundity and foulness of the land. Yet above all Caddy is the most enticing and most pathetic of Faulkner's nymphs. In the entire novel there is scarcely a scene in which Caddy does not appear in close conjunction with *water.* It is in the branch near the Compson house that she wets her dress and drawers on the day of Damuddy's death (19–22); it is in the same branch that Quentin and Caddy wash off the stinking mud of the pig trough after the Natalie incident (172);[46] and it is there again that Quentin finds his sister, sitting in the water, one summer evening, after the family has discovered her affair with Dalton Ames (186). Lastly, in the third section, Jason remembers her standing over her father's grave in a drenching rain (251). Throughout the novel, water is Caddy's element, and like Caddy herself, it is drawn into an extremely ambiguous symbolic pattern. In the branch scenes it is primarily the lustral water of purification rituals, and it would be easy to supply further illustrations of its cleansing function: Caddy, at fourteen, washing off the perfume to quiet Benjy (50); Caddy, washing her mouth after kissing Charlie in the swing (58); and, finally, Benjy pulling at his sister's dress, dragging her into the bathroom after the loss of her virginity (84–85). After these ritual ablutions, Caddy "smells like trees" again, except in the last scene where Benjy keeps on crying even after Caddy has bathed herself.

Water, however, is not only a symbol of purity. If it possesses a restorative power, at least in the eyes of the novel's characters, and if Faulkner at times suggests its function in Christian baptism (it rains on the night Benjy's name is changed), there are also many significant intimations of its erotic quality. Bathing, in particular, as evoked in the novel, seems to prompt a kind of soft, sensuous, almost sensual intimacy between water and flesh, and to prurient eyes the spectacle of this tender complicity may become both a scandal and a temptation. In the insidious caress of water, in the way it reveals the body in its embrace, there is something all but immodest which, even in the early childhood scene at the branch, disturbs and alarms young Quentin. For him, who then begins to act as guardian of Caddy's "honor," the sight of his sister and of the drenched dress clinging to her body is no longer an innocent spectacle. And when he slaps her for having undressed, he introduces by this very gesture the first suspicion of evil into a hitherto intact childhood world.

In Quentin's reminiscences and reveries, flesh and sex are repeatedly linked to suggestions of dampness and fluidity, and as the hour of his death draws nearer, it almost seems as if the waters were slowly rising, submerging his mind and memory, bringing him ever closer to the instant of his drowning. Thus, in the long

breathless memory sequence in which he relives his poignant encounter with Caddy at the branch and his subsequent meeting with
Dalton Ames near the bridge (185–203), water saturates the
whole atmosphere with a silent drizzle. Quentin inhales the smell
of the rain, breathes in the scent of honeysuckle wafted on the
humid warmth of twilight. And out of all this mugginess emerges
the body of his nymph-sister—water made flesh:

> . . . I ran down the hill in that vacuum of crickets like a breath
> travelling across a mirror she was lying in the water her head on the
> sand spit the water flowing about her hips there was a little more
> light in the water her skirt half saturated flopped along her flanks to
> the waters motion in heavy ripples going nowhere renewed them-
> selves of their own movement I stood on the bank I could smell the
> honeysuckle on the water gap the air seemed to drizzle with honey-
> suckle and with the rasping of crickets a substance you could feel
> on the flesh (186).

As in Faulkner's early sketch "Nympholepsy," woman's body—
"her hips," "her flanks"—is associated with running water, and
as Quentin watches his sister lying there, he cannot help thinking
back to the day long past when as a little girl she had soiled her
dress and drawers: "do you remember the day damuddy died when
you sat down in the water in your drawers" (188). Quentin himself is aware of the symbolic relationship between the two scenes;
in retrospect the childhood episode acquires a premonitory meaning, Caddy's muddy drawers becoming a symbol of her physical
and moral defilement, of what Quentin considers to be an indelible
stain on her honor: her fall from sexual innocence. This irreme-
diable loss is the focal point of Quentin's obsession, an obsession
eagerly feeding on every sense impression: the sight of flowing
water, the smell of rain and honeysuckle, the chirp of crickets,
shadows, warmth, moisture, everything melts into "a substance
you could feel on the flesh." It is clear that Quentin's obsession, as
it is described here, is by no means the abstract, disembodied mania
for which it has been all too often mistaken by critics. Experienced
at first in the sultry profusion of immediate sensations, the trau-

matic shock is relived by Quentin's memory with hallucinatory vividness and intensity.

There is no Proustian reunion, though, for Faulkner's hero. Caddy risen out of the past through the sortileges of memory is not Caddy recaptured. Memory only serves to exacerbate a sense of irrevocable loss. The past is recollected in fever and pain, never in tranquillity, and the camera obscura of memory turns out to be a torture chamber. It is never a shelter; happy memories have no place in it. As far back as it can reach, Quentin's memory encounters a Caddy *already* all but lost: as if she had resented her brother's jealous vigilance from the outset and were impatient to flee from the prison of innocence in which he would forever keep her, she is always seen rebelling against his demands, always on the point of running away. In this respect, the scene of the muddy drawers —one of the earliest among the childhood incidents recalled in his monologue—is equally prophetic: it marks the beginning of the ineluctable movement which is to separate him from his sister. From this childhood scene to Caddy's wedding, nearly all the fragments of the past which erupt into Quentin's mind are related to Caddy's gradual "betrayal," and each of his painful memories reenacts one moment in the process of her desertion.

Presence in absence, nearness in distance, nothing perhaps better sums up the paradox of Quentin's haunted memory than *odor.* A subtle emanation from things and beings, odor, as Jean-Paul Sartre writes, is "a disembodied body, vaporized, remaining entire in itself, yet turned into volatile essence."[47] Like memory, it is a diffuse presence, a felt absence, a tantalizing intimation of being. Like symbols, it acts by indirection, through allusion and suggestion: to the extent that it always has the power to evoke something other than itself, to point an absence, one might consider it a "natural" metaphor. Small wonder, then, that the fragrance of *honeysuckle* is the most pregnant and most poignant symbol in the Quentin section.

Quentin associates Caddy with the odor of honeysuckle, just

as Benjy associated her with the smell of trees. But whereas in the first section "she smelled like trees" functions as an index to Caddy's sexual innocence and vanishes as soon as the latter is compromised (see, for example, the perfume incident, 48–51), the meaning of honeysuckle in Quentin's monologue changes as Caddy changes, and its scent is irremediably corrupted when it comes to reek in Quentin's nostrils as the smell of her sex and sin. It is noteworthy that the term "honeysuckle," which occurs approximately thirty times in section 2, is nowhere as frequent as in the scene immediately following Quentin's discovery of his sister's loss of virginity (185–203): the scent of honeysuckle then becomes the pivot in a shifting complex of sense impressions. After blending into the uncertain grayness of twilight (119), it combines with the humidity of the atmosphere (189), "coming up in damp waves" (192) or drizzling like the rain (191). Through the cross-play of synaesthesia, honeysuckle is made to encompass and condense the entire field of sensory experience: something at once smelled, seen, and felt, it suffuses the whole scene. Yet, while metamorphosing and expanding across space, the smell also seems to flow back to Caddy as to its source, and Quentin refers to it as though it were a carnal secretion on the surface of her skin, a substance exuded from her flesh: ". . . the smell of honeysuckle upon her face and throat" (183); ". . . it was on her face and throat like paint" (188). Quentin thus comes to resent the cloying odor as a disturbing indiscretion, an almost obscene exuding of the innermost secrets of the flesh. Associated with Caddy's lovemaking in the swing by the cedars and eventually equated with Caddy herself, it symbolizes in his mind "the bittersweet mystery of sisterly sex"[48] as well as the unbearable scandal of its violation. It quickens his obsession, becomes the very emblem of his anguish and torment: ". . . after the honeysuckle got all mixed up in it the whole thing came to symbolize night and unrest" (211). In his confrontation with Caddy about Dalton Ames, his sister reminds him that he once liked the smell (190); now he hates it, cursing "that damn honeysuckle" (185; see also 190, 191). So hateful has it become to him that it even oppresses him physically, making him gasp for breath: ". . . I had to pant to get any air at all out of that thick grey honeysuckle" (188). The sweet "honey" of sisterhood, which Quentin so avidly "suckled" in his childish greed, has thickened into a suffocating substance, and now has the bitter taste of loss.

Trees, water, twilight, honeysuckle—all the nature imagery related to Caddy, so far from calling attention to itself as symbolic, seems to grow out of the soil of subjective experience while being at the same time inextricably bound up with the sensible world. It never hardens into the fixed patterns of allegory; its mobile and manifold symbolism originates in the dynamic exchanges between a self and its concrete environment. If some of these images run through several sections, they can never be separated from the singular voice in whose discourse they occur: they reflect the changing moods or the stubborn obsessions of a particular consciousness; they belong to the shifting landscapes of an individual mind.

Yet the central ambiguity to which all these images ultimately refer is that of Caddy herself. Caddy, as we have already seen, is first and foremost an image; she exists only in the minds and memories of her brothers. We can find out what she represents for Benjy, Quentin, and Jason; we never discover what she actually is. Hence her many and contradictory faces: she is in turn sister and mother, virgin and whore, angel and demon; she at once embodies fecundity and foulness, the nostalgia for innocence and the call to corruption, the promise of life and the vertigo of death. She is in fact what woman has always been in man's imagination: the figure par excellence of the Other, a blank screen onto which he projects both his desires and his fears, his love and his hate. And insofar as this Other is a myth and a mirage, a mere fantasy of the Self, it is bound to be a perpetual deceit and an endless source of disappointment. Caddy, to borrow a phrase from Paul Claudel, is "the promise that cannot be kept, and her grace consists in nothing else."[49]

Even so, she is more than the sum of these fantasy images. Faulkner's triumph in creating Caddy is that her elusive figure eventually transcends the abstract categories and rigid patterns in which her brothers attempt to imprison her, just as she escapes any facile sentimentalizing or demonizing on the author's part. Not that the reader is enabled to infer a "true" picture of Caddy from the information he is given in the novel. There is little doubt, of course, that she possesses the vitality, the courage, the capacity for love and compassion which her self-centered brothers and parents so sadly lack.[50] It is quite obvious, too, that she is both the tragic victim of her family and the unwitting agent of its doom. But to focus exclusively on Caddy's assumed psychology or to dwell at length on her moral significance is to miss the point. Caddy was elusive to her creator; so she is to her brothers in the novel, and so she must remain to the reader. She cannot be assessed according to the same criteria as the other characters. However complex her characterization (and it is indeed more complex than has been generally acknowledged), Caddy belongs in the last resort to another space, to what might be called the novel's utopia. "The true life is absent," Rimbaud wrote. In *The Sound and the Fury* Caddy is a pathetic emblem of that desired other life, while her fate poignantly confirms its impossibility in a world of alienation and disease.

Henry James thought that "a story-teller who aims at anything more than a fleeting success has no right to tell an ugly story unless he knows its beautiful counterpart."[51] The story of the Compsons is indeed "an ugly story"; Caddy, the daughter and sister of the imagination, the figure projected by "the heart's desire," is "its beautiful counterpart." Let us remember, however, that from the very beginning she was conceived of as "a beautiful *and* tragic little girl." Caddy is a dream of beauty wasted and destroyed. Her presence/absence at the center and periphery of the novel signals the unfulfillment of the writer's desire as well as the inescapable incompletion of his work. Caddy's beauty is the beauty of failure.

3

Benjy, or The Agony
of Dispossession

Quand les enfants commencent à parler,
ils pleurent moins.

JEAN-JACQUES ROUSSEAU

Echoing its Shakespearean title, the first section of *The
Sound and the Fury* presents itself as "a tale told by an idiot."
One would perhaps do well to keep the phrase between quotation
marks and to bear in mind its literary source, for if it applies to
Benjy's monologue, it does so literarily, not literally. Nothing was
further removed from Faulkner's intentions than to provide an
accurate record of what really goes on in an idiot's mind, and
his superb indifference to the tenets of naturalism is attested by
contradictions too obvious not to be deliberate: Benjy is dumb,
and yet he speaks; he is deaf, and yet he can hear. Which is to say
that he belongs with the idiots of literature, not with those of the
asylum. Like any character in fiction, but less hypocritically than

those one encounters in the realistic novel, Benjy is a set of conventions functioning in a verbal construct. Furthermore, his speech
immediately calls attention to itself as a literary artifact. From the
outset, the reader is jolted into the uncomfortable awareness of
a *text* that refuses to fit into his prior reading experience. Instead
of allowing us to settle cozily in the familiar world of make-believe
fiction, Faulkner points at once to the specific premises of his own
creation, compelling us to find out for ourselves by what rules it
is governed. Interestingly enough, it is in the first section that his
writing is at its most experimental, that the most radical departure
from the traditional novel occurs. There are modern novelists who
begin by lulling the reader into a false sense of security, and then
make him gradually realize the arbitrariness of their fictions. Faulkner's strategy here is far more abrupt and aggressive: the shock
comes without delay, and nowhere in the novel is the effect of
estrangement or "defamiliarization" (what the Russian formalists
called *ostranenie*) sharper than at its beginning. Benjy's monologue is not merely a technical *tour de force;* it is also a *coup de
force,* a brutal summons to give up our reading habits.

Not that section 1 defeats comprehension. Most sentences in
it are perfectly grammatical, and, taken one by one, nearly all of
them make sense. Moreover, reported conversation (by people of
normal intelligence) occupies more than half of Benjy's monologue—a monologue which, strictly speaking, is no monologue at
all but rather a *polylogue,* a mosaic or patchwork of many voices
seemingly recorded at random by an unselective mind.[1] Yet Benjy's
own idiolect stands out the more startlingly for being interwoven
with the speech of others. Throughout the section it forms a closed
system, a strictly private code, designed to suggest the functioning
of an abnormally limited consciousness. Privacy, in this case, does
not mean distortion and obfuscation, as it will in Quentin's monologue. In point of fact, what makes the Benjy section so disturbingly odd is rather an excess of simplicity. The idiot's vocabulary
is restricted to a minimum;[2] his syntax conforms to most elemen-
tary patterns and evinces an extremely rigid word order.[3] As Irena

Kaluza has pointed out, the typical Benjy sentence comes very close to what transformational grammar describes as *kernel sentences:* "simple, declarative, active, with no complex verb or noun phrase."[4] The impression of simplicity is further strengthened by the repetitiveness of the diction and by the systematic flattening out of the relationships between clause units, most of which are either asyndetic (mere juxtaposition) or paratactical (mere coordination). At first sight, there is indeed nothing to relieve the stark uniformity of Benjy's speech but the recurrence of a few phrasal motifs (e.g., "Caddy smelled like trees") and a number of unusual lexical combinations (e.g., "my hands saw it").

It is clear, then, that Benjy's code is primarily established through a process of ruthless *reduction.* Lexical variation and syntactic modulation are kept within extremely narrow bounds; language is consistently stripped to its barest essentials, generating a discourse as far removed from the formality of literary tradition as from the looser patterns of living speech. This type of discourse is usually referred to as "stream-of-consciousness"; in the present case, "stasis of consciousness" would probably be a more relevant phrase. It is true that we are allowed to travel through Benjy's kaleidoscopic mind and insofar as the logic of his mental processes is that of chance associations, his speech may be categorized as "interior monologue." Yet its overall effect is one of inflexible rigidity and ceaseless fragmentation rather than free, spontaneous flux. Benjy's words look fragile and frozen, as if they arose out of a wintry silence. They form sentences without ever developing into sequences of sustained reverie, let alone articulate thought. Each sentence hardens into a discrete unit, a brittle concretion of meaning, standing by itself in utter isolation, and as they accumulate, they become a random collection of atoms—all equal, adding together, never adding up.

The movement of Benjy's speech is most often one of slow dispersion, so steady and so even as to acquire at times the hypnotic quality of massive immobility. What is thus achieved is a very singular *monotone,* whereby the plurality of voices echoed in his monologue are muted and homogenized into a distant murmur. Faulkner's technique of linguistic reduction ends by creating an uncanny sense of neutrality (as befits a gelding), as though the section developed in a vacuum and were floating free of speaker, author and reader alike.

This impression of sustained flatness is mitigated, however, by subtle changes of pitch and tempo. On closer inspection, Benjy's speech even appears to follow a carefully modulated dramatic curve. The section begins at an almost leisurely pace with extended narrative units devoted to relatively minor incidents (3–15: the delivery of Uncle Maury's message to Mrs. Patterson on December 23, 1900; a trip to the cemetery in 1912). After reverting to the present (15–19), it then moves on to a fairly detailed account of the day of Damuddy's death in 1898 (19–47), interrupted with increasing frequency by memories of Caddy's wedding (23–26, 44–45, 45–46, 47–48) and of three other deaths in the family (33–35: Quentin; 35–38, 40–42: Mr. Compson; 93–40: Roskus). There follows a sequence of thematically related episodes centering on the process of Caddy's growing alienation from Benjy: Caddy uses perfume (48–51); Benjy must sleep alone at thirteen (51–52, 53–54); Caddy with Charlie in the swing (56, 57–58), the latter incident leading up to the parallel present scene with her daughter Quentin (58–62). Benjy's memories then focus more and more sharply on the agony of loss: the episode of his assault on the Burgess girl (62–64) is associated with his desire for Caddy's return as well as with the nightmare of his subsequent castration; the long scene of his renaming (68–88), on the other hand, is above all a poignant reminder of his sister's love and kindness. Moreover, the quick alternation of past and present scenes emphasizes the magnitude of his losses: Quentin's treatment of Benjy is contrasted with Caddy's; the happy memories linked with the name-change scene are set over against the atmosphere of nasty bickering prevailing in the Compson family under Jason's reign. As the past erupts into the present with ever-increasing urgency, Benjy's mind is set spinning. The feverish shuttling back and forth between his memories suggests an emotional crescendo, climaxing eventually in what is to Benjy as much as to Quentin the most unbearable of all memories: Caddy's loss of sexual innocence (84–85).

Beneath the still surface of Benjy's speech we can thus detect a wild undercurrent of emotional intensities, and its presence is intermittently felt in the very texture of his language. Whenever moments of extreme affective tension or utter mental confusion are recorded, the blank and rigid orderliness of Benjy's syntax breaks down. Words then begin to dash and crash into one another; ellipsis combines with staccato repetition to produce the kind of breathless and pathetic stammering we find, for example, in Benjy's account of his drunkenness on the day of Caddy's wedding (24), or in his recalling of the fateful incident with the schoolgirls (63–64).

The nature and limits of Benjy's language designate the nature and limits of his world. There is no central *I* through whose agency his speech might be ordered and made meaningful; in like manner, there is no sense of identity to make his experience *his*. The severe restrictions imposed on his linguistic abilities reveal the extent of his mental deficiencies. Benjy is an idiot, and all that is left to him is sensory and emotional response, perception without intellection, and a capacity for the raw intensities of pleasure and pain. He is humanity at its most elemental and most archaic, the zero degree of consciousness. His quasi-tropistic reactions to the conditions he meets are in fact all he *is*.

Benjy's monologue sends us back to the confusions of the pre-subjective, pre-logic, animistic world of infancy. Since there is no distinction between *I* and *non-I*, there can be no boundary between inner and outer space, and nothing to focalize what Benjy does, perceives or suffers. Hence the startling *eccentricity* of all his experiences: sensations, perceptions, and emotions are accorded exactly the same status as objects and occurrences in the outer world; everything is *out there,* in scattered fragments, and Benjy is at best the passive and uncomprehending watcher of what is happening to him.[5] His body is not any more his own than his mind; each part of it seems to act autonomously: his throat makes sounds of its own (48), his hand "[tries] to go back to his mouth" (72), and even the pain of burning is something external to him:

> I put my hand out to where the fire had been.
> "Catch him." Dilsey said. "Catch him back."
> My hand jerked back and I put it in my mouth and Dilsey caught me. I could still hear the clock between my voice. Dilsey reached back and hit Luster on the head. My voice was going loud every time (72).

Benjy's monologue is punctuated with cries of pain and his reactions to external stimuli are throughout extremely sharp. Yet his pain is nobody's pain; just pain, a blind discharge of impersonal emotion.

The world reflected by the Benjy section possesses a kind of oneness in that it seems to admit of no distinction, no differentiation, no distance. At first reading at least, it presses down upon us with all the weight of its *in-difference.* It does not take us long, however, to realize that Benjy's world is in fact a fractured world, a world in the process of falling asunder. There is nothing here to suggest the plenitude of experience which the Romantic tradition (mistakenly) attributes to primitives and small children. Even though Benjy is in many ways at one with his environment, his relationship with it is by no means symbiotic; and since, on the other hand, his condition prevents him from ever gaining any hold on it, he is bound to be the plaything of circumstance. Benjy is the quintessential victim, nakedly exposed to whatever blow fate or chance aims at him. Not that his life is one of unrelieved and uninterrupted misery. What gives it its basic rhythm is rather a perpetual oscillation between serenity and anguish. Benjy's sensibility knows no transition, no in-between, only abrupt switches

from contentment to pain, from pain to contentment, invariably
signaled by crying or silence:

> I tried to pick up the flowers. Luster picked them up, and they went
> away. I began to cry (66).

> "What you howling for now." Luster said. "Look there." The fire
> was there. I hushed (70) . . . the fire went away. I began to cry
> (71).

> "Here." Dilsey said. "Stop crying now." She gave me the slipper,
> and I hushed (74).

> "Take that cushion away, like I told you." Mother said. "He must
> learn to mind." The cushion went away. "Hush, Benjy." Caddy
> said (78).

All these scenes exemplify the same pattern. Jimson weed, fire,
the cushion and Caddy's slipper are things which Benjy likes.
When they "go away," he starts crying or howling; when they
"come back" (another recurrent phrase in his monologue), he
"hushes." Things and persons come and go, materialize out of
nowhere and vanish with magic suddenness: the jimson weed is
there or gone, and it is the same with the cushion (78), the bowl
(86) or any other object. Which is to say that there is at least
one distinction registered by Benjy's mind: the opposition of
presence and absence. They are the two categories into which his
whole universe is divided, and they make all the *difference*.
    Benjy's acute and unfailing responsiveness to the disappearance
and return of objects brings to mind the symbolic *fort/da* game
described by Freud in *Beyond the Pleasure Principle*. One day
Freud watched a little boy playing with a wooden reel: "What he
did was to hold the reel by the string and very skilfully throw it
over the edge of his curtained cot, so that it disappeared into it,
at the same time uttering his expressive 'o-o-o-o' [standing for
'fort' = 'gone']. He then pulled the reel out of the cot again by
the string and hailed its reappearance with a joyful 'da' ['there']."[6]
Freud's interpretation of the game is that by staging the disap-

pearance and return of the reel the little boy symbolized his "great cultural achievement—the instinctual renunciation . . . which he had made in allowing his mother to go away without protesting."[7] This is precisely what Benjy fails to do: he cannot renounce; he can only howl in impotent protest.

The pathos of his destiny lies largely in this total inability to master absence, especially the absence of the one person who matters to him: Caddy. His sister was not merely the focus of his life; she "was the whole world to him,"[8] so that with her departure his whole world has dissolved into emptiness. For Benjy all possible forms of presence and absence relate back to, and are metaphors of, the presence and absence of Caddy, and it is of course not fortuitous that all the objects mentioned above are in some way associated with her.

Everything in the first section hinges upon the brother-sister relationship, and as much could be said of the second and even, albeit to a lesser extent, of the third. For the first time in Faulkner's fiction this relationship becomes both thematic focus and structuring principle. The brothers—Benjy, Quentin, Jason—form the plural *subject* of the narration; the sister, as we have already seen, turns out to be its primary *object*. The former are present through their *voices;* the latter is the absent/present figure ceaselessly *evoked*—or *invoked*—in their monologues. Thematically, the brother-sister relation is just as central: it exemplifies the ambiguous relation of desire to its lost object, while functioning at the same time as a paradigm for most of the tensions and conflicts represented in the novel.[9]

The primacy of this relationship is no doubt as evident in Quentin's as in Benjy's section, yet it is in the opening monologue that its basic significance can be most easily grasped. For in the idiot's mind there are none of the obliquities and evasions, none of the ruses and rationalizations that characterize the (necessarily bad) conscience of the adult. Here again Faulkner's reductive procedures are at work: the first section reduces the novel's thematic concerns to a "kernel sentence," and in a sense the two following sections are merely elaborations of what Benjy at once exposes with absolute candor.

His monologue leads us straightaway into a world ruled over by what Faulkner was later to call "the blind self-centeredness of innocence."[10] Condemned to incurable childishness, unaware of good and evil,[11] Benjy has no links with his environment but those arising from his immediate needs. If infancy and innocence are interchangeable concepts, he is indeed an innocent. One should not forget, however, that the date of his monologue is that of his thirty-third birthday. If innocence has been preserved in him, it has been so at the terrible cost of degeneracy. Trapped in an adult body, his indestructible childhood, so far from being grace, exhibits the grotesque grimace of abjection.

What childhood means for Benjy is first and foremost a condition of utter helplessness, that is, of total dependence upon others. His wishes make no compromise with reality; his is the child's all-demanding desire as well as its radical impotence to achieve its aims. Benjy's predicament could be summed up in a single word: *lack*. His very being must be described in negative terms: self-less, devoid of intelligence and memory, deaf and dumb. Even the voice we hear is in fact only that in which he would speak if he could (*infans* = speechless).

It is remarkable too that most scenes in which he is directly implicated are scenes of dispossession. One of the earliest memories recalled in the section is the rainy November day in 1900 when his name was changed from Maury to Benjamin[12] at his mother's request: as often in Faulkner, the name change suggests a loss of identity, the more so as it is linked to Benjy's repudiation by Mrs. Compson. Another reminder of dispossession is the loss of the Compson pasture, sold by his father to finance Quentin's year at Harvard and to pay for Caddy's wedding. And eventually, after his assault on a schoolgirl, Benjy will even lose his sex.

The supreme loss endured by Benjy, however, was the loss of his beloved sister. Admittedly, he does not suffer from it in the same way as Quentin, and as he continues waiting for his sister at the gate, he hardly knows whom he is waiting for. In Faulkner's own words, Caddy, "that fierce, courageous being . . . was to him a touch and a sound that maybe he heard on any golf links and a smell like trees."[13] All he knows, or rather senses, is that someone or something is missing. Still, the seesaw movement, touched off by the merest sensation, which, again and again, tugs Benjy's mind back to the Caddy of his childhood, seems to bespeak an inarticulate obsession with a past forever vanished.

Critics have generally emphasized the timelessness of Benjy's vision, and so has Faulkner himself: "To that idiot, time was not a continuation, it was an instant, there was no yesterday and no tomorrow, it all is this moment, it all is (now) to him. He cannot distinguish between what was last year and what will be tomorrow, he doesn't know whether he dreamed it, or saw it."[14] To contest the general validity of this statement would be of course absurd, yet the question of Benjy's relationship with time deserves perhaps closer attention, for it is surely more complex than appears at first sight.[15] To begin with, his present lacks the fullness of presence. If Benjy existed, as has been argued all too often, in the perfect enclosure of an atemporal world, it would be hard to understand why the very sound of Caddy's name makes him whimper with grief. "The witless know only loss and absence," the narrator of *A Fable* remarks, "never bereavement."[16] But to sense loss takes at the very least a subliminal awareness of the difference between *was* and *is*. And if Benjy is not granted a minimal sense of the future, how to explain his waiting at the gate after Caddy's departure? True, it is routine waiting, one of Benjy's immutable rituals; it is waiting nonetheless, although, paradoxically, it is waiting for a return of the past, a way of negating time. Benjy has no consciousness of time, but his consciousness is in time. And if to him there is nothing before and nothing after the instant, this "nothing" forms a kind of halo around the present moment, contaminating it with its nothingness. Not unlike Quentin's, Benjy's present is in fact extremely thin ice, cracking at every step, and both brothers experience it as a perpetual falling or sinking in. Rather than in a seamless present, Benjy may be said to live in a temporal limbo, a no man's land *between* past and present, an empty but haunted space in which they echo each other in bewildering and agonizing confusion. Or one might liken his "time" to a creviced and pitted terrain, with holes that are so many traps laid by the past.

Benjy is the prisoner of his past, and forever exiled from it, forever "waiting at the gate." His whole monologue, erratic as it is, is like Quentin's a stubborn quest for the long-lost sister, or at any rate for the warmth, security, and order she represented to him.[17] A futile quest: if his memories of Caddy's tenderness are as vivid as ever, they give him no lasting comfort; and if he is occasionally allowed to relive past moments of happiness, it is remarkable that his speech dwells more readily on all the incidents presaging the final loss of his sister. Many of the remembered scenes record the progress of Caddy's sexual maturation and of her consequent estrangement from him: Benjy recalls the day when Caddy for the first time put on perfume and did not smell anymore like trees (48–51); he recalls the evening when he saw her in the swing with Charlie (56–58); he remembers being thirteen and Dilsey telling him he is too old to sleep with his sister (51–54); he remembers pulling at Caddy's dress to get her into the bathroom after she lost her virginity (84–85), and crying when he saw her in her wedding veil on the day of her marriage (23–26, 44–48). Most of the events recalled in the first section are either anticipations or consequences of Benjy's major loss, like the death of his brother Quentin and his own sexual mutilation. The image of Caddy projected by Benjy's monologue is primarily that of the beloved and loving sister; yet, because of her desertion and all its fateful effects, she can also be seen already as the unwitting instrument of disaster and the main cause of Benjy's present misery.

What the first section makes obvious, too, is the extent to which the brother-sister relationship is patterned on that of child and mother. For Benjy, Caddy is definitely a mother surrogate; it is she who replaced Mrs. Compson, the failing mother, and of all the family she alone appears to have cared for his well-being and to have given him genuine love. But for Caddy he would never have escaped from autistic isolation. As Faulkner himself put it:

> . . . the only thing that held him into any sort of reality, into the world at all, was the trust that he had for his sister . . . he knew that she loved him and would defend him, and so she was the whole world to him. . . .[18]

Benjy's love for his sister-mother is absolute, but, to forestall any sentimentalizing, let us add immediately that it is absolute only in its need and demand: the infantile dependence on which it is based precludes any authentic reciprocity. Benjy does not love Caddy so much as Caddy's love and in his fierce narcissism he would like this love to be given to nobody else. His keen jealousy, when Caddy begins to be "unfaithful" to him, leaves no doubt about the possessive character of his attachment. And his "love" is far from being innocent if by innocence we mean the absence of any sexual component in his relationship with her. Benjy would not be so extraordinarily alert to his sister's sexual development nor so preoccupied with her virginity if sexuality played no part in his own desire. His desire is innocent only inasmuch as, unlike Quentin's, it is free from any sense of inner conflict and guilt. Further evidence of this is provided by the Burgess girl episode. It is surely no accident that the scene of Benjy's unique attempt at sexual intercourse occurs at the very place where he used to meet Caddy when she too came back from school. Benjy once again confuses past and present, mistaking today's girl with yesterday's Caddy. The implications of his error should not be overlooked; if the Burgess girl functions as a substitute for Caddy, then Benjy's sexual aggression must be viewed as an attempt at incest. And the following castration then also assumes a new symbolic significance in that it becomes the inescapable punishment for the violation of the primal taboo. In the second section, we shall be told about another incident with a young girl, likewise equated with Caddy (Quentin calls her "sister"), and Quentin will be similarly accused of sexual misconduct. The parallelism, both dramatic and thematic, of the two scenes points to the many interconnections between the first and the second section, and it is interesting to note that the incest motif, so central to Quentin's monologue, already emerges here with its usual correlate, castration.

With Benjy, incestuous desire is not restricted to the field of fantasy as it is with Quentin. If left free to act, he would yield to his urges without the slightest sense of guilt. Is he then to be seen as a fictional embodiment of the Freudian id? Carvel Collins has argued that each of the first three sections of *The Sound and the Fury* may be viewed as a dramatization of one of the agencies of Freud's second "topography," the monologues of Benjy, Quentin and Jason corresponding respectively to the id, the ego and the superego.[19] It seems highly improbable that any such psychoanalytical allegorizing was in Faulkner's mind when he wrote the novel, and it would be preposterous to reduce his characters to dressed up Freudian concepts. Yet if handled with due caution, the parallel proves enlightening, especially with reference to the first section. Benjy's protracted infancy, his self-lessness, his utter amorality, and the uninhibited urgency of his sexual impulse in the Burgess girl episode are assuredly features relating him to the reservoir of drive energy which Freud designated as the id. Even more interestingly perhaps, his monologue recalls in many ways what Freud termed the "primary processes" of the unconscious. In contrast to verbalized, logically ordered conscious thinking, psychoanalysis describes these processes as nondiscursive, iconic, and illogical. Although the Benjy section is a verbal construct devised

Compreens as family unit

by a conscious mind, the mental functioning which it suggests comes pretty close to the processes Freud detected in dream-work and in the formation of neurotic symptoms. As we have already seen, Benjy's speech is indeed Faulkner's paradoxical attempt to write a nondiscursive discourse, to verbalize the nonverbal, and it reads indeed to an amazing extent like a text of the unconscious in its disregard of time and logic, its ignorance of negation and contradiction, and its evident reliance on the dream mechanisms of condensation and displacement.

There is more to it, however, even from a Freudian point of view. The emphasis in the first section falls on infancy, on the unconscious, on the id, yet the superego, the repressive agency, is also there. Not that it plays any role in Benjy's mind, but it is *represented,* externalized in physical space. Like Quentin's, Benjy's desire is already *barred;* what distinguishes them is that in the latter case the barrier is a plainly visible and tangible one. While Quentin's tragedy is played out on a purely internal stage, Benjy's drama is given a symbolic *mise en scène* in the outer world.

It is noteworthy in this respect that the space in which the idiot moves is a space of enclosure, rigorously circumscribed, bristling with defenses—a prefiguration of the state asylum at Jackson behind whose bars he will be eventually confined. His successive guardians—Versh, T. P., Luster—keep constant watch over him and control his every move. Confinement is suggested from the first words of Benjy's monologue: *"Through the fence,* between the curling flowers, I could see them hitting" (1, italics added). If he is allowed to look through the fence, he does not have permission to go beyond it. Yet what lies beyond is precisely one of the three things which, according to Faulkner,[20] he loves most: "Benjy's pasture," sold to pay off the family debts. The fence is thus a concrete token of dispossession and exclusion, while the closed-in pasture may be said to symbolize all that Benjy has lost. In the imaginary topography of his world, the pasture, since converted into a golf course, stands for the primeval Garden, access to which is henceforth forbidden; it reminds one too—ironically—

of the *hortus conclusus,* the enclosed garden of the Song of Songs. Its symbolic function is the more manifest as it is almost immediately connected with the memory of Benjy's sister: it is from the former pasture that he hears the sound of her name. And it is equally revealing that, a page later, as he tries to crawl through the honeysuckle-choked fence and his clothing snags on a nail, he relives for the first time a moment of his childhood with Caddy, the present scene suddenly dissolving to give way to a cold winter setting many years ago (3, first passage in italics). The fence is the limit separating the present from the lost Eden of childhood, and the many references to it throughout the monologue ("fence" occurs five times in the first paragraph alone, and thirteen times in the first three pages) make it an eloquent symbol of Benjy's captivity.

Benjy resents being fenced in and, as Lawrence E. Bowling has pointed out,[21] he constantly tries to break through various barriers. When he is inside the house, he wants to go outside; when he is in the yard, he runs down to the gate:

> "Couldn't keep him in." Versh said. "He kept on until they let him go and he come right straight down here, looking through the gate" (6).

"Gate" is another key word of the first section. It belongs to the same set of symbols as the fence, but contrary to the latter the gate is not only a limit and an obstacle; it can also become an opening and give access to the *other* world. As a promise of escape, it exercises an irresistible attraction over Benjy. Every day he runs down to the gate and stays there like a sentry on duty or, to use one of Jason's animal metaphors, like an imprisoned bear clutching at the bars of its cage (see 315). As long as Benjy is confined to this cage, he never stops whining and whimpering; as soon as he is let out, his crying ceases. Thus, on Easter Sunday, before leaving for church with Dilsey, he is wailing "quietly and steadily" (360), and nothing, apparently, can console him. Yet once he has gone through the gate, he hushes, as if suddenly delivered from his unnameable torment: "They passed out of the gate. 'Now den,' [Dilsey] said. Ben ceased" (361). The gate symbolizes Benjy's blind yearning for freedom, but let us not forget that this yearning is one with his desire for Caddy's return.[22] If he continues to wait there for her every day, it is because he thinks she may come home again as she used to as a schoolgirl. His ritual waiting is actually propitiatory magic: "He think if he down to the gate," T.P. explains to Mrs. Compson, "Miss Caddy come back" (63). "Nonsense," the latter replies, and nothing indeed could be more nonsensical than Benjy's obstinate denial of time and mute reaffirmation of the lost kingdom of desire.

Only once does Benjy find the gate unlocked and manage to escape the adults' vigilance:

> It was open when I touched it, and I held to it in the twilight. I wasn't crying, and I tried to stop, watching the girls coming along in the twilight. I wasn't crying.
> "There he is."
> They stopped.
> "He cant get out. He won't hurt anybody, anyway. Come on."
> "I'm scared to. I'm scared. I'm going to cross the street."
> "He cant get out."
> I wasn't crying.
> "Dont be a 'fraid cat. Come on."
> They came on in the twilight. I wasn't crying, and I held to the gate. They came slow.
> "I'm scared."
> "He wont hurt you. I pass here every day. He just runs along the fence."
> They came on. I opened the gate and they stopped, turning. I was trying to say, and I caught her, trying to say, and she screamed and I was trying to say and trying and the bright shapes began to stop and I tried to get out. I tried to get it off of my face, but the bright shapes were going again. They were going up the hill to where it fell away and I tried to cry. But when I breathed in, I couldn't breathe out again to cry, and I tried to keep from falling off the hill and I fell off the hill into the bright, whirling shapes (63–64).

This is Benjy's retelling of the Burgess girl episode and, if we may say so, his personal interpretation of what happened on that fatal day. What did Benjy want of the two girls? The close repetition of "trying to say" stresses the urgency of his desire: to seize the unexpected opportunity of communication and so break the isolation in which Caddy's departure has left him. This desperate need for communication is expressed here by the wish to speak and be heard, the very wish Benjy's monologue is at pains to fulfill. For is not the entire first section a "trying to say"?[23] One could even go further and extend the meaning of the phrase to the whole of the novel. Is *The Sound and the Fury* not more than any other of Faulkner's works the one in which he tried and failed to say what he wanted to? It is perhaps no mere coincidence that when, years later, Faulkner spoke of his "failure," he used the very terms he had attributed to Benjy.[24] But while it is interesting to speculate upon the wider implications of the phrase, it is also necessary to attend to its ambiguity within the immediate context of the scene. Apart from a few details ("I caught her," "she screamed"), nothing here suggests a sexual assault. Yet it is as such that Benjy's behavior is construed by the girls and by the adults who are told about the incident. And Faulkner's comments leave no doubt either as to the sexual character of the attempted "communication."[25] That it should be obscured in the text hardly surprises us: sex and violence are often treated elliptically in Faulkner's fiction, and more explicitness would have been inconsistent with Benjy's general inability to articulate his emotions. What is more amazing is that an attempt at sexual intercourse should be masked as a wish for verbal communication.

"Trying to say" (mark the intransitive use of the verb) thus refers at once to the writer's creative endeavor and to the character's crude sexual impulse. Beyond Benjy's story, it brings to mind what we know about the psychological circumstances of the novel's birth, confirming our assumption that *The Sound and the Fury* is itself an extended metaphor for a nameless desire. Exploiting the duplicities of language, taking advantage of its gaps,

Faulkner's fiction *reveals* itself as a desire for utterance—"trying to say"—and *conceals* at the same time what it is in essence: an utterance of desire, a discourse endlessly spiraling around the focus of its secret fascination—the unspoken, the unspeakable, the dark and mute powers of sex and death.

In Benjy's monologue sex and death are never far away and are always seen in close conjunction. Thus in Benjy's memory the Burgess girl scene (sexual aggression) and the castration scene (sexual death) are significantly juxtaposed. Furthermore, the operation depriving Benjy of his manhood is itself suggested through extremely ambiguous imagery. Everywhere else in the section "the smooth, bright shapes" are associated with euphoric sensations: the fast flow of houses and trees during his drives to the cemetery (11, 13), the sight of fire that Benjy so loves (69, 78), and above all the memory of going to sleep with Caddy (13, 92). Here the luminous shapes also herald sleep, but a sleep that is suffocation ("I couldn't breathe out again"), falling ("I fell off the hill into the bright whirling shapes"), descent into death.[26]

This ambiguous interweaving of images of life and death is typical of Benjy's section. Throughout, without ever being named, death is a haunting presence. Thus, the earliest episode, the water splashing incident at the branch, which Benjy harks back to more frequently and lengthily than to any other,[27] is overshadowed by the event of Damuddy's death. From the memory of this death Benjy's mind slips imperceptibly to all the other deaths that have occurred in the family: the return of Quentin's body after his suicide at Cambridge (33–35), Mr. Compson's death and funeral (35–38, 40–41), the death of Roskus, Dilsey's husband (39–40). In his chaotic memory, these successive deaths are so entangled as to resemble an obsessive harping on a single occurrence, a ritual homage to Death. To this must be added the macabre image of Nancy, the mare shot by Roskus and devoured by the vultures, whose carcass Benjy glimpsed in a ditch one moonlit night (40, 42). Benjy's mind is of course not death-ridden in the same way as Quentin's is; death is something that he cannot comprehend, no more than little Vardaman can understand his mother's death in *As I Lay Dying,* but there is ample evidence that its mystery weighs very heavily on his mind. Moreover, Benjy senses the imminence and presence of death with an infallible animal instinct. When Mr. Compson dies, he howls at death like Dan, the dog, and even before his father dies, he "smells" his impending end (40–42). Benjy's uncanny divination powers in this field are indeed as keen as in the sexual one.

Lastly, there is Benjy's curious penchant for graveyards. The visit to the family cemetery is one of the first scenes recalled in his monologue (9–13), and it is on another of these funeral trips that the novel ends. The cemetery is invariably the goal of the only outings allowed Benjy; ironically, his contacts with the external world are restricted to the immutable Sunday ritual of the pilgrimage to the family dead. The special significance that the place has for him is further emphasized by the fact that one of his favorite games is playing with what Dilsey and Luster call his "graveyard" (67–68)—a blue bottle, perched on a little mound, into which he sticks stalks of jimson weed. As Edmond Volpe notes, Benjy's private graveyard may be taken as a derisory symbol of all his losses.[28] The nasty smell of jimson weed has come to replace the clean smell of trees associated with Caddy. Considering that the weed was used by Southern Negroes in contraception and abortion, and that it was given obscene names by the hill people of Mississippi because of its phallic form,[29] it is tempting to regard it also as an ironic symbol of lost manhood. Benjy's game is a mourning rite, a primitive commemoration of loss and death. The miniature graveyard and its fetid flowers condense all the ambiguities of his crippled and shrunken world—a world as close to its beginnings as to its end, forever arrested in its blind innocence, no sooner born than dead.

"He was a prologue," said Faulkner of Benjy, "like the grave-digger in the Elizabethan dramas. He serves his purpose and is gone."[30] At first sight none could qualify less for such a role than

Benjy, and the choice of an idiot's point of view was obviously something of a gamble. Yet Benjy does serve his purpose, or rather his purposes, with admirable efficiency. "I was trying," the author explained later, "to tell this story as it seemed to me that idiot child saw it."[31] So the first section was to create the illusion of a mind registering what happens or recalling what happened without understanding in the least the multiple connections between the events. The illusion works: reading Benjy's section, we see the world through the eyes of early childhood. To use again a comparison often made by critics, the idiot's mind seems to function like a camera or a tape recorder out of human manipulation and control. This is to say that Benjy is in a sense the most reliable narrator one can dream of: insofar as the recorded facts escape manipulation, his monologue achieves an objectivity in sharp contrast to the following sections. Yet what ensures his trustworthiness is paradoxically also what compromises his narrative competence. As he is unable to order his memories and perceptions in a consistent temporal perspective, his point of view is actually no *point* of view at all, and his telling of the Compson story is the very negation of narrative.

There is, then, a definite loss in the kind of immediate intelligibility that most readers expect from fiction and that many will claim as their due. There are substantial gains and subtle rewards, however, for those who are willing to play the novel's game, that is for those who consent to the emotive immersion and are capable of the imaginative openness and intellectual alertness which the first section and, for that matter, the whole novel demand. It is true that Benjy provides no orderly dramatic exposition, but if one pays close attention to Faulkner's identification devices—the changes in typeface to indicate time-shifts,[32] the names of Benjy's successive guardians, the carefully planted verbal clues[33]—a broad outline of the story will emerge, and in fact no section supplies as much information about the childhood and adolescence of the Compson children as the first. Benjy's monologue might be defined as information shorn of explanation and undistorted by subjectivity, or as a narrative held in timeless suspension, waiting for the reader to give it form and meaning: it does not tell a story but creates within us the possibility of telling one—or several.

This does not mean, as was insinuated by Faulkner's early critics, that the first section is nothing but a perverse puzzle. That the burden of narrative organization and interpretation is transferred from narrator to reader does not imply that the latter is confronted with mere confusion, nor that he is free to arrange the material he is given at his will. The seeming chaos of Benjy's section conceals what might be termed a *vertical* order, an order, that is, in which the horizontal linearity of external chronology is replaced by a synchronic patterning of internal relationships. The compressed series of juxtapositions to be found in the monologue constitute virtual superimpositions through which similiarities as well as differences come to light. As can be seen, for instance, from the juxtaposition of the two scenes in the swing, the one with Caddy, the other with her daughter Quentin (see 56–59), the past may be turned into an implicit comment upon the present, the present into an ironical reminder of the past. Throughout the section past and present as well as distinct time-units within the past are counterpointed in such ways as to suggest both continuities and contrasts. Scenes separated in time tend to fall into groups and to form chains by reason of their common elements: thus the Caddy scenes, the death scenes, the dispossession scenes. And these chains are integrated in their turn into larger complexes of meaning. So the linking of four death episodes with Caddy's wedding (8–48) points to the common significance of those events for Benjy in terms of loss, and foreshadows at the same time the metaphoric equivalence of sex and death underlying the second section. Clearly, then, the arrangement of narrative data, random though it may seem, does possess a logic and a purpose. Its disconcerting effect upon the reader is easy to account for: traditionally fiction relies on syntagmatic (or metonymic) developments; here the ordering is paradigmatic (or metaphoric).[34] In marked opposition to the literalness of its linguistic texture, the overall structure of Benjy's discourse is therefore essentially *symbolic,* allowing thematic configurations to emerge much more forcibly than would have been possible within the sequential framework of conventional narration.

In the first section, narrative exposition is deliberately subordinated to thematic implication, granting the reader an intuitive foreknowledge of the issues at stake in the novel even before he has been able to piece the story itself together. What is more, we are at once engaged in the process of interpretation. Benjy appears from the outset as a key-figure and even more so in retrospect. He is only a mirror, but mirrors do not lie. What his monologue tells us is the truth, albeit not the whole truth. It is against Benjy that all the other characters of the novel are measured; as Lawrence Thompson states, he is "a mirror of moral conscience, in which the various members of the family can see their own actions reflected and implicitly evaluated."[35] This thematic function has been so abundantly analyzed by critics that no further comment is required.[36] One must add, however, that this is not his only function. Benjy is not only the touchstone and revelator of the Compson family; the supreme irony is perhaps that he is also its living emblem. Admittedly, he is an outsider; being an idiot, he cannot be held responsible for what he is and judged according to the same criteria as the other Compsons. Yet once we have become aware of the many interconnections existing between the novel's first three sections, we cannot fail to be struck by the many ways in which Benjy anticipates Quentin and even Jason. It is quite true that, as Faulkner himself notes, he is not "rational enough even to be selfish,"[37] but at the same time there can be no question either that, to resume another of the writer's phrases, "the blind self-centeredness of innocence"[38] is the very core of his emotional being. As we shall see later, the same phrase also applies perfectly to Quentin and Jason, the only major difference between them and Benjy being that they refuse to outgrow their "innocence" whereas the idiot is forever doomed to it. Benjy and his brothers are alike in their basic narcissism, their refusal of change, their denial of life's motion—disquieting innocents, all of them.

The first section—the story of the miserable child-man—may thus be said to represent the whole Compson drama in reduced form. It tells us almost all there is to know, but it does so with a deceptive mixture of opaqueness and transparency. To yield its rich harvest of ambiguities and ironies, the prologue must be read again—as an epilogue.

4

The Young Man, Desire, and Death

Brother-Sister relationship

Denk: es erhalt sich der Held, selbst
    der Untergang war ihm
Nur ein Vorwand, zu sein: seine letzte
    Geburt.

RAINER MARIA RILKE

En somme, la mort, c'est un peu comme
un mariage.

FERDINAND CELINE

IF BENJY'S MONOLOGUE SERVES as a prologue to the whole novel, it is obviously with the section immediately following it that it has its closest affinities. Again Caddy is "the center on the horizon," the remote and haunting figure in which death and desire meet and merge; again everything revolves around the brother-sister relationship, and one may well wonder whether, fundamentally, its function and significance are not much the same as in the previous section: like his retarded brother's, Quentin's love for Caddy is jealous, exclusive, excessive; like his, it can only be described in terms of lack and loss. Yet, while Benjy's desire barely emerges from the primitive demands of need and can be stilled by specific objects, Quentin's is desire in its fullest, or rather emptiest, sense: a desire never to be satisfied, incommensurate with any real object, gliding from substitute to substitute down to the very last—death. In Benjy's childish attachment to his sister there is little more than an indiscriminate hunger for love; Quentin's feelings are rooted in the same archaic soil, but they are refracted through the deceptive prism of an adult or at least adolescent mind, and must be traced through a far more devious discourse. His monologue does not so readily reveal the hidden pattern of its disorder.   *vibeology*

To switch from section 1 to section 2 is to pass from the simple to the complex; it means leaving the limbo of blank innocence to be thrust into a private hell of anguish and guilt. Quentin certainly remains an innocent inasmuch as innocence may be equated with "blind self-centeredness." But in opposition to the all but mindless Benjy, he suffers rather from an excess of consciousness and conscience, and although he eventually proves incapable of making an ethical choice, he does possess an extremely keen sense of good and evil. As a consequence, his relationship to Caddy is a much more intricate affair, raising psychological and moral issues totally alien to Benjy's world. The idiot's helpless dependency on his sister is just an aspect of his stunted growth, the result of blocked mental development. With Quentin the blockage is of a subtler kind, and it is only toward the end of his adolescence that its negative implications come to be fully felt. Benjy's love for Caddy hardly strikes us as abnormal once we know that he is fated to perpetual childhood; Quentin's on the other hand, develops into a morbid passion whose outcome can only be death.

These differences account for the changes intervening at this point in the novel's thematic development. In the first section the dual reference to desire and death never becomes explicit; it must be inferred by the reader from the symbolic patterning of the idiot's monologue. In the second section, the two poles of Benjy's inarticulate anxiety are no longer submerged: desire and death can be easily identified in Quentin's double obsession with *incest* and with *suicide*.

Neurotic obsession is not only what his monologue expresses; it informs and deforms the very texture of his language, being at once the root of its disorder and the key to its twisted logic. Like Benjy's idiocy, it operates up to a point as a reductor, de-rationalizing speech by its disruptive impact on the hierarchical structures of grammar.[1] Linguistically, there are obvious similarities between the two monologues, and especially when Quentin records "present" actions and perceptions, he often uses strings of one-unit kernel sentences strongly reminiscent of Benjy's speech:

> When I finished breakfast I bought a cigar. The girl said a fifty cent one was the best, so I took one and lit it and went out to the street. I stood there and took a couple of puffs, then I held it in my hand and went on toward the corner . . . (102).

But the disjointedness characteristic of Quentin's monologue does not derive exclusively from the neutral juxtaposition of minimal sentences. With him the breaking up process is taken a step further: syntactic order is not only reduced to elemental patterns but repeatedly torn apart; there is not only an impoverishment in grammatical and logical relationships, the clauses themselves tend to fall asunder or are abruptly broken off before completion:

> . . . *getting the odour of honeysuckle all mixed She would have told me not to let me sit there on the steps hearing her door twilight slamming hearing Benjy still crying Supper she would have to come down then getting honeysuckle all mixed up in it* (160).

In such passages the absence of punctuation and the disintegration of syntax lead to an almost complete breakdown of language. Nowhere in the first section is there so much confusion. Which does not mean that all of Quentin's monologue is chaotic. His is in fact the most subtly modulated speech in the novel and the one that offers the greatest flexibility in tone and style, ranging as it does from clear and orderly narrative prose to opaque stream-of-consciousness, and from Benjy's "reduced" syntax to Faulkner's rhetorical manner. Quentin is at times a standard first-person narrator (mainly in recounting the events of his last day, but also in reporting certain scenes of his past); the point is that he proves unable to fulfill his narrative function with sustained consistency, and that whenever painful private memories or fantasies surge forth he loses control over his words. Again and again Quentin attempts to tell his story in orderly fashion; again and again his narrative gets caught in the vortex of his obsessions. Many paragraphs in the second section begin quite conventionally as controlled narration, only to end in uncontrolled interior discourse. And this entropic tendency also characterizes the monologue as a whole. The closer one gets to its emotional climax (Quentin's decisive encounter with Caddy at the branch, 186–202), the less Quentin masters his language; the deeper he moves into his monologue, the less he *speaks* and the more he *listens* to the myriad voices of the past. That these effects were all carefully calculated by the author can be easily seen from the significant changes which he made in revising his manuscript. Formally, the latter is still fairly traditional in many respects: unpunctuated passages are rare, reported speech is generally presented between quotation marks, speakers are easy to identify, and it almost looks as if some of the unconventional devices used in this section had been gradually discovered during the process of composition, to be systematized once the manuscript was completed. Thus, in the manuscript version of the climactic scene with Caddy, the suppression of punctuation marks occurs later than in the final version (p. 77 in holograph, beginning with "All right let go"; cf. p. 200 in published text), and the removal of capitals occurs even later (p. 78 in holograph, beginning with "anytime he will believe me"; cf. p. 202 in published text). It is clear, then, that in revising the manuscript Faulkner radicalized the experimental character of his writing and thereby emphasized the dream-like "interior" quality of Quentin's monologue.

What the confusion thus achieved is meant to render is of course Quentin's emotional turmoil, but paradoxically it also testifies to his greater intelligence: his mind works hardly more logically than Benjy's, yet it works at higher speed, and ranges over a far more extended network of private associations. There are twice as many time shifts in the second section (about two hundred) as in the first (about one hundred), and the shuttling back and forth between past and present is at times so swift as to convey the impression of a mind running on several tracks at one and the same time.

Contrasting with the deliberateness of his external actions, Quentin's mental activity betrays throughout a feverish restlessness. Erratic, elliptical, full of unexpected detours and sudden turnabouts, his thought processes are those of a frantically busy mind. At the same time, however, they also reveal a captive mind, compulsively racing within the closed circle of its fantasies and obsessions. While Benjy's memory seldom repeats itself, Quentin's is ceaselessly driven back to the same painful scenes of the past, and the persistent recurrence of identical words (*Caddy, water, shadow, door, honeysuckle,* etc.) and identical phrases and sentences (*Did you ever have a sister?—One minute she was standing there—Father I have committed*) gives his monologue the incantatory rhythm of a litany. From first to last, the syntax of fragmentation is counterbalanced by a closely patterned rhetoric of repetition,[2] a rhetoric suggesting, as so often in Faulkner, stasis as well as motion, "fury in itself quiet with stagnation."[3]

These repetitive patterns are an index to the specific quality of Quentin's experience. His present, as we shall see, is a reenactment of his past; his future is past in waiting. Contrary to Benjy, however, Quentin has a history. Yet the preliminary question one must raise is whether he can be considered in any strict sense the *subject* of this history. In point of fact, the speech attributed to him can hardly be called *his,* for it is not any more than Benjy's the discourse of a single person. Again, many voices, past and present, are heard, and within this polyphonic ensemble Quentin's own enjoys no special privilege.[4] The very fragmentation of his speech, its dreamlike incoherence and obsessive redundancy belie the postulate of a stable "I" presiding over it. What Quentin's "monologue" actually records is the process through which the entire fabric of a self is unraveled and comes apart. Insofar as there is still an ego at play, it is not at all the agent of mediation, integration, and adaptation which it is supposed to be by American ego psychology. Modern French psychoanalysis might prove more helpful here, for the redefinition of the ego concept it proposes is much more relevant to what we find in section 2: an ego which is the locus of alienating identifications rather than the location of identity.

Quentin's drama is that of the "poor player," trying out various roles without ever finding any that he is able to appropriate and sustain. His quest for selfhood amounts to little more than a desperate search for models to imitate and parts to play. Like the other members of his histrionic family (except Benjy and Caddy), Quentin attempts to dramatize and dignify his existence by projecting himself into ennobling roles, and Mr. Compson as well as Shreve, Spoade, and Herbert Head are quite aware of his roleplaying.[6] The characters he would impersonate are those provided by the repertoire of his culture: Jesus, the saint of Christian tradition (St. Francis of Assisi), the medieval knight (Galahad), the Romantic hero (Byron), the Southern gentleman. That there should be so many literary echoes in his monologue is hardly surprising; the quixotic Quentin lives in a world of words and books, a museum of romance, an echo chamber of "fine dead sounds" (217), and his existence is thus doubly fictive: he is a character acting characters, an unsubstantial "I" lost in the maze of its fictions and myths.[7]

Subjectivity, then, is at best a theatrical creation. The core of
Quentin's being is deceit, division, nonidentity. Nothing in him
and around him seems real. His speech drags us into a space cor-
roded by absence, a space inside out and outside in, with neither
landmarks nor boundaries, just as it plunges us into a time out of
time, collapsing rather than elapsing, in which the self is shattered
by the reciprocal exclusion of *being* and *having been* (216). Besides, isn't this monologue a posthumous speech? As if to underscore how little reality he bestows upon him, Faulkner makes
Quentin speak once he is dead. As Sartre writes, "all Faulkner's
art aims to suggest to us that Quentin's soliloquy and his last
walk are already his suicide."[8] The voice we listen to in the
second section is a voice out of nowhere—nobody's voice.

What is offered instead is the tormented landscape of a mind,
an interlacing of tracks and traces, a palimpsest of desire and
memory. Deciphering it is no easy matter, yet, reading and rereading it, we eventually make out the pattern of a trajectory,
tortuous, shadowy, paradoxical, headed for death, and we also
come to see where and when this lethal course began.

Quentin's fate arises from what Faulkner calls elsewhere "the
tragic complexity of motherless childhood."[9] Like Darl, the un-
loved son in *As I Lay Dying*, Quentin, strictly speaking, never
had a mother, and in his monologue there are several suggestions
that, had he not been deprived of motherly love, his whole life
might have taken a different direction: *"If I could say Mother.
Mother"* (117), or again "... *if I'd just had a mother so I could
say Mother Mother"* (213). And the same poignant sense of
abandonment is revealed by Quentin's remembrance of the picture
in the story book:

> When I was little there was a picture in one of our books, a dark
> place into which a single weak ray of light came slanting upon two
> faces lifted out of the shadows. . . . I'd have to turn back to it until
> the dungeon was Mother herself she and Father upward into weak
> light holding hands and us lost somewhere below even them with-
> out even a ray of light (215).

Quentin's projection of the family situation onto this scene of darkness and confinement is eloquent evidence of the parental neglect from which the Compson children suffered. Both parents failed them, but in this Rorschach test it is significantly the mother who is equated with the dungeon. The cold, egotistical Mrs. Compson has become a lightless prison to her children, keeping them captive, as securely as she would have by possessive love, through what she denied them. Or, to borrow another of Quentin's metaphors, she poisoned them once and for all: "Done in Mother's mind though. Finished. Finished. Then we were all poisoned" (214–16).

For this poison there is no cure; from this darkness, there is no escape. None of the Compson children will ever succeed in fleeing from it, whatever their individual responses to the original trauma. Quentin had no mother, but he had a sister. Like Benjy, he turned to her for the love his mother denied. His attachment to her is an all-consuming passion, just because of its deep roots in infancy. Yet in shifting his affective allegiance from the mother to the sister, he has perhaps also transferred to her his early resentment of the mother's betrayal. It is worth noting that even in the earliest childhood scenes he appears as a moody, introverted boy with a very ambivalent attitude toward his sister, and it is equally remarkable that this ambivalence is matched from the outset by a curious suspiciousness with regard to sex.

The most revealing episode in this respect is certainly the scene in which Quentin and Natalie, a neighbor girl, are "dancing sitting down" in the barn (168–69). When Quentin sees his sister standing in the door watching their little love game, he immediately breaks off and hurls abuse at Natalie: "Get wet I hope you catch pneumonia go on home cowface" (169). Then he jumps into the hog wallow:

> I jumped hard as I could into the hog-wallow the mud yellowed up to my waist stinking I kept on plunging until I fell down and rolled over in it . . . mud was warmer than the rain it smelled awful (169–70).

Telling Caddy that he was "hugging" Natalie, he expects her to be offended, but his sister does not "give a damn" about what happened. Upset by her indifference, he then angrily smears mud from his own body onto hers, while she scratches at his face. After which, reconciled at last, the two children go to the branch and sit down in the water, washing off the malodorous mud.

There is scarcely a detail in this childhood scene that does not in some way anticipate Quentin's future actions and attitudes. His leap into the hog wallow is the enactment of an old Puritan metaphor, the symbolic performance of what his first and no doubt last sexual experiment means to him: yielding to the urges of the flesh equals wallowing in filth.[10] Mud becomes quite literally the substance of sin: it is water (and as such related to the whole complex of water symbolism pervading the novel), but with its transparency gone, its fluidity thickened into sticky stinking matter —a concrete image of sexual nausea. Just as in *Light in August,* where it is associated with the thick, black, putrid water in the sewers, sexuality here is linked with the unclean and the viscous, and, through the implicit reference to pigs, with loathsome animality.[11]

The hog wallow scene dramatizes the sudden revulsion that followed Quentin's timid attempt at sexual initiation. The ritual mudbath is both a symbolic reenactment of the previously mimed sexual act and its exorcism, its nullification; it is intended to operate as homeopathic magic.[12] In much the same way as Joe Christmas, after his discovery of woman's "periodical filth," shoots a sheep and steeps his hands in "the yet warm blood of the dying beast,"[13] Quentin, by wallowing in the mud, magically cures evil by evil and cleanses himself from defilement. One might add, too, that his strange ritual on this occasion is strongly reminiscent of the defense mechanism well known in the study of obsessional neuroses as "undoing."

At once a confession of guilt, an act of penance, and a purification rite, Quentin's gesture foreshadows the magical actions through which he will attempt time and again to ward off the threats of the world, not only during his childhood and adolescence, but up to and even *in* his suicide. Magical too is the code by which he lives and acts: in the last analysis all his perception of good and evil comes down to that of the pure and the impure. The summum bonum is equated in his mind with his sister's intact virginity; his nostalgia for lost innocence is above all the dream of a sexless life. In his monologue Quentin recalls Versh's story about a self-castrated man (143). But castration—an idea which haunts him and a possibility he must have envisaged for himself —does not appear to him as a satisfactory alternative. Castration would simply be a *pis aller,* so to speak, for it would not obliterate the memory of having had a sex:

> But that's not it. It's not not having them. It's never to have had them then I could say O That That's Chinese I dont know Chinese (143).

The correlate of this deep aversion to sex is misogyny. Quentin's is the Puritan version of the Fall: Eve was the beginning of evil; it was through her that the innocence of Eden was lost. Although he clings to the Southern myth of Sacred Womanhood, and will defend Woman's honor to the last (as is shown by his fight with Gerald Bland a few hours before his suicide), Quentin's faith in her purity has been shattered by his sister's sexual misconduct. His monologue reverberates with Mr. Compson's cynical remarks on women, and for all his protests and denials he has apparently come to acknowledge the bitter truth that "women are never virgins" (143), that they are by nature impure, that is, impure like Nature herself. One quickly senses that the revered and radiant image of the Immaculate Virgin screens a darker one— not very far removed, in fact, from Jason's definition of women as bitches. Quentin shrinks from so much candor, yet womanhood, in his monologue, is constantly linked to suspect images and sensations—softness, warmth, wetness, darkness—and particularly to dirt.[14] As with other male characters in Faulkner's fiction, we find in Quentin a morbid concern with the physiological evidence of woman's "impurity," menstruation:

> Because women so delicate so mysterious Father said. Delicate equilibrium of periodical filth between two moons balanced. Moons he said full and yellow as harvest moons her hips thighs. Outside outside of them always but. Yellow. Feet soles with walking like. Then know that some man that all those mysterious and imperious concealed. With all that inside of them shapes an outward suavity waiting for a touch to. Liquid putrefaction like drowned things floating like pale rubber flabbily filled getting the odour of honeysuckle all mixed up (159).

Woman's delicacy and suavity are a decoy; the sanctuary of her body hides an ignoble secret: the filth of sex, at once the periodically renewed promise of fecundity (hinted at by the references to the moon and to harvests, and by the symbolism of yellow) and the threat of mortal engulfment. In Quentin's diseased imagination, the menstrual flow and "liquid putrefaction" are confused in the same obscene streaming.

"*Templum aedificatum super cloacam*": Tertullian's horrible definition of woman perfectly sums up Quentin's view. The equation of woman with dirt in his mind is confirmed, moreover, by at least three of the female figures evoked in the second section: Caddy, Natalie, and the little Italian girl whom Quentin meets at Cambridge on the day of his suicide. Caddy is the girl with the "muddy drawers,"[15] and in Quentin's memory, Natalie too is a "dirty girl": twice he recalls Caddy's sarcastic remark when he teased and taunted her about her first kiss: "I didnt kiss a dirty girl like Natalie anyway" (166). As to the "present" episode with the Italian girl, it alternates significantly with the account of the Natalie scene and one of the links between the two scenes is precisely the "dirty girl" motif: Quentin's new "sister" is also "a dirty little child" (155), and in his descriptions of her there are references to "her dirty dress" (158), her "dirty hand" (163), and "her filthy little dress" (165). The dirt is made even more repellent by moisture and warmth: "She extended her fist, it un-curled upon a nickel, moist and dirty, moist dirt ridged into her flesh" (157). And the suggestion of disgust is further strength-ened by animal similes: "Her fingers closed about [the two cop-pers], damp and hot, like worms" (159); "She had a funny looking thing in her hand, she carried it sort of like it might have been a dead pet rat" (159).[16] All these touches lend the scene of Quentin's encounter with the girl a faintly nauseous atmosphere, and emphasize the eerie, almost ominous effect of her silent pres-ence at his side. The girl is an echo of the past and a prefiguration of the future; while taking Quentin back to his childhood as the ironically rediscovered sister, she is also, in her uncanny silence, her dark stare, and her inexplicable stubbornness in following him everywhere, a symbol of Fate, an avatar of "little sister Death," and she is finally another metaphor for soiled innocence, a re-minder of the defilement whose unbearable memory is soon to be washed away by the waters of the Charles River.

In Quentin's daily behavior this concern with purity and im-purity is reflected by a magic need for order and cleanliness. Spots and stains make him uneasy, and nothing annoys him more than other people's slovenliness.[17] Even as a child, he resented the fact that Louis Hatcher's lantern was not spotlessly clean (141). Similarly, during his interview with Herbert Head, his sister's vulgar fiancé, he is anxious lest the lighted cigar which the latter has put on the mantel should cause a blister (135–37),[18] and after his fist-fight with Gerald Bland, his first question is not about possible injury but about the blood stains on his vest (204). At no moment, however, is his preoccupation with cleanliness and order more conspicuous than during the elaborate prepara-tions for his suicide. After lamentably failing to put order into his life, Quentin sets very methodically about putting order into his death:

> I laid out two suits of underwear, with socks, shirts, collars and ties, and packed my trunk. I put in everything except my new suit and an old one and two pairs of shoes and two hats, and my books.

I carried the books into the sitting-room and stacked them on the table, the ones I had brought from home and the ones *Father said it used to be a gentleman was known by his books; nowadays he is known by the ones he has not returned* and locked the trunk and addressed it. The quarter hour sounded. I stopped and listened to it until the chimes ceased.

I bathed and shaved. The water made my finger smart a little, so I painted it again. I put on my new suit and put my watch on and packed the other suit and the accessories and my razor and brushes in my hand bag, and wrapped the trunk key into a sheet of paper and put it in an envelope and addressed it to Father, and wrote the two notes and sealed them (99–100).

Quentin is determined to leave everything in impeccable order. His death, at least, shall be no mess. As if to reassert *in extremis* the aristocratic code he failed to live by, he wants his exit to be a gentleman's. Hence the fastidious care he takes of his personal hygiene and clothing. Here he is, on the last morning of his life, taking a bath, shaving, donning a new suit. Later, at the close of his monologue, this funeral toilet is resumed and completed: after his altercation with Bland, Quentin returns home, cleans his blood-stained vest with gasoline, washes his face and hands, changes his collar, shirt, and tie (213–14). The record of his very last gestures is the following:

The last note sounded. At last it stopped vibrating and the darkness was still again. I entered the sitting room and turned on the light. I put my vest on. The gasoline was faint now, barely noticeable, and in the mirror the stain didnt show. Not like my eye did, anyway. I put on my coat. Shreve's letter crackled through the cloth and I took it out and examined the address, and put it in my side pocket. Then I carried the watch into Shreve's room and put it in his drawer and went to my room and got a fresh handkerchief and went to the door and put my hand on the light switch. Then I remembered I hadnt brushed my teeth, so I had to open the bag again. I found my toothbrush and got some of Shreve's paste and went out and brushed my teeth. I squeezed the brush as dry as I could and put it back in the bag and shut it, and went to the door again. Before I snapped the light out I looked around to see if there was anything else, then I saw that I had forgotten my hat. I'd have to go by the

postoffice and I'd be sure to meet some of them, and they'd think I
was a Harvard Square student making like he was a senior. I had
forgotten to brush it too, but Shreve had a brush, so I didn't have
to open the bag any more (222).

In its tedium of detail Quentin's flat, factual report faithfully
reflects the manic meticulosity of this ultimate inspection. Yet behind the mechanical succession of seemingly controlled gestures,
one senses a consciousness no longer fully present to itself and to
the world, registering the actions of the body as if from a distance,
a consciousness more than ever astray, and it is remarkable that
for all the scrupulous attention given to his final preparations,
Quentin twice nearly forgets a detail. Is it because he cannot help
thinking of his imminent suicide? And does he go through all
these futile motions to avert the thought of death? It seems safe
to assume that they are a last diversion maneuver, but perhaps all
this absent-minded fussiness testifies even more to a radical incapacity to welcome death, an inability to *want* it at the very moment when it appears most desirable.[19]

Besides, it is not at all evident that Quentin desires it, and if
we were not informed of his design and alerted by the chilling
flatness of his tone, his actual intentions might be easily misinter-
preted. In the extreme care he lavishes on his body and clothing
there is a suggestion of coquetry, a touch of narcissistic self-
concern that one would hardly expect from a man on the point of
committing suicide. Quentin spruces himself up as if he were
going out for a date. The ambiguity is hardly ambiguous: Quentin's suicide is indeed, as we shall soon see even more clearly, a
lover's date.

To grasp its deeper significance, it is necessary to retrace the
long and complex process that has led Quentin to choose death.
Let us return for a moment to the prophetic hog wallow scene.
Quentin's game with Natalie was the beginning of his initiation
into sex. Now it is worth noting that *before* Caddy's return to
the barn he enjoys the game and apparently feels no compunction

about his pleasure. Only when Caddy comes back and surprises him hugging the girl, does the love game make him feel guilty and distraught. Then he begins to panic, for then he suddenly realizes (although his realization remains subliminal) that the intrusion of sex into his life threatens to compromise forever his unique relationship to Caddy. In order to stave off this menace, it becomes indispensable that his sister should acknowledge its seriousness by a firm disavowal of what she has seen. As Caddy does not react in the expected way, he smears her body with mud. Symbolically he thus drags her down with him into the mire of sin, forcing her to share his assumed guilt and so reestablishing —in evil—the intimacy that his game with Natalie had put in jeopardy. After that, quits, they can both go to the branch and purify themselves in its water: the illusion of innocence is provisionally restored.

Quentin's puzzling behavior in the course of this ritual defilement and purgation clearly shows that what most matters to him—at this point as well as later on—is not so much the preservation of sexual innocence, whether his own or Caddy's, as the safekeeping at any cost of the absolute mutuality of a dual relationship. Innocence to him is a means rather than an end, and if he is so anxious to preserve it, it is firstly because it is a token of isolation, safety, and peace. Conversely, if he distrusts sexuality and recoils from it, it is primarily because it imperils his exclusive bond to his sister. Even at this early stage Quentin is virtually prepared to go to any lengths to keep her out of the world's clutches; no price seems too high, and he is quite willing to pay even that of sin provided that the sin committed is a common sin and that they suffer common punishment. In this childhood scene, he compels his sister to share his mudbath. When, later, Caddy is "soiled" by the loss of her virginity, he insists no less on restoring their intimacy, but it is his turn then to join the fallen virgin in the filthy waters of sin.

From the sex game in the barn to the ritual cleansing in the branch, the episode is also prophetic and paradigmatic in that

it involves a *triangular* relationship. It foreshadows situation patterns with which Quentin is confronted time and again—except
that in the later scenes the roles are ironically reversed. Here the
triad consists of Quentin, Natalie, and Caddy, and tension arises
as soon as it is formed, that is, from the moment when Caddy
appears in the doorway of the barn. The little drama for three
characters which then takes place curiously resembles a banal
adultery story: Quentin, Natalie, and Caddy virtually play the
parts of husband, mistress, and betrayed wife. At least it is along
these lines that Quentin seems to interpret the situation. Expecting
Caddy to be jealous of her rival and shower reproaches on her
faithless partner, he stands ready to go into the dock and plead
guilty. The actors, however, do not play the roles they had been
given in his private script. In hoping that his sister would play the
outraged partner, he has in fact cast her for his own role, one
which was already to some extent his in the first branch scene (the
splashing incident), and which he will play with ever more
pointed jealousy in his subsequent encounters with Caddy: the
quarrel after her first flirtation with a "darn town squirt" (166),
the long pathetic colloquy about her affair with Dalton Ames
(185–203), and the last meeting in her room on the eve of her
wedding (151–54). In all those scenes, just as in the early Natalie scene, there are three persons involved, but sex is no longer
a childish game and the actors have been allocated different roles:
Caddy has replaced Natalie in the part of the "dirty girl," her
lovers have supplanted Quentin, and it is he who now plays the
thankless role of the *terzo incommodo*.[20]

Insofar as it proceeds from concurrent desires with Caddy at
stake, this triangular relationship is bound to generate conflict.
In point of fact, from the yet harmless squabbles of childhood
to the poignant confrontation before Caddy's wedding, all the
scenes just referred to are scenes of potential or overt violence, and
each time Quentin turns out to be its agent or its cause.

Most often Quentin's aggressiveness is aimed at Caddy herself: he slaps her, at fifteen, for having kissed a boy, just as he

did, at seven, after she had taken off her dress in the branch; he smears her with mud after the incident with Natalie, and in the climactic scene about Ames, he even takes out his jackknife and points it at Caddy's throat.[21] On the other hand, he shows persistent hostility to his sister's lovers: he tries to hit Dalton Ames when he meets him near the bridge (200), and during his interview with Herbert Head, he deliberately antagonizes his future brother-in-law (133–37). The same conflictual pattern reemerges ironically in the two major episodes of Quentin's last day. The episode with the Italian girl culminates in a grotesque inversion of roles. Charged with "meditated criminal assault" (174), Quentin is willy-nilly cast in the role of the seducer, while Julio, the girl's older brother, successfully assumes the part that Quentin could not play—that of defender of his sister's honor: small wonder that Quentin is convulsed with hysterical laughter on realizing the irony of the situation. As to the second episode, the fight with Gerald Bland, it is likewise based on a tragicomic quid pro quo, since it arises from Quentin's unconscious identification of Bland with Caddy's first lover.

The targets of Quentin's aggressiveness do not change, and what it constantly aims at is either the elimination of the hated rival or the punishment of the beloved sister. To recapture the object of his love, he will try anything, from physical intimidation to the subtler stratagems of persuasion. His are in fact all the desperate ruses of the frustrated lover. One of his favorite tactics is vilifying his rivals: *"that blackguard Caddy. . . . A liar and a scoundrel Caddy was dropped from his club for cheating at cards got sent to Coventry caught cheating at midterm exams and expelled"* (152). By exposing Head's disreputable past, Quentin hopes he can induce Caddy not to marry him, and there are similar motives to his caustic comments on Caddy's first boyfriends (166) and on Dalton Ames (113). The point is of course that none is more dishonest here than Quentin himself: what worries him is not so much that Ames and Head are no gentlemen as the threat they pose to his love, and he objects to them as he would to any other man taking Caddy away from him.

Quentin is the one who cheats most, and if he cannot deceive others, he deceives himself. Another of his tricks, related to the magic rituals we have already noted, is *denial*. When faced with unpleasant facts, Quentin refuses to acknowledge them or tries at least to twist the evidence so as to minimize their significance. Thus he persuades himself and attempts to persuade Caddy that her "infidelities" were not committed of her own free will but forced upon her. Hence his resentment when, questioned about her first kiss, Caddy admits with blunt candor: "I didnt let him I made him [kiss me]" (166). Later, when he learns about her affair with Ames, he wants Caddy to admit that she has been raped, and his greatest fear then is that his sister might love her seducer:

> do you love him
> her hand came out I didnt move it fumbled down my arm and she held my hand flat against her chest her heart thudding
> no no
> did he make you then he made you do it let him he was stronger than you and he tomorrow Ill kill him I swear I will father neednt know until afterward and then you and I nobody need ever know we can take my school money we can cancel my matriculation Caddy you hate him dont you dont you (187).

It should be clear by now that Quentin's desire is above all a desire for Caddy's desire. What is unbearable to him is not that his sister lost her virginity but that she consented to lose it, that she willingly gave herself to Ames and still wants his embraces. What he desperately denies is that she eludes him as *subject* of desire. This is to say that, contrary to what most commentators and Faulkner himself (Appendix, 411) have contended, Caddy's virginity is not simply an abstract concept, a symbol of Quentin's idealistic concern for the Compson honor. So far from being a mere emblem, it is of vital interest to him in that it guarantees both Caddy's inaccessibility to another's desire and the innocence of his own. As long as this double insurance works, Quentin feels safe and pure, and can love his sister as his undisputed property. Conversely, once Caddy's virginity is lost, everything is lost: the closure of Quentin's private world forever fractured, the trustful mutuality of the dual relationship irremediably destroyed.

Then his *passion* truly begins. Its immediate cause is the intrusion of the hateful third party and the ensuing clash of rival claims on Caddy, yet much more than mere rivalry is involved. The intruder is of course at once abhorred and feared as a potential ravisher, but he also acts as mediator, revealer, and catalyst. While portending the breakup of Quentin's intimacy with Caddy, he is also instrumental in dispelling the illusion of its "purity." To Quentin as much as to his sister, his entrance upon the stage means the end of innocence. For even though he will never confess to it, Quentin recognizes in the rival desire a reflection of his own, and as Caddy's body becomes attractive to others, it ceases to be sexless to him.[22]

Hence the extreme ambivalence of Quentin's attitudes toward his rivals. He hates them as Caddy's seducers; he admires and envies them for the virile potency and daring he lacks. Dalton Ames and Herbert Head realize by proxy his unavowed and unavowable wish: the sexual possession of his sister. No wonder then that he should be such a poor avenger of her outraged honor. His weakness vis-à-vis Caddy's lovers is of the same order as Hamlet's hesitation to kill the usurper of the royal bed:[23] unconscious identification with the successful competitor prevents his wreaking vengeance for the insult.

Quentin's two contradictory wishes—disposing of the rival while becoming like him and taking over his role and prerogatives —thus come to merge in the fantasy of complete substitution, that is, the fantasy of consummated incest:

... it was I it was not Dalton Ames (97–98).
... you thought it was them but it was me (185).

Quentin's desire at this point becomes an imitation of his rival's, just as in the oedipal situation the son's desire is patterned on the father's. It is noteworthy too that the two male figures who most excite his animosity and admiration—Dalton Ames and Gerald Bland[24]—are to some extent father images: in their ability to seduce and dominate, their sexual potency, physical strength, and sporting prowess (shooting in Ames's case; shooting, rowing, and boxing in Bland's), they embody alike the ideal of *mastery* which Quentin pretends to despise because it is out of his reach.[25]

The most amazing thing about this father image is that it never coincides with the image of the real father. Not that the latter's role is marginal. Far from it. It is to his father that Quentin addresses himself at the beginning and end of his monologue, as though he (had) expected of him an answer to his questions, an alleviation of his anguish. If Caddy is the primary object of his discourse, Mr. Compson is to a very large extent its implied *receiver*. The whole of the monologue, frequently punctuated with "Father said," could almost be defined as an imaginary conversation between Quentin and Mr. Compson, a running debate between father and son. In his function of interlocutor *in absentia,* the figure of the father occupies indeed a key position, and it is significant that when Faulkner revised the manuscript of *The Sound and the Fury,* he saw fit to give him an even greater role.[26]

Quentin, Caddy, Mr. Compson: another triad comes to light, and it is without any doubt the most crucial in the second section, the one that brings us closest to the young man's complex and tragic fate.

An oedipal triangle? Quentin's relations with his father breathe mutual trust and affection. The father/son conflict, so often evoked in Faulkner's fiction, is apparently missing here. Indeed, Quentin feels so close to his father that he makes him his confidant.[27] In his distress and disarray, he turns to Mr. Compson as the one who *knows,* and whose knowledge should help him to find a *raison d'être.* But the father's wisdom is a knowledge of death, not of life. His "philosophy," a garrulous nihilism distilled into cynical aphorisms on the absurdity of the human condition, has undeniably left a deep mark on Quentin's own thinking. Its only effect, however, has been to thrust him more irretrievably into despair.

Through his disillusioned *fin-de-siècle* rhetoric Mr. Compson has attempted to rationalize his personal failure; to him it has been a refuge in much the same way as alcohol or his reading of Horace and Catullus. And the one thing his son inherits from him is precisely his failure—a failure which he had likewise inherited from his own father. For, as Faulkner himself was to point out in an interview, in the Compson family failure is congenital:

> The action as portrayed by Quentin was transmitted to him through his father. There was a basic failure before that. The grandfather had been a failed brigadier twice in the Civil War. It was the—the basic failure inherited through his father, or beyond his father.[28]

These comments by Faulkner put Quentin's story in a genealogical perspective—a perspective barely outlined in the novel itself, but which had already begun to emerge in *Sartoris* and which was to be further explored in Faulkner's great inquiries into the Southern past, *Absalom, Absalom!* and *Go Down, Moses.* Admittedly, *The Sound and the Fury* lacks the historical dimension of the latter novels, yet it is clear that Quentin's fate is not simply that of a neurotic young man. Not unlike Isaac McCaslin in *Go Down, Moses,* he is an *heir* figure, and his tragedy is a tragedy of inheritance. Beyond his individual failure lies the bankruptcy of at least two Compson generations (Appendix, 408–9), and beyond that again the disease and decay of a whole culture.

What Mr. Compson represents to his son is all this past, and through this past he has a hold over him. Mr. Compson is weak, and yet, regardless of what he is or does, he has power—a power originating in his *priority.* And because he comes *after* his father, Quentin is inevitably caught up in a test of fidelity. Through his father, he is heir to the Southern tradition, to its code of honor with all the aristocratic and puritanical standards it implies. When this pattern of values is passed on, however, it has already lost its authority, the more so in this case as the appointed transmitter of the Southern creed is an inveterate skeptic. Quentin clings to it with desperate obstinacy, because to him it is the only available recourse against absurdity, and because its very rigidity seems a safeguard of order and integrity. Yet while transmitting the code, his father's voice has taught him its inanity. Quentin's fidelity is an allegiance to values long dead, and in making them his he chooses defeat. The Southern code has failed; the failure of tradition has become a tradition of failure. In refusing to break with it (as some later Faulkner heroes do), Quentin can only repeat the fatal errors of his fathers.

Why such a sequence of failures? How is one to account for the curse on the Compsons? For what crime is it the punishment? Faulkner gives us a clue in the sequel to the comment quoted above:

> It was a—something had happened somewhere between the first Compson and Quentin. The first Compson was a bold ruthless man who came into Mississippi as a free forester to grasp where and when he could and wanted to, and established what should have been a princely line, and that line decayed.[29]

If Faulkner is to be believed, Quentin's most redoubtable antagonist is none other than this pioneering ancestor, the long-dead founder of the family line; the decisive contest opposes the last of the Compsons to the first, four generations apart, and it is in the "something" that happened between them that we are asked to seek the deeper causes of Quentin's failure. His tragedy is indeed the tragedy of the son, but if we follow the author's suggestions, the overpowering paternal figure with whom Quentin is confronted is not at all his real father: it is embodied in the daunting features of the founding father. The quick sketch of him that Faulkner gives us here (see also the Appendix, 404–5) at once brings to mind other ancestor figures of his fiction: Colonel John Sartoris (briefly referred to at the close of section 2), Carothers McCaslin, the patriarch of *Go Down, Moses,* and Thomas Sutpen, the demonic hero of *Absalom, Absalom!*—men of daring, rapacious and ruthless like Quentin MacLachan Compson, and like him founders of an ill-starred dynasty. In the light of these resemblances, the secret kinship between Quentin and all the other victims of those legendary ghosts can be easily seen, and it becomes more understandable too why Faulkner chose Quentin as principal narrator for *Absalom, Absalom!*: through the history of another Southern family, it is his own he attempts to decipher, and if he identifies so readily with the young Henry Sutpen, it is not only because of their common obsession with incest, but also because both of them are enthralled by the same formidable father figure.

Death has raised these figures to the heights of myth, setting them at an unbridgeable distance and turning them into indestructible specters. The ancestor finds in death an extra power over the living; absence makes him godlike. Yet he is a cruel and culpable god: discharging his own guilt by the curse he heaps upon his descendants, he watches jealously over the perpetuation of the "original sin," and so ensures the inexpiable nature of the past.

True, in *The Sound and the Fury* the almost theological implications of this drama are never dwelt upon, and the importance which Faulkner accords retrospectively to the Compson ancestor is by no means evident. The latter plays no visible role in the novel, he is not even mentioned, so that the suspicion grows that Faulkner unwittingly reads his later books into the earlier one. Yet to discount Quentin MacLachan Compson altogether leads one to misunderstand the complex issue of the father-son relationship. For Mr. Compson's weakness may be said to derive primarily from the fact that he too, just like his son, is a powerless hostage of this ancestral shade. In other words, he too has never stopped being an impotent son, and is consequently unfitted to exercise his paternal prerogatives. His failure as parent is symmetrical with Mrs. Compson's: while she refuses to play the part of the love-dispensing mother, he evades the sterner duties of the father.[30] Quentin is thus torn between two equally negative father images: on one hand, the genitor, the living father of the present, weak and kindly, a mere transmitting shaft in the cogs of fate, much too close to his son to be anything else than an elder brother showing him the way to defeat; on the other hand, the dead and mythicized Father, omnipotent and fiercely repressive, because of whom fatherhood has become an impossibility and sonhood the curse of impotence.[31]

Quentin's drama can therefore have no solution—except in death. The real battle, to paraphrase one of Mr. Compson's remarks, is not even fought. It's no use fighting ghosts. Between the living and the dead the match can never be even. To Quentin the Ancestor is a mute and massive transcendence, crushing him with all his invisible weight, fating him to helpless paralysis. Nor can Quentin rise up against his real father, for the latter is just as elusive in his weakness as the great-grandfather in his hidden power.

This impasse of the father-son relationship is perhaps the major cause of Quentin's incapacity to live. It is as fatal to him as his incestuous attachment to Caddy, and the two relationships are in fact closely interdependent. Within the oedipal structure the primal function of the father is to declare the Law and guarantee its authority, and inasmuch as it is his task to deflect desire from its first object, the mother, he assumes a crucial role as interdictor. Now it is precisely as lawgiver that Mr. Compson fails his son. Quentin's tragedy is, as we have already seen, originally determined by the absence of the mother—a gap provisionally filled by Caddy and reopened by her desertion, but it can be traced back as well to a rift in what Jacques Lacan has termed the *Name-of-the-Father*, that is, in the symbolic function identifying the person of the father with the agency of the Law.[32]

Not that Quentin is law-less. But everything happens as if the distance separating the legislative figure of the Ancestor from the person of the genitor had become impossible to bridge. Though this hiatus does not cancel the Law, it radically alters its operation by precluding the process of exchange and transmission which would normally lead to the mutual *recognition* of father and son.[33]

For Quentin the Law functions in a vacuum, absolutely, and instead of being accepted as a prerequisite of order and sought after as a protection against the vertigo of forbidden desire, it is suffered as arbitrary and destructive violence. The failure is indeed a failure of *tradition:* as it is no longer *handed over* by the living, the legacy of the dead has become deadly.

Deprived as it is of its regulating function, the Law no longer ensures the normal transition from the *imaginary* register (marked by the prevalence of the dual mother-infant relationship) to the *symbolic* order (marked by the advent of mediated relationships).[34] To Quentin the mirror hall of narcissism has become a nightmare, yet for want of an intercessor he can find no way out of it.

His incest fantasy testifies to this entrapment, but one should note that in his circuitous strategies it serves several purposes. To interpret it as a resurgence of a repressed wish is plainly not enough. For the point about the incest with Caddy is that it is at once conceived as *confessed* to the father, and what Quentin secretly intends by confessing it to him is to challenge paternal authority, to provoke Mr. Compson into acting at last as the punishing father. The gamble which Quentin considers is a desperate one, but it is not without hope: the hope that the flagrant transgression of the primal taboo would entail a reaffirmation and restoration of the Law, that the very scandal of his sin would set its dialectic into motion again.

Or, to put it into more specifically Freudian terms, in attempting to provoke paternal retaliation. Quentin may be said to seek the symbolic castration which would free him from his bondage to the incestuous wish. Yet here again one must beware of oversimplification: there are as many reasons to construe his fantasy as an unconscious ruse to be spared castration. For it is certainly noteworthy too that the fantasy is conjugated in a past tense, that incest is referred to as an accomplished fact: "*I have committed*

incest I said Father it was I . . . " (97–98). Quentin's is actually
"the fantasy of having acted out the fantasy,"[35] typical of the
obsessional neurotic: "[For him] it is a question of composing his
oedipal fantasy *as if it had already been enacted:* the father already killed, the mother already possessed. In return for which
castration need no longer be considered; only guilt persists; this
is the reason why it can be so intense with him."[36] If we retain
this hypothesis in Quentin's case, our first reading of his fantasy
has to be reversed, not to be invalidated but rather to allow for
a new contradiction: the imaginary confession of incest should
then be interpreted as *both* defiance and escape—castration simul-
taneously sought after and fled from.[37]

Quentin's highly overdetermined obsession with incest is a
symptom of regression as well as an index to potential rebellion
and liberation. Like his other fantasies, it is multivalent and reversible—a skein of many interweaving threads. And as so often
with Quentin, it provides a magic answer to a real dilemma. Halted
on the threshold of adulthood, unwilling and unprepared to encounter reality, terrified by the unpredictable changes the future
holds in store for him, Quentin would do anything to turn the clock
back and revive the closed and sheltered world of childhood. There
are many hidden motives to his incest wish, but as he conceives
of it, its consummation would serve above all as a kind of pro-
phylaxis, folding his family back on itself and sealing it off
against the troublesome outsiders.[38] More specifically, as has been
suggested before, it would also allow him to reestablish his exclusive relationship with Caddy: *"Then you will have only me then
only me then the two of us amid the pointing and the horror
beyond the clean flame"* (144). And the same wish for isolation
recurs in his later (imaginary) reply to his father: "It was to
isolate her out of the loud world so that it would have to flee
us of necessity and the sound of it would be as though it had
never been" (220).[39]

The paradox is twofold, however: it is not simply a question of wresting from sin what innocence failed to preserve, but to regain innocence by way of the greatest guilt and of the everlasting punishment that this guilt entails: in hell Quentin would "guard [Caddy] forever and keep her forevermore *intact* amidst the eternal fires" (Appendix, 411. Italics added).

Far from being irreducible, it appears then that to Quentin the contradiction between the demands of his conscience and those of his desire is only provisional, and in some measure it is his very puritanism that leads him to consider the unforgivable sin of incest. His ethics is a *morale du pire:* the incest once committed, the honor of the Compsons would be rescued through the very excess of disgrace, and evil exorcised by the very enormity of his sin.

To state it again in Freudian terms: in the last resort the energy of the id is confiscated by the superego and used by the latter to further its own ends. And, as we shall soon see, Quentin's suicide is likewise a triumph of the id *and* the superego. His incest wish and his death wish both spring from the interplay of the same psychic agencies, from their confrontations and compromises: in fact, they are the opposite sides of the same coin.

Quentin's route from desire to death in many ways resembles the process of "melancholy mourning" analyzed by Freud.[40] In this process the libido, instead of reaching out toward another object, withdraws within the ego, where it serves to establish a narcissistic identification with the lost object. The ambivalence toward the object is preserved, if not strengthened, during that identification, and the conflict between the latter and the ego is then transformed into a conflict between the ego and the superego: the other is being attacked through the self, the self through the other, and by way of this reversal, the murderous impulse may be turned into a suicidal wish. In Quentin's story a similar process can be traced from the initial trauma of loss to the ultimate surrender to death.

Melancholia is closely bound up with narcissism. As we pointed out earlier, Quentin's love for Caddy is from the outset a highly ambivalent form of self-love. The loss of his sister is the fatal wound inflicted upon his narcissism; the ensuing "work of mourning" is Quentin's response to it.[41] An identification then occurs with the lost object, internalizing the conflict, transferring it to another stage, and owing to this displacement, aggressiveness is transformed into masochism. The shift is already indicated in his fights with Dalton Ames and Gerald Bland: in front of the former, he ends by fainting "like a girl" (201),[42] and his fight with the latter ends just as lamentably. In looking for trouble with men he knows to be stronger than himself, Quentin satisfies his quixotic sense of honor, but also tries to gratify his need for humiliation and punishment—a need fostered by complex guilt feelings, and reinforced by the self-hatred that has gradually come to replace his resentment toward Caddy. In the early childhood scenes Quentin was most often the aggressor; once he realizes that Caddy is irrevocably lost, his hostility is turned against himself, and henceforth he is both provoker and provoked, accuser and accused, torturer and victim.

A parallel movement of inversion and introjection converts his murderous impulses into a suicidal drive. None probably kills himself who has not begun by wishing the death of another. Quentin is no exception: before his death wish is fulfilled in suicide, it is directed at each of the three points of the triangular relationship. Sometimes it is aimed at the rivals: murder threats against Ames ("I'll kill you," 189),[43] and murderous fantasies about Herbert Head on the eve of his marriage to Caddy ("Quentin has shot Herbert he shot his voice through the floor of Caddy's room," 130). Sometimes its object is Caddy herself: "I wish you were dead" (195) says Quentin to his sister when she returns from her date with Ames, or again: "I'll kill you do you hear" (196). Yet in the scene with the knife just before this, the death wish has already begun to turn inward. It matters little whether Quentin actually proposed a "suicide pact" to Caddy or not; the point is that he envisioned it, and as we shall see, symbolically his death by drowning is indeed a *double* suicide.

Not that he has ever seriously considered killing his sister. At the crucial moment in this scene, he drops the knife (190), unable to carry through his gesture. His dreams of revenge and murder are only dreams, and whenever it is really a matter of action, Quentin falters—or faints. Just as he shrinks from murder, he recoils from incest, contenting himself with the thought of it, afraid of committing the act (220). Like the three boys encountered on his last day whom he overhears discussing the money they would get by selling a trout they haven't yet caught, he makes "of unreality a possibility, then a probability, then an incontrovertible fact, as people will when their desires become words" (145). Like the boys', his is a childish world of wishful thinking, of magic and make-believe, a world in which you can always say "calf rope" (166). Only Quentin's last fantasy is *deadly* serious, yet it is significant that the sole act of which he proves himself capable is precisely one that frees him for ever from any responsibility or obligation. And it is probably not mere chance that makes him choose the most passive form of death: death by water. His suicide, however well prepared, is less an act of will, a free decision than an entranced surrender.

Still, if Quentin's death is not a voluntary death, if from the outside it appears to be nothing else than his final admission of failure, the last resort of his impotence, one should not infer that it is devoid of meaning and finality. In much the same way as his incest wish, his suicidal urge results from multiple and contradictory motivations, and aims at resolving their conflict.

Quentin's death completes the destructive work of his relentless superego.[44] In ending his days, he expunges his guilty desire and appeases his need for self-punishment. Water delivers him from his "shadow," from the curse of being burdened with a body and a sex; it dissolves the foulness of the flesh and returns his bones to the mineral chastity of sand:

> And I will look down and see my murmuring bones and the deep water like wind, like a roof of wind, and after a long time they cannot distinguish even bones upon the lonely and inviolate sand (98).

In trying to imagine afterlife, Quentin reverts spontaneously to the water imagery associated with the ritual cleansings of his childhood and adolescence. What he expects from his suicide is a final purgation, washing him of the sin of existence, effacing the very trace of his having been alive. Only then will his guilt be absolved, the debt paid, the Law restored.

In Quentin's death reveries, water thus renews its promise of obliteration, oblivion, and peace, and yet it also retains to the last the ambiguity of its sexual implications. We have seen that throughout section 2 Caddy's body is metonymically and metaphorically linked to water and wetness. Water is a figure of desire, of its seductions but also of its dangers: in Faulkner's fiction the perils of sex are often described in terms of engulfment, and drowning is a recurrent metaphor for the vertigo of lust.[45] In Quentin's destiny the metaphor comes true *to the letter*. However solitary, his end evokes a Romantic *Liebestod,* a reunion with the forbidden sister in death: his suicide is incest at last consummated. It is not only the consequence of Caddy's marriage; it is its symbolic counterpart. "Is it a wedding or a wake?" (100): Shreve's question when he sees Quentin dressed up on the morning of his last day could hardly be more to the point.[46] After Caddy lost her virginity, Quentin for the first time thought of rejoining her in death; his dive into the waters of the Charles River is another attempt to recover possession of the sister-naiad of his lost childhood.

And beyond the sister of his childhood his reveries carry him back to the mother of his birth. The lethal waters soon become maternal waters. The river is lost to sea, a sea which Quentin imagines as an underworld full of caverns and grottoes (111, 139, 217). Everything is eventually soothed and stilled in the cosmic motherhood of Thalassa. Quentin's death marks the ultimate regression: to the quiescence before birth or, better still, to the stasis before life; to the one and to zero; to the all and to nothingness. Eros and Thanatos are the two powers that tore Quentin's life apart. Through his death their reconciliation is at last accomplished.[47]

5

Of Time and the Unreal

Le temps est le sens de la vie (sens:
comme on dit le sens d'un cours d'eau,
le sens d'une phrase, le sens d'une étoffe,
le sens de l'odorat).

PAUL CLAUDEL

IF THE BAFFLING DIALECTICS of desire and death in Quentin's section has seldom been given close attention, the thematic relevance of
time has been perceived by critics from the very beginning.[1] The
first to recognize its importance in the novel was Jean-Paul Sartre.
His influential essay on *The Sound and the Fury*, first published
in 1939, was the earliest analysis of the theme, and though it has
often been contested and is indeed very debatable, it remains to this
day an indispensable point of reference.[2] As a critical description
it is brilliant and perceptive, unfortunately, it goes astray in its
premises and in its conclusions. That Sartre was particularly interested in the second section is understandable enough, since this is
where the issue of temporality is most in evidence. But he mistook
the part for the whole in commenting upon *The Sound and the*

Fury as though it consisted only of Quentin's monologue. His second error was the familiar confusion of the author's point of view with that of one of his characters: in his essay he never hesitates to attribute Mr. Compson's philosophizings to Faulkner himself, who thus finds himself saddled with a "metaphysics of time" which is by no means his.[3] Similarly, if Sartre is quite justified in stressing the thematic implications of Faulkner's technique, he seems to forget that this technique varies from one section to another, and that time is actually a function of the narrator-character. Quentin's monologue does not exemplify a preconceived concept of time, but suggests time as experienced by an individual consciousness. Even supposing that Quentin's concern with time reflects Faulkner's own, there is no valid reason to assume that he is his spokesman. Besides, to Quentin time is much more than a concern: an obsession, one among several, and we should not dissociate it from the complex neurotic configuration within which it occurs and from which it derives its meaning.

Quentin is time-haunted, as can be seen from the very beginning of his monologue. Here again the second section stands in sharp contrast to the first, a contrast emphasized by the significant opposition between Benjy's falling asleep and Quentin's awakening. Section 1 closes with Benjy slipping peacefully into the happy unconsciousness and timelessness of sleep; Quentin, on the other hand, wakes up at the opening of the second, and to him being reborn with the day is to fall once again into the nightmare of time:

> When the shadow of the sash appeared on the curtains it was between seven and eight oclock and then I was in time again, hearing the watch (93).

Hardly has he woken when Quentin's consciousness redoubles itself as consciousness of time, of being trapped in time, and this painful awareness is all the more acute as the hint of dawn Quentin sees at his window is the dawn of his last day. The countdown has begun: from now on each hour, each minute will bring him closer to

June Dremel, 1910

The shadow of the sash fell across the curtains between 7 and 8 oclock, and then I was hearing the watch, again, ~~and I~~ and I lay there looking at the window bar across the way and motionless curtains, listening to the watch. Hearing it, that is. I dont suppose anybody deliberately listens to a watch or a clock. You can be oblivious to the sound for a long while, then in a second of listening it can create in the mind unbroken the long diminishing parade of time you did not hear. Whens up the long and lonely annunciation of light rays you might us Jesus walking, blue. The Inner Son of Man: he had no sister. Messieurs and Mesdames and Virginian, they had no sister, one minute she was

Beyond the wall Shreve's bedsprings complained thinly, then his carpet slippers on the floor. I got up and went to the dresser and slid, Had no sister my hand along it and touched the watch and went back to bed. Quisze as I knew I couldnt as if that content speculation as to what mechanical terms it in what cause to be a part I was content wasn't mind, at rest again. All right. I words what time it is. What about it? Because and Benoni and Virginian. ~~Because~~ Damballah then the wheels

Ye utter none of ye concertos: _____
upon away by a minute the clicking of little wheels

the moment of death. From the very first sentence of his monologue, Quentin's time is a time-for-death or even (insofar as his
voice reaches us from beyond life) a time-in-death.

Yet Quentin does not yield at once to the vertigo of imminence. Resorting again to magic tricks, he tries at first to outwit
time. Could he manage to forget it, he would be saved: his suicide
would then lose its *raison d'être*. Time, however, will not let itself
be forgotten:

> I dont suppose anybody ever deliberately listens to a watch or a
> clock. You dont have to. You can be oblivious to the sound for a
> long while, then in a second of ticking it can create in the mind
> unbroken the long diminishing parade of time you didn't hear
> (93–94).

Quentin's demented time awareness projects itself onto the external world, temporalizing space, spatializing time. Everything becomes a virtual signal or metaphor of time; the whole world is
transformed into a gigantic chronometer. The shadow of the sash
on the curtains in the room where Quentin wakes is the first of
these time symbols. Throughout his last day *shadows*,[4] lengthening
or shortening according to the position of the sun, constantly re-
mind him of the ineluctable flight of time, and Quentin watches
them, fascinated, as though their slow creeping movement were
time itself:

> The shadow hadn't quite cleared the stoop. I stopped inside the
> door, watching the shadow move. It moved almost perceptibly,
> creeping back inside the door, driving the shadow back into the
> door (100).

But it is his own shadow that most intrigues him. His ambiguous
attitude toward it recalls all the symbolism traditionally associated
with the *double*.[5] Yet contrary to primitive and popular lore, according to which a man's shadow is primarily a representation of
the immaterial and immortal soul, Quentin rather interprets it as
an image of the body, and it is worth noticing that he even gives it
an anatomy by referring to its belly (119, 124), its bones (118),

and its head (165). To him it is first and foremost a haunting reminder of his mortal bodily self. Its darkness partakes of the darkness of sex, sin, and guilt;[6] it stands for the part of himself he is determined to deny and destroy.[7] Hence his persistent hostility toward his dark twin brother: on many occasions he tramples on his shadow (118, 119, 124, 129, 138, 149) or attempts to "trick" it (110, 114, 118, 166), and when he looks down at his shadow on the water, he dreams of holding it under and drowning it (111). These absurd gestures and childish fantasies provide further evidence of Quentin's self-division and of his deep need to punish and be punished. It goes without saying that they also "foreshadow" his suicide: the shadow—a fleeting form without substance—is obviously also a symbol of death.[8]

Time, flesh, death, all of Quentin's obsessions intersect in the shadow image. Among these obsessions time is perhaps not the deepest, and if it is more often and more openly admitted than the others, it is perhaps just because it is more admissible than the others, and also because in the hours preceding his suicide Quentin has come to identify time as his supreme enemy, the nameless and invisible power that has reduced his dreams to naught and hurls him on to death. Yet the obsession has always been with him and can be traced back to his childhood: already at school Quentin had the habit of counting the seconds and minutes to the bell sounding the end of classes (108–9). In the narrative of his last day, the obsession is expressed by a profusion of explicit temporal references, especially numerous at the beginning and end of his monologue, and by frequent allusions to anything suggesting time, from natural time indicators such as shadows, the position of the sun in the sky and the angle of its rays, to man-made instruments of time measurement such as clocks and watches.

Nearly all of Quentin's senses are alerted to time. Time is not only something measured by the eye and registered by the mind; its law is inscribed in the organic depths of the flesh, in its rhythms and routines: "Eating the business of eating inside of you space too space and time confused Stomach saying noon brain saying eat oclock" (129). And when time stops being visible, its inescapable progress continues to claim Quentin's attention by the regular repetition of bells chiming and, even more insidiously, by the implacable ticking of his watch. Hence his various attempts to occult or silence time. In the morning, on waking, he begins by turning his watch upside down so as not to see the two hands (94). A little later, he breaks its crystal and twists off the hands:

> I went to the dresser and took up the watch, with the face still down. I tapped the crystal on the corner of the dresser and caught the fragments of glass in my hand and put them into the ashtray and twisted the hands off and put them in the tray. The watch ticked on. I turned the face up, the blank dial with little wheels clicking and clicking behind it, not knowing any better (98–99).

The symbolic significance of Quentin's gesture is obvious enough, and just as manifest is the irony of the scene: what it reveals is not only Quentin's refusal of time but the utter futility of his refusal. For in breaking his watch Quentin hurts no one but himself, and thereafter, throughout the day, the ticking goes on, pursuing him to the very end.

There is as much irony in the ensuing scene: Quentin's visit to the jeweler's shop. He walks past its window at first, feigning not to notice it ("I looked away in time," 102); then, as he sees a clock "high up in the sun" (102), he becomes aware of time again, turns back and enters the shop on the pretext of showing the craftsman his broken watch. But what he really wants to know is whether "any of those watches in the window are right" (103). The negative answer finally given him by the perplexed jeweler[9] is precisely the one he hoped for: if each of the watches tells a different time and none of them is correct, the case of their deception is proven. A last look at the window as he leaves confirms Quentin's conviction of their falseness:

> There were about a dozen watches in the window, a dozen different hours and each with the same assertive and contradictory assurance that mine had, without any hands at all. Contradicting one another.

I could hear mine, ticking away inside my pocket, even though nobody could see it, even though it could tell nothing if anyone could
(104).

Immediately afterwards Quentin recalls his father's words:

Father says clocks slay time. He said time is dead as long as it is
being clicked off by little wheels; only when the clock stops does
time come to life (105).

These reflections of Mr. Compson's refer to a polarity underlying
the entire second section and brought into evidence by Faulkner's
very technique: the seemingly irreducible opposition between the
time of clocks and calendars and the time of consciousness and
sensibility—what Sartre calls "the time of the heart."[10] The former
is a contrivance of man's intelligence, a "symptom of mind-func-
tion" (94), a quantitative concept abstracted from reality; the latter
constitutes the dense and dynamic medium of our psychic experience. This distinction between spatialized, mechanized, objective time and subjective duration is of course strongly reminiscent
of Bergsonism. Let there be no mistake, however: in Quentin's
case at any rate, there is no ontological benefit in shifting from one
to the other, no access to some "truer" dimension of being. Faulkner's rendering of his character's predicament strikes us as "truer"
in that it manages to suggest the achronological quality of inner
experience, yet for the character himself the immersion in "real"
time only means further disarray and dislocation. Time does "come
to life" for him, but only to kill him.

    To some extent Quentin's experience of time may no doubt be
said to reflect common experience, but insofar as it is conditioned
by his neurotic alienation, it possesses specific traits one cannot
afford to disregard. Contrary to Sartre's contention, what his
monologue points to is not so much a metaphysic as a pathology of
time. Isn't neurosis also a failure to come to terms with temporal
existence, resulting from a fixation to the past which prevents
adjustment to the present and mortgages the future? Quentin's
exacerbated chronophobia is above all an index to his immaturity

and confusion, as is also the utter disconnectedness of his inner time.

No one has described more judiciously than Sartre this dismantled, exploded time. Only, he forgets to specify that the *present* he analyzes is Quentin's, not Faulkner's:

> One present, emerging from the unknown, drives out another present. It is like a sum that we compute again and again: "And . . . and . . . and then." Like Dos Passos, but with greater subtlety, Faulkner makes his story a matter of addition. Even when the characters are aware of them, the actions, when they emerge in the present, burst into scattered fragments.[11]

One of the most arresting features of this present is indeed the way in which it crumbles away, the jerky movement of its *dispersal*. Bergsonian river metaphors will hardly do here: there is nothing to suggest the unbroken flow of a *durée*. Quentin's present is a line, but it is a dotted one. Moments swirl up out of an opaque emptiness and vanish again, following one another without merging into a continuity. On the linguistic level, this disjointedness is reflected, as Sartre again notes (taking the scene of the broken watch as an example), in the splitting up of Quentin's discourse into a multiplicity of short, simple clauses, and the "and" supposed to connect them rather operate as disconnectors, so that each statement seems to be closed in on itself, and that large portions of Quentin's narrative produce an uncanny staccato effect.

The other characteristic of Quentin's present is what Sartre aptly calls its *sinking*:[12] no sooner has it surged up than each moment sinks like a stone into the past; no sooner does it recede than it congeals. Hence the self-contradictory impression of time endlessly marking time, of time standing still:

> Beneath the sag of the buggy the hooves neatly rapid like the motions of a lady doing embroidery, diminishing without progress like a figure on a treadmill being drawn rapidly offstage (154).

It is true that suggestions like this are quite frequent in Faulkner's novels,[13] but in Quentin's monologue arrested time seems to be the very medium of experience. Oscillating as it is between evanescence and solidification, his present is in fact no present at all. His consciousness never adheres to the *now;* it perceives it as a flickering shadow and registers it distractedly. Quentin moves through the present like a sleepwalker; he does not live in it, turned as he is toward the past. To him the present comes to life only when it is dead; only when it is past does it gain sense and substance. Time is thus reduced to just one of its dimensions: the past enjoys absolute dominion, and not content with eating up the present, it rules out any projection into the future. Instead of being a possibility, Quentin's death takes on even before it happens the incontrovertible finality of a *fait accompli.*

Present, past, future are apprehended indiscriminately by way of *memory,* and memory bewitches all time into a turbulent stasis. It invades the whole mind and becomes its exclusive function. Much like Benjy, Quentin does not *have* a memory; to a large extent, he *is* his memory. So much so that he not only tends to forget the pastness of the past, but that the hallucinatory reactivation of memory-traces sometimes totally obliterates the present moment. Consider, for instance, his fight with Bland: the scene is recounted not by Quentin but by his friend Shreve; Quentin no longer knows why he tried to hit Bland (206); he seems to emerge from the fight as from a confused bad dream, and everything indicates that he is scarcely conscious of what has happened to him. But we learn later that before the incident Bland had spoken disrespectfully of women, and that before striking him Quentin had asked: "Did you ever have a sister? did you?" (206). A year earlier Dalton Ames had likewise offended feminine honor, and Quentin had then asked exactly the same question (199). Without being aware of it, Quentin has identified Bland with his sister's first lover, and this identification has sufficed to tip the present into the past. While being beaten up, Quentin relives a scene of his past, and the drubbing he is given by Bland revives once again the humiliating experience of his utter helplessness before his rivals.

Quentin's monologue reads like a palimpsest. Almost every moment of his life opens, backwards and/or forwards, onto other moments resembling it. The similarity may be due to the return of an earlier situation (as in the fight with Bland and all the triangular scenes), to the reappearance of an identical background (all the water scenes) or it is suggested even more subtly through the recurrence of identical motifs in different spatio-temporal contexts. Thus the equation of the Quentin-Bland scene with the Quentin-Ames scene is surreptitiously prepared by the association bird-water-broken sunlight[14] used in the narrative of Quentin's walk along the river with the little Italian girl:

> There was a bird somewhere in the woods, beyond the broken and infrequent slanting of sunlight (168).
>
> The bird whistled again, invisible, a sound meaningless and profound, inflexionless, ceasing as though cut off with the blow of a knife, and again, and that sense of water swift and peaceful above secret places, felt, not seen not heard (168-69).
>
> . . . I looked off into the trees where the afternoon slanted, thinking of afternoon and of the bird and the boys in swimming (182-83).

The same motif reemerges in the remembered scenes with Ames and Caddy:

> . . . behind him the sun slanted and a bird singing somewhere beyond the sun (199).
>
> I heard the bird again and the water (201).
>
> her face looked off into the trees where the sun slanted and where the bird . . . (203).

All these echoes and cross-references induce a disturbing sense of *déjà vu:* we are caught with Quentin in a spell-binding set of mirror images in which things and events are perpetually duplicated through the giddy interplay of reflections. Quentin's is a world where the present is but a mirror held up to the shadows of the past, a theater of ghosts where nothing is ever first, where nothing ever begins. All Quentin's actions, including his suicide, are simply re-beginnings, compulsive, Sisyphus-like repetitions of an ineffaceable past. No newness is produced, no difference can occur, or rather the only possible alteration is a gradual degradation in the dreary round of sameness.

The greater the pressure of this memory-ridden time, the emptier Quentin's world. For if the past weighs on the present and shapes it inexorably in its image, it is hardly more real to him. In much the same way as Benjy, he seems to exist "between" the present and the past, that is, in the similarity between the two. Unlike the characters of Joyce and Virginia Woolf, Quentin experiences no epiphany, no "moment of being." Contrary to Proust's world, there is here strictly speaking neither time lost nor time recaptured. The past haunts the present, it never comes to inhabit it. In Proust memory can be a source of illumination; remembering is far more than a moment of the past relived: "something which, common to both past and present, is much more essential than either of them,"[15] crystallizes in the mind, touching off a transtemporal experience, an ecstasy that allows the self, the "true" self, to rise above the contingency of mere duration and to recognize itself in the plenitude and permanence of its identity. To Quentin there is no such transcendence of time within time; for him, the encounter of present and past, instead of achieving a happy fusion, can only result in painful confusion. And in this confusion there is nothing to sustain a stable sense of selfhood. Quentin is so irretrievably lost in it, so racked between past and present that he no longer knows whether he *is* or *has been*. *"Non fui. Sum. Fui. Nom* (sic) *sum"* (216) : coming almost at the close of his monologue, these Latin words epitomize his total failure to reconcile becoming and being, time and identity. Ironically, Quentin then turns at last to the future, the future he had so far chosen to ignore. But the only future he considers is actually a nonfuture, a simple promise of extinction: "And then I'll not be. The peacefullest words. Peacefullest words" (216).

Since he can neither be himself in time nor escape alive out of time, Quentin seeks refuge in death. But even as he prepares to relinquish the world of the living, he has already begun to die to it or—to be more faithful to the subjective quality of his experience—the world has already begun to die to him. Space has become a place of exile and restless wandering, secretly conquered by *emptiness:*

> The houses all seemed empty. Not a soul in sight. A sort of breathlessness that empty houses have. Yet they couldnt all be empty (164).
>
> The road curved on, empty (165).
>
> The entrance to the lane was empty (165).
>
> The road went on, still and empty, the sun slanting more and more (168).

Quentin is a lonely traveler in a deserted space whose very atmosphere becomes rarefied:

> Even sound seemed to fail in this air, like the air was worn out with carrying sounds so long (140).

In Quentin's disenchanted gaze, the New England scenery which forms the décor of his last day shrivels to a "waste land," stirring up by contrast nostalgic recollections of the generous summers of his home country:

> Only our country was not like this country. There was something about just walking through it. A kind of still and violent fecundity that satisfied ever bread-hunger like. Flowing around you, not brooding and nursing every niggard stone. Like it were put to makeshift for enough green to go around among the trees and even the blue of distance not that rich chimaera (140).

In retrospect, the South has come to stand for the lost Eden, the motherland of plenty. New England, on the other hand, reflects Quentin's present state of starvation. Thin colors, thin air, a landscape drained of all vigor; everything bespeaks a world on the verge of exhaustion. Becoming their own replicas, depthless and weightless, things look like "ghosts in broad day" (100). Halfway between life and death, Quentin wanders in a spectral space; even before he left his home country for Harvard, his world had dissolved into a grey limbo of mocking shadows:

> I seemed to be lying neither asleep nor awake looking down a long corridor of grey halflight where all stable things had become shadowy paradoxical all I had done shadows all I had felt suffered taking visible form antic and perverse mocking without relevance inherent themselves with the denial of the significance they should have affirmed thinking I was I was not who was not was not who (211).

As much as through shadow imagery this process of derealization is suggested through the motif of the *mirror*.[16] In Benjy's section, the mirror functions as a beneficent object, associated with the brightness of fire, with Caddy's loving and protecting presence, and the safety of a stable and orderly world: "refuge unfailing in which conflict tempered silenced reconciled" (211). In the second section its symbolic meaning is reversed: mirrors are no longer linked with light and fire but with darkness and water, and instead of giving shelter, they become disquieting presences, partaking like shadows of the uncanny nature of the double. In Quentin's memory, the mirror is an emblem of Caddy's departure (95, 100); in his present experience, it stands as a symbol of his wounded narcissism. In the course of his comings and goings on his last day, Quentin looks several times at his reflection: in the morning he stares at his shadow in the river (110); after his fight with Bland, he tries to look at his face in a basin of water (203); later, in the trolley car on the way home, he catches sight of his reflection in a window (209), and before committing suicide he looks at himself in the mirror of his dormitory room for the last time (222).[17] It is worth noting that, except in the last instance, all Quentin's mirrors are unstable ones: the quivering surface of water or a windowpane reflecting his face "on the rushing darkness" (214)—liquid mirrors, mirrors silvered with night, reducing everything to a mere flicker of appearances. They only heighten Quentin's sense of unrest and impermanence: in much the same way as his shadow, his mirror image materializes the division of his self and portends its imminent destruction. In his reflection he sees himself as other—unreal, imaginary, dead. "Isn't looking at oneself in a mirror thinking of death?" Paul Valéry asks.[18] The image of his body which Quentin glances at is indeed nothing but the reflection of a reprieved corpse.

Instability, fragmentation, unreality: these are also, in Quentin's quasi-posthumous perception of the world, the essential attributes of *light*. Caught in the ever-renewed interplay of shadows and reflections, light is ceaselessly divided and refracted, scattering through space in myriads of luminous atoms: trees lean over the wall "sprayed with sunlight" (140); the shade of trees is "dappled" (149, 151); "the river [glints] beyond things in sort of swooping glints (137), and Quentin sees "the last light supine and tranquil upon tideflats, like pieces of broken mirror" (211). Light resembles a swarming of ants: "Sunlight slid patchily across his walking shoulders, glinting along the pole like yellow ants" (152). Or it is held in quivering suspension like a butterfly: ". . . light began in the pale clear air, trembling a little like butterflies hovering a long way off" (211). And by a sudden reversal of the simile, "yellow butterflies flickered along the shade like flecks of sun" (151; see also 175).

One is almost tempted to read these suggestive evocations of light and shade as a passing tribute to the beauty of the natural world—Quentin's farewell to the sun before his descent into darkness. The profusion of reflections and refractions, glints and glimmers reminds one at times of the effervescent luminosity of impressionist painting. Yet the multiplying omens of death hardly allow the enchantment to work. The movement of light here is not fluid expansion so much as infinite dispersal, and nothing better defines the space of its reverberation than the image of the *broken* mirror (211).[19] This sense of brokenness combines with Quentin's sharp awareness of obliquity or *declivity*[20]—a spatial cognate, as it were, to the temporal notion of decline: most of Quentin's descriptions include allusions to oblique and downward movements, and obliquity also characterizes the direction of light, often referred to as "slanting" (149, 151, 168). The sun always

sheds its light at an angle, and the slant of its beams measures for
Quentin the advance and decline of the day, reminding him like
the hands of his watch of the irreversible passing of time and the
ineluctable approach of death.

The sense of an ending increases as the light of day decreases
into *twilight*.[21] As in *As I Lay Dying* human death is symbolically
associated with the dying of the day—an association emphasized
by Quentin's transferring the waning of light to himself:

> As I descended the light dwindled slowly, yet at the same time with-
> out altering its quality, as if I and not light were changing, decreas-
> ing, though even when the road ran into trees you could have read
> a newspaper (209).

As though he had already reached the threshold of death, Quentin
then feels the burden of time getting lighter:

> . . . I could see the twilight again, that quality of light as if time
> really had stopped for a while, with the sun hanging just under the
> horizon (209-10).

The closeness of Quentin's end is equally hinted at through the
association of twilight and water:

> . . . the road going on under the twilight, into twilight and the sense
> of water peaceful and swift beyond (210).
>
> I could feel water beyond the twilight, smell (210).

The onset of night and the proximity of water both portend death.
But for Quentin they are also reminders of the past, stirring the
memory of other scenes connected with greyness and wetness: it
was in the same "grey light" (187, 192, 195) that he met his
sister at the branch, after finding out about her affair with Ames;
it was also in the abetting shadows of twilight that Caddy joined
her lovers. Quentin's twin obsessions with sex and death thus
merge one last time, and again he comes to brood on what has
become the major symbol of his torment, the odor of honeysuckle:

> When it bloomed in the spring and it rained the smell was every-
> where you didnt notice it so much at other times but when it rained

the smell began to come into the house at twilight either it would rain more at twilight or there was something in the light itself but it always smelled strongest then until I would lie in bed thinking when will it stop when will it stop (210).

Shadows and reflections, the flickerings of daylight and the uncertainties of twilight—all these images of instability and impermanence are signs of a world disjointed and adrift. They symbolize for Quentin the ceaseless movement of becoming, of flux and change, and to him all changes are changes for the worse and all becoming is but a hemorrhage of being.

Reverberating through the final pages of his monologue, the word "temporary," "the saddest word of all" (222), points accusingly to the ultimate cause of Quentin's tragedy: time, the universal destroyer, the irresistible agent of defeat and death. His individual experience is thus virtually raised to broader significance; Mr. Compson's rhetoric, at any rate, tends to present the pathetic destiny of the young suicide as an extreme exemplification of our common condition. Quentin's father articulates in abstract terms what his son suggests through a chaos of broken images and fragmented memories, namely that man's curse is to be shackled to time:

> Father said that a man is the sum of his misfortunes. One day you'd think misfortune would get tired, but then time is your misfortune Father said (129).

Time means sundering. It removes us ever further from the plenitude of the origin and brings us ever closer to death. And indefatigably it secretes in us that other form of death, forgetfulness:

> . . . Father said That's sad too, people cannot do anything that dreadful they cannot do anything very dreadful at all they cannot even remember tomorrow what seemed dreadful today (98).

It dulls and degrades our affections and wears away even our sorrows:

. . . It is hard believing to think that a love or a sorrow is a bond purchased without design and which matures willynilly and is recalled without warning to be replaced by whatever issue the gods happen to be floating at the time no you will not do that until you come to believe that even she was not quite worth despair (221).

Mr. Compson's reflections on time unquestionably add a new dimension to Quentin's monologue and invite the reader to consider his despair and suicide in a philosophical as well as psychological perspective. Yet the nihilistic aphorisms of the old drunkard no more express Faulkner's convictions than they provide the key to Quentin's suicide. Mr. Compson implies that his son is considering suicide because he cannot bear the idea of being robbed of his very despair. Now it is true that Quentin clings to it as if its sheer intensity were a protection against nothingness,[22] and that he is alarmed at the prospect of losing even his sense of loss. However, even admitting that his death is *also* a gesture of protest against an absurd world, Quentin dies above all because of his inner weakness, and nothing in his monologue allows one to assume that at the point of death his blind confusion has yielded to tragic lucidity. Quentin *lives* the absurd in the narcissistic vertigo of his obsessions and fantasies; to the end he lacks the power of detachment which would convert his experience into awareness and so make his suicide a death *against* the absurd. Quentin's is not a philosophical suicide but the predictable end of his long journey into night.

The crux of the matter in section 2 is not time; it is Quentin's relationship to time. And as if to belie his failure to live and to invalidate Mr. Compson's a priori rationalizations of it, the monologue itself intimates the possibility of different relationships. One of these is hinted at through the image of the *trout*, whose shadow Quentin watches in the water:

I could not see the bottom, but I could see a long way into the motion of the water before the eye gave out, and then I saw a shadow hanging like a fat arrow stemming into the current. . . . The arrow in-

creased without motion, then in a quick swirl the trout lipped a fly
beneath the surface with that sort of gigantic delicacy of an elephant
picking up a peanut. The fading vortex drifted away down stream
and then I saw the arrow again, nose into the current, wavering
delicately to the motion of the water above which the May flies
slanted and poised. . . . The trout hung, delicate and motionless
among the wavering shadows (144-45).

Conjoining stability and suppleness, gravity and grace, the trout
stands for a mode of being in which self-possession does not pre-
clude adjustment to a changing environment. The fish achieves
balance in the vortex, immobility in motion, eternity in time. Just
as Ben, the Bear in *Go Down, Moses,* has always escaped the
hunters, the old trout has defied all the fishermen in the area for
over twenty-five years (145). Like Ben, the "great ancestor" of the
wilderness, it symbolizes endurance, and it is perhaps because it
represents to Quentin himself his not yet totally extinguished desire to live on that he asks the three boys to leave it alone (148).[23]
It is significant, though, that in his thoughts (the interpolated
italicized passage in the description of the trout) this image of life
is instantly reversed into a vision of death: the liquid shadow of
the fish becomes in his reverie a flickering flame, water turns to
fire, the living depths of the river are replaced by the abyss of hell
where Quentin imagines himself burning eternally with Caddy
(144). Quentin fails to understand the parable of the trout; he can
conceive of no immobility other than death.

The obvious parallel to the fish suspended in the water is the
bird poised in the air:

. . . in a break in the wall I saw a glint of water and two masts, and
a gull motionless in midair, like on an invisible wire between the
masts (110).

As the aerial counterpart of the trout, the *gull* is another model
of grace, delicate poise, and dynamic immobility. Yet its meaning
for Quentin is more ambiguous. On the one hand, the gull seems
to hover above the flux of time:

I could hear my watch and the train dying away, as though it were running through another month or another summer somewhere, rushing away under the poised gull and all things rushing (149).

On the other hand, the association of its outspread wings with the hands of a clock turns it into yet another time symbol:

> The hands were extended, slightly off the horizontal at a faint angle, like a gull tilting into the wind (105).

Moreover, the gulls are repeatedly described as if they were hanging in space on "invisible wires" (110, 129). Is this to suggest that their freedom is only a deceptive appearance? The image is actually one of *hampered* flight, reflecting Quentin's wish for escape but also its frustration.

As for other Faulkner heroes, the air comes to represent for Quentin the element par excellence of the immaterial, the boundless, the timeless, and is thus set in sharp contrast to earth and water. The latter are the emblems of human finiteness; the air stands for the infinite. Hence the positive valuations given in Quentin's dualistic imagination to ascent and flight: to fly is to be free of earth's gravity, to conquer both flesh and time.[24] Nowhere is this striving for transcendence, this desire to rise above the world more eloquently expressed than in Quentin's envious and admirative vision of Gerald Bland rowing:

> . . . all things rushing. Except Gerald. He would be sort of grand too, pulling in lonely state across the noon, rowing himself right out of noon, up the long bright air like an apotheosis, mounting into a drowsing infinity where only he and the gull, the one terrifically motionless, the other in a steady and measured pull and recover that partook of inertia itself, the world punily beneath their shadows on the sun (149).

In this amazing description we discover another aspect of Quentin's imaginary world, what one might call its positive pole. The imagery that prevails in his monologue is the negative imagery of descent, dispersal, and darkness. Here we find its reverse: the evocation of a solitary and glorious ascent toward the ethereal

regions of infinity. The nightmare of time ("all things rushing")
and the nausea of matter give suddenly way to a bright dream of
escape out of the "puny" world.

It is of course not fortuitous that the fulfillment of this sun-
dream is granted not to Quentin but to the "royal" son/sun figure
of Bland.[25] The heroic transfiguration which the latter embodies
in this scene is clearly not for him. Still, as his father suggests in
commenting upon his projected suicide, Quentin too is thinking
of an "apotheosis":

> . . . you are not thinking of finitude you are contemplating an
> apotheosis in which a temporary state of mind will become sym-
> metrical above the flesh and aware both of itself and of the flesh it
> will not quite discard you will not even be dead (220).

Contrary to Bayard Sartoris, Quentin lacks the energy to match
his dream of "apotheosis" in death. He dies as lamentably as he
lived. But he too seeks in death a form of immortalization, and
one of the many paradoxes of his suicide is that self-destruction
becomes a way to self-aggrandizement. For what the suicide is
meant to accomplish is the expunction of the abhorred carnal self,
and it is in order to get rid forever of his body that Quentin takes
care to weight it with two flatirons before diving into the Charles
River. Yet in his imaginations of death the destruction of the body
is no total annihilation. In the passage already quoted in which he
speculates upon his posthumous destiny and evokes his bones at
the bottom of the sea, he puts himself in the position of a beholder:
"I will look down and see my murmuring bones . . ." (98). Sur-
viving his own death as a disembodied I/eye, Quentin projects
himself into afterdeath to be witness to his own dissolution; seeing
himself dead, he will not be dead altogether. So what Quentin
actually expects from his suicide is not at all a state of not-being
but rather an *ek-stasis,* that is, literally, a standing outside and
beyond his self—without any self-loss.

A divided self, a dual death:[26] in his suicide Quentin is once
again split into two distinct halves: while the gross corporal self

is given over to nothingness without any regrets, the ideal self, having managed to get rid at last of its cumbersome twin brother, gains full access to the perfect immobility of the timeless. This ultimate scission, though, by no means diminishes the magic virtues and curing powers which Quentin attributes to his suicide. As his father rightly notes, the death he is seeking does not even imply a complete renouncement of the flesh nor a total abrogation of time. Quentin's "apotheosis" is in fact a compromise with eternity: flesh restored to innocence rather than immolated; time arrested rather than abolished; the ego unburdened and exalted rather than destroyed.

It goes without saying that this miraculous resolution of all contradictions is purely *imaginary:* Quentin's suicide is the ending of an elaborate play performed from first to last in a mock theater, among shadows and reflections, and staged by a Narcissus enthralled by his own image. The passage through the looking glass is eventually achieved by drowning: a reentry into the waters of death/birth, a return of self to self, blotting out all otherness and erasing all difference. But by *whom* is the mirror traversed? An unanswerable question. Quentin tries to make the limits of his ego coincide with the absolute limit of death; he would cross the boundary and pass to the *other* side without ceasing to be himself. It cannot be done. Identity is no more found in death than it was in life. Quentin's rapport to death is an impossible one; his suicide turns out to be a fool's bargain.

For the protagonist of Tolstoi's story, "The Death of Ivan Ilyich," the prospect of death means first of all a return to the solitude of the self, but it also reveals to him his existence as irremediably his own: Ivan comes to acknowledge time and to accept death, taking it into himself as the most intimate of possibilities, and is therefore allowed to salvage his banal life from pretense and absurdity before he dies. For Quentin, on the other hand, death is never a possibility, but a faked certitude. He keeps playing at hide and seek with himself to the very end, and his game with life and death is throughout a double game. Quentin's encounter with death is in fact nothing more than an ultimate lure, the final mirage before the mirror is shattered. The last of his fictions.

Quentin's story can be read as an ironic version of the familiar journey of the Romantic ego:[27] from descent into a private hell to glorious resurrection, from self-loss to self-aggrandizement. Goethe's Werther, Chateaubriand's René, Byron's Manfred, Shelley's Prometheus, and a host of lesser Romantic figures at once come to mind. There is of course nothing heroic about Quentin, but his tortured egotism, his alienation from the actual world, and his yearning for the purity and perfection of absolutes are assuredly Romantic traits. Like Horace Benbow, Gail Hightower, and Ike McCaslin, he is longing for the stasis and permanence enjoyed by the lovers on Keats's Grecian urn.[28] And like his spiritual cousins, he belongs with Faulkner's potential artist or poet figures.[29]

As such he is also, as Faulkner himself came to admit, a self-projection of the author.[30] Quentin has been created out of the depths of the novelist's emotional experience, and he is undeniably the most complex portrait of the artist as a young man.[31] There can be no question either that his haunted vision, his anguish and suffering are at the very center of the novel. Yet even though Faulkner called him "that bitter prophet and inflexible corruptless judge of what he considered the family's honor and its doom" (Appendix, 412), Quentin hardly qualifies for the role of "moral agent" which so many critics take to be his.[32] Not simply because he is too weak and too confused to take significant action, nor because his despair is rooted in neurosis, but because there is nothing behind his moralistic poses and family pieties but plain, unmitigated narcissism. Faulkner himself points out that Quentin is "incapable of love" (Appendix, 412): there could be no more damning comment. No doubt he is "a sensitive young man," yet seldom has "the sensitive young man" been more thoroughly demystified; no doubt he is a Romantic, but in the last resort his Romanticism comes down to glorified infantilism. Rip off the noble mask, and you'll find Benjy's whining baby face. For all the autobiographical elements that went into the character, Faulkner holds him at a distance, and subjects his loveless, life-denying egocentricity to ruthless exposure. What is perhaps most admirable about Quentin's monologue is a unique combination of empathy and critical detachment. For in exposing Quentin's blindness, Faulkner gives the full measure of his own insight and of the extraordinary self-knowledge he must have achieved by the time he wrote *The Sound and the Fury*.

Quentin, the writer's *alter ego* and *pharmakos,* eventually dies of his fictions. Faulkner, by writing them into a fiction of his own and capturing them in the mirror of a novel, succeeds here for the first time in making his art a vehicle of living truth.

April 5th, 1928

Once a bitch always a bitch what I say. I says dont blame me if you cant do anything with her. You never could do anything with any of the others, how do you expect to have tried to do anything with her, have she you expect to begin this late, and whenever I tried to you ... what I got. I says crying even here until do any good, either stop worrying about her or ... either stop worrying, over-her and napping at me about her, or keep your hands off and let me do it. I'll have to have. What she needs and all she needs is a good whipping. When people have nigger ways, no matter who they are the only thing to do is to treat them like a nigger. Then she says they own flesh and blood it more up and curses me. She says You are the one not one that isn't a reproach to me, Jason. And I says what else do you expect, from these Compsons, and went on downstairs and left you're lucky if her playing out of school is all that worries you. I says she ought to be down there in that kitchen right now, instead of me suppos a kitchen full of niggers that could stand up out of a chair unless they're put a pan full of her cold bread and meat to balance them. And she says "But to have the school authorities think that I cant control her, that I cant ———"

"Well." I says. "You cant, can you? How can you expect to do anything with her," I says — You can have tried to do anything with her, I says, "how do you expect to begin this late?" She thought about that for a while. "But to have them think that .... did you sign that report to have?"

"Did I sign it?" I says, "I even knew she ever had one. She's meant them to let me know she had me; I'd a known what she was up to

I didnt even know she had a report card. She told me last fall that they weren't using them anymore. And now for Professor Junkin to call me up and tell me if she's absent one more time, she will have to leave school. How does she do it? Where does she go to? You're down here all days you ought to see her if she stays on the streets."

"Yes." I says, "if she stays on the streets. I dont reckon she'd be playing out of school just to do something she could do in public." I says.

Then she began to cry again, talking about how her own flesh and blood rose up to curse her. "You are the one not one of them that isn't a reproach to me," she says.

"Sure." I says. "I am bound have to be. I am bound have to go to Harvard or drown myself into the ground. I had to walk. But of course if you want me to follow her around and see where she goes, I can argue with old ... I can quit the store and get a job as nightwatchman. You can use Ben for the night shift."

"I know I'm just a trouble and a burden to you." she says, crying on the pillow.

"I ought to." I says, "You've told me that enough. Even Ben ought to know it now. Do you want me to say anything to her about it?"

"Do you think it will do any good?" she says.

"Not if you come down there interfering," I says. "If you want me to control her, just say so and keep your hands off. Every time I try to, you come butt in, and she goes both of us the laugh."

"Remember she's your own flesh and blood," she says.

6

Jason, or The Poison
of Resentment

The petit bourgeois is the man who has
preferred himself to all else.

MAXIM GORKI

Once a bitch always a bitch, what I say. I says you're lucky if her playing out of school is all that worries you. I says she ought to be down there in that kitchen right now, instead of up there in her room, gobbing paint on her face and waiting for six niggers that cant even stand up out of a chair unless they've got a pan full of bread and meat to balance them, to fix breakfast for her (223).

IN ITS SARCASTIC BLUNTNESS the opening paragraph of Jason's monologue signals straightaway the distance separating the third section from the previous two. Nothing here like Benjy's incoherent babble, nothing like Quentin's tortuous reminiscences and reveries. Another voice is heard now, harsh, vulgar, petulant, a voice hysterically self-assertive. From the interior monologue, with the unpredictable meanderings of its private logic, we switch to the plainer and louder language of the dramatic soliloquy; despite occasional use of associative patterns, Jason's section owes in fact much more to the tradition of oral narrative than to the Joycean stream-of-consciousness.[1] At times it is as though one overheard the unpremeditated talk of someone thinking aloud; more often it is as if one read the verbatim transcript of an impromptu oral account. Contrary to Benjy's "trying to say" and to Quentin's self-absorbed musings, Jason's discourse at once emphasizes the narrator's awareness of himself in the very act of speaking (through the countless interpolated *inquits:* "I say(s)," "like I say," "what I say") and suggests time and again the presence of an addressee, the silent complicity of a listening *you,* often explicitly referred to in the text.[2] For all its self-consuming fury, the rhetoric of Jason's monologue points to an eagerness to communicate, a desire to win over his implied audience which has no parallels in Quentin's or Benjy's section.

What is more, with Jason the novel reverts to its traditional narrative function. A story gets told, and Jason assumes the role of storyteller with almost histrionic glee. As a consequence, there are no longer any barriers to our understanding: the presentation of events is most often in chronological sequence, and the very few time-shifts occurring in the section are handled in such a careful way as to reduce the risk of confusion to a minimum.[3] Although Jason is by no means a reliable narrator, the narrative thus gains clarity and coherence, many gaps in the reader's information are filled in, and the fragments of the Compson story collected in the previous sections begin at last to fall into an intelligible pattern.

Similarly, traditional models reassert themselves in the characterization of the narrator-protagonist. Jason is one of Faulkner's most superb creations, and he is surely a far more complex character than has been generally acknowledged. Yet, sharply individualized as he is, he acts above all as the comic villain of the piece, and in this role he turns out to be an original combination of several standard types supplied by tradition. With the third section, *The Sound and the Fury* moves into the vicinity of folk comedy—a vein Faulkner was to explore more fully in *As I Lay Dying,* the Snopes trilogy, and *The Reivers.* In his racy colloquial language as well as in his antisocial attitudes, Jason reminds one of the vernacular figures created by the humorists of the Old Southwest. His lineage can be traced back to Simon Suggs and Sut Lovingood,[4] characters whose pungent wit and brutal candor are close to his, and who are his peers in cruelty and meanness. Moreover, insofar as his mental and emotional life is reduced to a small set of *idées fixes* and stock responses, Jason also presents affinities with the "humor" in the sense defined by Ben Jonson, and most richly illustrated in fiction by Dickens. And lastly one may see him too as a distant country cousin of the great railers and misanthropes of Western literature—Homer's Thersites in the *Iliad,* Shakespeare's Timon and the many malcontents of Elizabethan drama, Molière's Alceste, and the Gulliver of the last voyage.[5] To compare Jason to these imposing figures is to do him perhaps too much honor, yet like them he is in his own petty provincial way an implacable man-hater, and in like fashion, too, he takes the role of the satirist,[6] venting his rancor in floods of invective and sarcasm, and exposing human folly with merciless eloquence.

Jason equally resembles these famous railers in being both agent and target of the satirical thrust. His whole monologue may be read as a brilliant variation on the classical theme of the satirist satirized.[7] Faulkner's irony here kills two birds with one stone: it works at Jason's expense, since his speech clearly shows him to be a rogue and a fool, but at the same time it operates through his agency at the expense of the other Compsons, reducing the drama of their downfall to the ludicrous proportions of a madhouse chronicle:

> I haven't got much pride. I can't afford it with a kitchen full of niggers to feed and robbing the state asylum of its star freshman. Blood, I says, governors and generals. It's a damn good thing we never had any kings and presidents; we'd all be down there at Jackson chasing butterflies (286).

Jason has throughout a sharp eye for the incongruous and the grotesque, and as satirist he is all the more redoubtable because Faulkner—the satirist behind the scenes—lends him his own talents for the role. Described without nuance, stripped of everything that might earn them understanding or pity, the protagonists of the family drama become in his monologue the typecast actors of a burlesque Southern melodrama halfway between Caldwell and Tennessee Williams: alcoholics for a father and an uncle, a whining hypochondriac for a mother, a trollop for a niece, and a drooling idiot for a brother, such are the dramatis personae in section 3. Small wonder that the tale of their mishaps, including Jason's own, turns to Gothic farce.

All these alterations induce quite naturally a different relationship between the reader and the narrator-character. In Quentin's monologue our first response is identification, and it is only on second thoughts that we come to view the character critically; with Jason, on the contrary, the possibility of identification is undercut by the novelist's irony. The distance between Jason and all those he rails at is paralleled by the distance of revulsion and derision separating Jason from the author. To Faulkner, Jason represented, in his own words, "complete evil," and in the same interview he added: "He's the most vicious character in my opinion I ever thought of."[8] It should be noted, however, that as narrator and commentator Jason possesses at times an almost demonic power of persuasion. He is indeed a villain, but he is a very disturbing one, and as John Longley notes, "he is disturbing because we all know he lurks in us."[9] The reader's response to Jason is therefore an extremely ambivalent one: to the extent that he is held up to ridicule and contempt, identification with him is deflected toward a sense of comic exhilaration arising from the conviction of our moral superiority; we side with Faulkner against Jason or, as Wayne C. Booth puts it, "we take delight in communion, and even in deep collusion, with the author behind Jason's back."[10] This is not to say, however, that identification is totally precluded.

The very violence of the reader's recoil from such a character is in itself suspect, and one may well wonder whether it is not unconsciously intended to prevent the shock of recognition. For insofar as Jason voices and acts out our own aggressive emotions, he becomes a magnified mirror image of our own rancorous selves— an image both repellent and fascinating from which we hastily escape into derisive laughter and comfortable contempt.

In this connection it may be tempting to speculate upon the relationship between Jason and his creator. Apparently, the character stands for everything Faulkner abhorred. Yet it seems safe to assume that identification and distancing were at play here just as they were in the second section. To interpret Quentin in merely biographical terms and to equate him with the author is to yield to romantic fallacy. But conversely it would be quite as wrong to believe that, contrary to Quentin, Jason is a pure fictional construct, a grotesque figure projected in cool satirical detachment. That Jason was removed from Faulkner by the whole range of the novelist's irony is obvious enough. Yet his presence in the book is without any doubt as immediately felt as Quentin's; perhaps it is even more compelling in the raw power of its fury. Could it be so compelling, so hallucinatingly "real," if Jason were not somehow related to the deeper springs of Faulkner's creation?

When asked about *The Sound and the Fury* in 1953, Mrs. Maud Falkner, the novelist's mother, made the following comment: "Now, Jason, in *The Sound and the Fury*—he talks just like my husband did. My husband had a hardware store uptown at one time. His way of talking was just like Jason's, same words and same style. All those 'you know's.' He also had an old 'nigrah,' named Jobus, just like the character Job in the story. He was always after Jobus for not working hard enough, just like in the story."[11] If we are to believe this testimony, the sources for Jason are not far to seek, and the possibility that this villainous character may have been at least partly modeled on Faulkner's own father is indeed a very intriguing one. Years ago Carvel Collins suggested that Jason may be viewed as a fictional embodiment of the superego; it is interesting to know that his voice in the novel is perhaps quite literally the voice of the father. One could of course press the point and interpret the third section as an oedipal settling of accounts. Yet if it was a literary parricide, it was also an act of identification, and in the father the son probably recognized another of his potential selves.

Just as there was a Stavrogin or a Smerdyakov in Dostoevski, there must have been a Jason in Faulkner.[12] But our concern here is not to find the counterparts of his characters in real life nor even to determine how the characters are related to the ambiguities and complexities of the novelist's psyche, but rather to apprehend them from within the work itself, to see how they relate to one another, and how they function within the thematic structure.

Thematically there is no major break between section 3 and the preceding sections. But the treatment of themes is set in a very different key and undergoes radical changes. It almost looks as if they had been turned inside out. Thus in Jason's monologue, the brother-sister relationship, though hardly less central than in Benjy's or Quentin's, changes its sign from plus to minus: what Jason feels for Caddy is hatred, a hatred as intense and uncontrollable as Benjy's love or Quentin's love-hate. To him as to them she is a rankling memory; for him as for them she has been the instrument of disaster. Not that he misses his sister as his brothers do, but the loss he has suffered is directly related to her: Herbert Head, Caddy's fiancé, had promised him a job in a bank—a promise broken because of her misconduct. The child she had to leave him as a hostage has therefore become in his eyes "the symbol of the lost job itself" (383–84), and it is on his niece that he will take out his hatred. What differentiates Jason from his brothers is essentially his response to loss: Benjy howls in blind protest; Quentin commits suicide; Jason, on the contrary, carefully nurses his resentment and is determined to take revenge.

Yet the differences are perhaps less significant than the resemblances. "Because like I say blood is blood and you can't get around it" (303): when Jason invokes the family heritage to account for his niece's promiscuity, he is ironically unaware of how much his statement also applies to him. In his monologue he poses as the only sane and sensible man in a world of fools and lunatics, and prides himself on his worldly wisdom and his capacity to cope with reality. He believes and would have us believe that he has nothing in common with the other Compsons. This belief, however, is given the lie by his behavior and is just one of his many delusions about himself. In a sense, it is true, Jason is indeed an outsider and has been one since his early childhood. His mother considers him a true Bascomb (225, 244, 249), and seemingly cherishes him as her only child. Not unlike Jewel, Addie Bundren's favorite son in *As I Lay Dying,* Jason has been deeply marked by his mother's preferential treatment, but as Mrs. Compson is incapable of loving any one except herself, he has been little more than a pawn in the destructive game she has been playing with the family.[13] All she has accomplished is to mold Jason in her likeness, and, by not allowing him to think of himself as a Compson, she has been quite successful, too, in alienating him from his father, his brothers, and his sister. Of all her children he is undeniably the one most like her in his mean-spirited egoism, his imperturbable smugness, and his petit bourgeois concern for propriety. On closer examination, however, it becomes clear that Jason has inherited as much from his father as from his mother. Mr. Compson's cynical philosophy has left its mark upon his mind as it has upon Quentin's: in spite of his undisguised contempt for his father, Jason has adopted his principles and erected them into a rigid rule of conduct. His inflexible logic is Mr. Compson's skepticism hardened into dogma, and by pushing it to preposterous lengths, he unwittingly exposes its contradictions and provides the final proof, *per absurdum,* of its impracticality.[14]

Even more surprising: Jason turns out to be in many ways Quentin's homologue. On the face of it, the two characters are of course poles apart, and it seems safe to assume that Jason was originally conceived to serve as a foil to his brother. Beside Quentin, Jason is no doubt a buoyant extrovert. Whereas Quentin, in his adolescent romanticism, flees from "the loud, harsh world," Jason, even though he does not feel at home in it, is bustling about with pugnacious energy and desperately scrambling for success. Most critics have noted the contrast between Quentin's quixotic idealism and Jason's hard-nosed pragmatism. What has been less often noted is that the former's idealism and the latter's pragmatism are equally spurious, and that behind these deceptive façades one finds the same amount of self-centeredness and the same capacity for self-delusion, or, to use again Faulkner's more ambiguous term, the same irreducible "innocence." Jason is in fact merely the negative of his brother—a tougher Quentin who, instead of becoming a suicide, has turned sour.

They do not fly together, but birds of a feather they surely are. Throughout, their actions and attitudes reveal startlingly similar patterns. With both there is a persistent refusal of the Other, an unfailingly hostile response to anything or anyone likely to threaten the closure of their narcissistic world. Only—and it is here that the differences show—while Quentin's aggressiveness turns finally against his ego and ends in self-destruction, Jason's strikes out in sadism.

Jason misses no opportunity to inflict pain upon others, and as Cleanth Brooks has pointed out, in its sophisticated meanness his cruelty goes well beyond that of a Popeye or a Flem Snopes.[15] Its roots are in his childhood, as can be seen from the early episode recorded in the first section in which he cuts up the paper dolls which Caddy had made for Benjy (79).[16] Similarly Jason takes a perverse pleasure later in subtly frustrating Caddy's desire to see her daughter (254–55), or in tormenting poor Luster when he burns the two circus tickets before his eyes (317–18). In his own way Jason, just like Benjy and Quentin, remains true to his childhood,[17] and Dilsey is well aware of the childish perversity

hidden beneath his adult meanness when she scolds him at the
end of the circus ticket scene: "A big growed man like you" (318).

Within the family circle Jason can indulge his petty tyrannical
bent and his sadistic whims in full safety. Outside, in his social
and professional relations, prudence would normally commend a
measure of vigilance and restraint. Yet Jason's animosity is so
irrepressible that it breaks out at the slightest provocation and impels him to antagonize whoever comes his way. In all the conversations recalled in his monologue, his own words are nothing but
gall and vinegar: he ceaselessly taunts Earl, his former business
partner (in fact, his employer since Jason withdrew his money
from the business to buy a car), and treats his customers with
haughty condescension; he tells off the telegrapher for not keeping
him right up to date with the stock reports, quarrels with the
sheriff who refuses to help him catch his runaway niece, and provokes an old man into assaulting him in Mottson. Projecting his
own malevolence and dishonesty on to others, Jason senses treach-
ery everywhere, suspects everyone, and regards the whole world
as his personal enemy.[18] And on Easter Sunday, during the frantic
chase after his niece and the carnival man with the red tie, his
morbid suspicion develops into a positively delirious sense of
persecution.

If Quentin's divided self is close to schizophrenia, Jason's
conspiracy and persecution fantasies belong with the symptoms
of paranoia.[19] The world, as seen and experienced by him, is—
in much the same way as for Quentin—the mirror image of his
own neurotic self; it is full of hostility and malice, and his relationship to it is one of permanent warfare. As Jason describes
the conflict, one might think that he only fights for survival in
an unfriendly environment, and that his aggressive behavior is
dictated by the necessities of self-defense. It soon appears, however, that Jason himself writes the script and stages the show,
albeit unconsciously, and it becomes quite evident too that his behavior patterns are determined beforehand by the contradictory

demands of his paranoid condition. By using every opportunity to antagonize his family and his acquaintances, Jason, while finding release for his pent-up rage, also provokes retaliation from those he abuses and assaults. The expected counter-attacks of his opponents are indeed an integral part of his singular game, and they serve in fact several purposes: (1) they provide him with a posteriori justifications for his own aggressions; (2) supply new food for self-pity by confirming him in the role of victim, and (3) gratify as well an obscure need for punishment, as can be seen from the way he courts disaster in the final pursuit episode. To Jason, then, persecuting and being persecuted are complementary, and the compulsive pattern of his internal drives requires that he be alternately agent and sufferer. Which is to say that his bellicose behavior is not just unmitigated sadism. Although Jason may seem to be a simpler character than his brother Quentin (an impression ironically reinforced by Jason's image of himself in the monologue), his antagonistic relationship to others involves likewise complex processes of exchange and transference, and points to the devious workings of a residual sense of guilt. True, with Quentin masochism and self-destruction prevail while with Jason the emphasis is on aggressiveness, yet in both cases one has to make allowances for the intricate play of displacements, reversals, and occultations from which each character derives his many-layered ambiguities.[20]

The difference between the two figures lies not so much in the psychological components of their personalities as in the dynamics of their working out. The basic features are almost identical, but differently combined and differently stressed. This identity-in-difference can also be traced through the subtle modulation from private obsessions to collective fantasies that occurs in section 3. Contrary to Quentin's extreme estrangement from society (not to speak of Benjy's autistic isolation), Jason's relation to it is a very odd mixture of rebellion and conformity. His paranoid resentment is surely boundless, and for his ever-ebullient malice any available target will do. It is noteworthy, however, that his animosity flows so many times into the fixed channels of common prejudice.

In its lighter moments Jason's sardonic wit is leveled at such harmless stereotypes of folk humor as misers, small-towners, old maids, parsons (241, 308, 310, 311), and, more significantly, intellectuals:

> Like these college professors without a whole pair of socks to their name, telling you how to make a million in ten years . . . (311).

Anti-intellectualism generally goes along with xenophobia, and Jason is no exception to the rule:

> But I'll be damned if it hasn't come to a pretty pass when any damn foreigner that cant make a living in the country where God put him, can come to this one and take money right out of an American's pockets (239).

A champion of Americanism, hostile to foreigners, Jason also feels quite naturally anti-Yankee as a Southerner:

> . . . maybe your damn company's in a conspiracy with those damn eastern sharks (270).

Not surprisingly either, his national and regional prejudices are coupled with ethnic prejudice, as evidenced by his strong anti-Jewish feeling—a feeling he expresses with the hypocritical qualifications and reservations that have always been characteristic of the more "respectable" forms of anti-Semitism:

> "I give every man his due, regardless of religion or anything else. I have nothing against jews as an individual," I says. "It's just the race. You'll admit that they produce nothing. They follow the pioneers into a new country and sell them clothes" (237-38).

And it goes without saying that Jason holds nothing but scorn for blacks:

> What this country needs is white labour. Let these damn trifling niggers starve for a couple of years, then they'd see what a soft thing they have (237).

> Like I say the only place for them is in the field, where they'd have to work from sunup to sundown. They cant stand prosperity or an easy job. Let one stay around white people for a while and he's not worth killing. They get so they can outguess you about work before your very eyes, like Roskus the only mistake he ever made was he got careless one day and died. Shirking and stealing and giving you a little more lip and a little more lip until some day you have to lay them out with a scantling or something (312-13).

The black, the Jew, the foreigner, the intellectual: as many avatars of the despised and detested Other. In accordance with the standard procedures of bigotry and racism, Jason congeals them into rigid categories and reduces their being to a small set of unalterable predicates: Jews are mercantile and parasitic, Negroes lazy and thievish, etc. Once petrified by prejudice, they become safe objects for Jason's hatred and contempt, and afford him moreover ready assurance against his own mediocrity.

The spectrum of Jason's preconceptions and phobias would of course not be complete without sexual prejudice. Jason is as much a sexist as he is a racist, and, just as on Jews and blacks, he has on women his stock of rancid clichés to neutralize their humanity. One index to this dehumanizing process is his use of animal imagery: Jews are likened to sharks (270), Negroes to monkeys (315), and women to bitches (223, 329). Another is the way in which Jason objectifies behavior and classifies actions. Whatever a woman may do, she can do nothing that will not fit neatly into his ready-made deterministic patterns: "Just like a woman," he declares when Caddy's check reaches him six days late (236). Yet his assumed knowledge and foreknowledge of feminine behavior do not immunize him against its perils. The trouble with women is that only their unpredictability is predictable; they are so illogical in their arguments, so fickle in their moods and motivations that anything can be expected any time: "I dont know why it is I cant seem to learn that a woman'll do anything" (303). That is why woman becomes for Jason the supreme enemy, the first object of his hatred and resentment: she is to him the most perverse embodiment of irrationality, and therefore a permanent challenge to his schemes and calculations, an ever-present threat impossible to avert. And ironically the development of the action in the novel seems to prove Jason right in his fears: he is twice flouted by a woman, the first time by Caddy, whose promiscuity prevents him from getting the promised job, the second time by her daughter Quentin who, by running away with the money he had so artfully and so painstakingly stolen from her, again reduces his hopes and projects to nothing.

Jason's misogyny differs from Quentin's in that it does not imply a total repudiation of sexuality. Yet, arising from the same deep-seated suspicion, it leads him likewise to arrest woman in an arbitrary concept of womanhood. Desexualized and idealized in romantic fashion, woman becomes to Quentin the white idol of the inviolate Virgin, but we already know how little this image is to be trusted and how little Quentin trusts it himself. Jason turns Quentin's gyneolatry inside out, spelling out what "the champion of dames" had suspected all along but refused to acknowledge, namely, that all women are bitches. For Quentin this is an unbearable truth which he does his utmost to conceal under the noble trappings of courtly idealism. Jason, on the other hand, seemingly adjusts to it by choosing "a good honest whore" (291) for a mistress. This is not to say, of course, that he is less deluded about women than his brother: the whore is simply the reverse or correlate of the virgin—another mythic fabrication to rationalize women out of existence and to prevent the possibility of a true encounter. By debasing woman to the function of a marketable commodity, Jason thinks he can keep his distance from her, the more so as he is careful to establish his liaison with Lorraine on a contractlike commercial basis.

Yet Jason's crass and cynical "philosophy" about women, so readily translated into action with his docile mistress, no longer operates as a safe and efficient strategy where Caddy and her daughter are concerned. Here emotional involvement takes the upper hand, as becomes pretty obvious in Jason's dealings with his niece. Quentin II is the favorite target of Jason's rage and hatred; money is the sole object of his love. Both passions, it should be remembered, are closely related to his sister. Caddy plays the role of money-provider: potentially, insofar as her marriage was to assure Jason a respectable position at her husband's bank; actually, since for fifteen years he has been stealing from her two hundred dollars a month. In other words, it is from Caddy that Jason expects the gratification of his dearest wishes, and in this respect he reminds one again of his brothers and especially of Quentin: in Jason, one might argue, Quentin's ambivalence toward Caddy, instead of being internalized, has been dissociated and displaced. This hypothesis is the more plausible as displacement manifestly underlies Jason's relationship to Quentin II, and as the latter nearly comes to occupy in his monologue the central place which her mother held in the previous sections.

It is most remarkable, too, that Jason's relationship to his niece parallels Quentin's relationship to his sister in such a way as to become its parodical reenactment. Jason is indeed as compulsively preoccupied with his niece's promiscuity as Quentin was with Caddy's. The reasons given are no doubt different, yet between Quentin's sense of honor and Jason's concern for respectability there is only a difference of degree. Furthermore, Jason is so sincerely outraged by the girl's escapades that a hypocritical care for propriety will hardly do for an explanation. Here again Jason's attitudes are extremely inconsistent, and once more his actual behavior gives the lie to the thoughts and feelings he professes. At one moment he pretends to be indifferent to Quentin's fate:

> Like I say, let her lay out all day and all night with everything in town that wears pants, what do I care (300).

But immediately after his indignation and anger explode:

> These damn little slick-haired squirts, thinking they are raising so much hell, I'll show them something about hell I says, and you too.

I'll make him think that damn red tie is the latch string to hell,
if he thinks he can run the woods with my niece (301).

Jason rails at "those damn town squirts" (243) just as Quentin
did, and it is revealing that both should use the same colloquial
phrase of abuse (see section 2, 166: "It's for letting it be some
damn town squirt I slapped you"). His fury here is strongly
reminiscent of his brother's resentment of Caddy's early dates. Similarly, in the scene where he confronts his niece at the beginning
of section 3 (227–35), his brutality parallels—even in particular
gestures such as grabbing her arm—Quentin's aggressiveness toward Caddy in many of the scenes described in section 2. The
parallel is further emphasized by the girl's defiant attitude, and
when she threatens to tear her dress in front of Jason, one is irresistibly reminded of the scene at the branch on the day of
Damuddy's death, when young Caddy took hers off as a challenge
to Quentin. In both scenes the gesture of undressing is felt as a
provocation, and its effrontery maddens Jason just as it outraged
Quentin's prudery. Their being both scandalized by the sight of
naked female flesh is a clear index to their puritanical recoil from
sex. To Jason as to Quentin, sex is associated with the darkness
of sin, and in his monologue woods—the bewitched area that
haunted Hawthorne's Puritan sinners—become once again the
secret abode of shameful lust: "Are you hiding out in the woods
with one of those damn slick-headed jellybeans? Is that where
you go?" (229). Significantly too, sexual obsession and ethnic
prejudice overlap in the image of the promiscuous Negro girl:
". . . I'm not going to have any member of my family going on
like a nigger wench" (234). And it is precisely the same puritan
and racist imagery that expresses Quentin's anxiety over his sister's
lost honor: *"Why must you do like nigger women do in the pasture the ditches the dark woods hot hidden in the dark woods"*
(113–14).

The ambiguity of such attitudes and such language need hardly
be stressed again. While professing to be shocked and disgusted
by his niece's outrageous make-up[21] and slovenly deshabilles, Jason

feels secretly titillated and barely manages to conceal his lecherous thoughts:

> . . . if a woman had come out doors even on Gayoso or Beale street when I was a young fellow with no more than that to cover her legs and behind, she'd been thrown in jail. I'll be damned if they dont dress like they were trying to make every man they passed on the street want to reach out and clasp his hand on it (289).

There is an unmistakable touch of prurience and voyeurism about Jason's constant spying on his niece (again reminiscent of Quentin's attitudes toward Caddy), and what impels him to chase her around the countryside through ditches and poison oak is not only the desire to get his money back but also the hope to catch her in the act. In Jason's relationship to Quentin II hatred prevails, but its sheer intensity points to the depth of his emotional involvement, and it is probably not going too far, as one critic suggested, to relate it to a "deeply repressed incestuous attraction."[22]

The recurrence of similar if not identical situations, attitudes, gestures, as well as the many verbal echoes of section 2 in section 3, provide conclusive evidence of the very close affinities between Quentin and Jason. Yet they also emphasize the contrast between past and present. Instead of the pathetic confrontations recalled in Quentin's monologue, we find here scenes of harsh vulgarity which show how deep the Compsons have sunk under Jason's rule. In the third section everything takes on a more sordid color. Perhaps too a truer color, revealing Quentin as well as Jason in a clearer light. For after all, Quentin's influence upon his sister was no less damaging than Jason's on his niece. More insidiously, his perverted love produced the same results as outspoken hatred. "If I'm bad," says Caddy's daughter to Jason, "it's because I had to be. You made me. I wish I was dead. I wish we were all dead" (324). Before her, Caddy voiced the same resigned despair, the same awareness of being "bad" (196), and instead of invoking destiny, she could well have accused Quentin of corrupting her. The victims, one of a jealous brother, the other of a vindictive uncle, Caddy and her daughter both recognize themselves eventually as damned in the maleficent mirrors held up to them by their pitiless judges. Quentin and Jason are doubtless not alone in working their wretched fates, but as prosecutors and persecutors they are undeniably instrumental in turning them into "lost women." In the last resort the novel pits the two brothers back to back: Jason is Quentin the censor become torturer; Quentin is Jason with the alibi of high-minded idealism. The third section, in this respect, is not simply a grating repetition of the second; it is also a radical demystification of Quentin's fevered romanticizing.

Because of their extreme self-absorption and self-delusion, Quentin and Jason alike are destructive to themselves and to others. For the same reasons, they also fail to come to terms with reality, and nothing illustrates this better than their common failure to conquer time. With regard to time as in other matters, the seeming opposition between the two brothers should not blind us to the congruence of their attitudes. Jason, it is true, does not break his watch; he is not haunted by the past as Quentin was, and shows nothing but sneering contempt for tradition. Yet, as we have already seen, he is trapped in the past as his brothers are, and even though memory plays no prominent part in his life, the "outrage" he suffered when Caddy deprived him of the promised job is still an open wound. In Jason's monologue, flashbacks are far less numerous than in Quentin's, but in the one major shift to the past, his thoughts return significantly to his sister (251–56). What sets him apart is that instead of brooding endlessly on Caddy, he takes active steps to make good the affront. Where Quentin was haunted by the past, Jason is obsessed with the future. The future, to him, is above all a call to vengeance; it is what will allow him to settle his account with the past. Tomorrow becomes the antidote to yesterday.

For him, then, it is not so much a question, apparently, of escaping from time as of catching up with it. From the continual

shuttling between store, telegraph office, and home related in the
third section to the mad pursuit described in the last, Jason's life
is nothing but a long and exhausting race against the clock. A
ludicrous race as well: Jason's compulsive bustle reminds one of
the incongruous frenzy of actors in the early silent movies; like
them, Jason is transformed into a grotesquely gesticulating puppet
by the jerky acceleration of movement. Always on the alert, always
in a hurry, dashing convulsively from place to place without ever
getting anywhere on time, Jason spends all his energy in sheer
waste. Unforeseen and uncontrollable incidents occur at every
turn and develop into a series of exasperating contretemps: Jason
arrives at the telegraph office an hour after the cotton market has
closed; he has run out of blank checks when he needs them to
deceive his mother once more; he "just misses" catching his niece
and her carnival lover, and so on. Jason never has time enough
to master time. The more he works himself up for action, the
farther behind he gets: the tantalizing distance between the empty
present and the bright, avenging future will never be bridged.

Jason is like a trotting donkey, with a carrot forever dangling
beyond his reach. While Quentin dreams of a vertical eternity
above time, Jason's eternity is an ever-receding mirage lying *ahead,*
on the horizontal line of duration: paradoxically, like all naïve
believers in "progress," it is in time that he flees time. "Just let
me have twenty-four hours" (329), he pleads at the end of his
monologue. Those twenty-four hours measure the gap that sep-
arates him from the realization of his covetous dream—a dream
not far removed, after all, from Quentin's: both are actuated by
the same narcissistic and regressive wish to retain, to possess, to
lay in a treasure-store and to shelter it from the law of change.
For Quentin the "treasure" to be hoarded is Caddy's virginity; in
Jason the same hunger for self-extension through safe and exclusive possession manifests itself more prosaically in the love of
money, and finds its most eloquent metaphor in the strongbox
where he keeps the dollars stolen from Caddy. But Jason loses

his savings just as Quentin lost his sister. All his calculations, ruses, and precautions cannot save him from disaster.

In the Appendix to *The Sound and the Fury* Faulkner tells us that Jason is "the first sane Compson since before Culloden," and defines his character as "logical rational contained" (420). It should be clear by now that Faulkner's statements about him are to be taken ironically. In point of fact, the way in which Jason reacts to people and events is every bit as emotional as that of Quentin or, for that matter, Benjy, and his attempts to force experience into a rigid order of his own, far from distinguishing him from his brothers, only confirm the likeness. True, cold rationality is what he is striving for, as can be seen from his meanly legalistic approach to all practical questions and from his propensity to reduce all relationships to business arrangements. But even more than by the unpredictability of events his need for rational order is flouted by the irrationality of his own impulses. Not only does his reason betray him time and again in his dealings with his family; even in business matters, it abandons him whenever an important decision is to be made. His performance as a businessman is indeed a poor one, and for all his cupidity and cynicism, he fails miserably in his enterprises. As old Job points out to him, the very excess of his suspiciousness turns against him:

> "You's too smart fer me. Aint a man in dis town kin keep up wid you fer smartness. You fools a man whut so smart he cant even keep up wid hisself," he says, getting in the wagon and unwrapping the reins.
> "Who's that" I says.
> "Dat's Mr Jason Compson," he says (311-12).

Jason ends up trapped by his own machinations, and his actions all bear out Job's shrewd remark. Consider his cotton speculations (237-40, 270-71, 281-83, 303-8) or his sporting bets (314): they establish beyond any doubt that so far from being reached through cool reasoning his decisions are invariably dictated by whim or vanity or the most puerile spirit of contradiction.

Too suspicious to believe in luck, too impulsive to adhere to logic, Jason is doomed to lose out at every turn.

As reflected in his monologue, Jason's thinking is in itself a shabby travesty of rational thought. "Once a bitch always a bitch": the opening sentence of his speech exemplifies from the outset the kind of sophistry that vitiates his reasoning throughout; it is the first of the many unwarranted generalizations that allow his prejudices to posture as plain objective truths. Most of Jason's ideas and opinions belong in the same category of false induction: they are little more than the rough and ready rationalizations of preconception and rancor. His ratiocinative mania (another trait of his paranoid personality) demands that every fragment of experience be coerced into procrustean mental patterns and that nothing be left unexplained. But for Jason it is not so much a matter of explaining as of explaining *away,* of reducing complexity to simplicity, of converting otherness into sameness. What he looks for is the magical surrogate of a logical system—a system proving the world to be a vast and sinister conspiracy and thus buttressing his sense of outraged martyrdom.

Jason, however, is not a very imaginative paranoiac, and his mind is far too shallow and conventional to devise a system of its own. What he thinks is seldom what *he* thinks. His ideas are all second-hand, and, as we have seen, they all come from the threadbare ideology of his cultural environment. The very texture of his speech testifies to his mental barrenness: its diction is repetitious; its syntax multiplies subordinate clauses but never masters them, and its whole language tends to freeze into formulas.[23] Jason's grammar is hardly better than his logic, and provides evidence not only of his lack of education but also of his abysmal vulgarity. True, his blustering rhetoric has an acrid flavor of its own, yet fundamentally his language is dead and deadening: it immobilizes everything and everyone in a hideous grimace, creating the arrested image of a world in which a woman will always act "just like a woman," and where Negroes will be forever "niggers." Behind this accumulation of pseudo-logic and tauto-logic, one senses an atrophied intelligence, frantically feeding on the meager diet of its stale truisms and stereotyped fantasies. A nauseous compound of clichés, a dreary dictionary of *idées reçues:* in the last analysis Jason's monologue has nothing else to offer.

Such concepts as rationalism, realism or pragmatism, then, appear totally irrelevant as far as Jason is concerned. They refer to what he would be, not to what he actually is. His tough-minded stance is just a protective pose, a fragile barrier erected against the world and against his own folly, and bound to break down in times of stress. The final chase of Miss Quentin is a case in point. Jason's irrationality, hitherto contained, then erupts in a most spectacular way: in the course of his pursuit, he drops all his pretensions to sense and sanity, throws prudence and moderation to the winds, and rushes headlong toward disaster. The madness of the Compsons, so often the butt of his jibes, has obviously not spared him, as even Jason himself comes to realize in his very rare moments of lucidity:

> Me, without any hat, in the middle of the afternoon, having to chase up and down back alleys because of my mother's good name . . . there I was, without any hat, looking like I was crazy too. Like a man would naturally think, one of them is crazy and another one drowned himself and the other was turned out into the street by her husband, what's the reason the rest of them are not crazy too (289-90).

Jason is "crazy too," and his madness can be seen at its furious climax on Easter Sunday, after the disappearance of his niece with the money from the strongbox. Wild fantasying then comes to obliterate his precarious sense of reality in ways reminding one again of Quentin. Nothing is left of Jason's cocksure aggressive stance, and he now plays the victim and wallows in self-pity. Yet at the same time, as a true Compson, he projects himself into heroic imaginary characters to sustain and strengthen his vacillating self-image. Quentin thought of himself as the last medieval knight and likened his imminent death to the sacrificial death of

Christ; similarly assuming that his petty private affairs are of universal moment, Jason casts himself in the Romantic part of the heaven-storming rebel. In his delirious megalomania his burlesque misadventures are given operatic scale and raised to tragic significance; his opponents are no longer a little slut and a vulgar showman but "the opposed forces of his destiny" (384), while Jason himself is suddenly transmogrified into a provincial Prometheus or a seedy Satan:

> From time to time he passed churches, unpainted frame buildings with sheet iron steeples, surrounded by tethered teams and shabby motorcars, and it seemed to him that each of them was a picket-post where the rear-guards of Circumstance peeped fleetingly back at him. "And damn You, too," he said, "See if You can stop me," thinking of himself, his file of soldiers with the manacled sheriff in the rear, dragging Omnipotence down from His throne, if necessary; of the embattled legions of both hell and heaven through which he tore his way and put his hands at last on his fleeing niece (382).

The return to reality is triggered off by the harrowing experience of physical humiliation, in the scene of Jason's tangle with the old man at Mottson—a scene which, as Duncan Aswell has judiciously pointed out, "might have come straight out of Quentin's day,"[24] and closely parallels the latter's fight with Gerald Bland. Quentin tries to hit Bland to avenge a woman's honor; Jason acts no less absurdly in provoking an old man he has never seen before and who has nothing whatsoever to do with his troubles. In both scenes there is a kind of quid pro quo, of tragicomic misunderstanding, the person attacked being each time a surrogate for the real antagonist out of reach. If Jason considers himself less quixotic than his brother, his blind anger leads him eventually to the selfsame tilting at windmills. His fight, like Quentin's, is shadowboxing in a shadow world, the more ludicrous as he falls and hits his head on a rail before the furious old man has had a chance to get near him with his rusty hatchet. Several other details of the scene further underscore the irony of repetition: references to blood (203–4, 388), inviting comparison with Quentin's bleeding nose, and the question asked by the witness of the inci-

dent who believes it was a suicide attempt (388) and asks Jason
if the girl he is looking for isn't his sister (289).

The clinching irony, however, comes at the end of the episode,
when Jason finds himself a victim so wretched that his plight
recalls not only Quentin's impotence but also the utter helplessness of his idiotic brother Benjy. His energy drained and his
bravado gone, Jason is now like a puppet with its strings broken,
and we see him crushed, annihilated by the bitter humiliation of
total defeat:

> He sat there for sometime. He heard a clock strike the half hour,
> then people began to pass, in Sunday and Easter clothes. Some
> looked at him as they passed, at the man sitting quietly behind the
> wheel of a small car, with his invisible life ravelled out about him
> like a wornout sock (391).

Through Jason's lamentable failure Faulkner makes a kind of
poetic justice triumph. Situations and roles are reversed according
to the standard patterns of farce and comedy: Jason's story is that
of the robber robbed, the persecutor persecuted, the victimizer
turned victim. As in the puppet theater, one would be tempted to
clap the downfall of the villain, had not the novelist changed his
attitude in the meantime. In the final scene of the chase, when
Jason, alone and abandoned, slumped behind the steering wheel
of his little car, is patiently waiting for one of the despised Negroes
to drive him home, he is no longer a laughable figure. Not that
he suddenly enlists our sympathy. But the contempt heaped upon
him throughout the novel gives way now to that respect mingled
with pity that Faulkner had grace enough to grant each of his
creatures at the hour of extreme solitude or impending death, be
they as vile as Popeye, Flem Snopes or Jason.

From blustering bullying self-affirmation Jason is thus brought
down to abject impotence. By the end of the novel he has been
exposed to the core of his being, with no corner of his tortuous
mind left unsearched. He now stands before us as a living embodiment of Evil, yet with Faulkner Evil is never simple: Jason's vil-
lainy is not to be explained away by the facile assumptions—

whether metaphysical, psychological or sociological—that he was born bad and predestined to play the villain. As Faulkner portrays him through the ambiguities of his speech and the contradictions of his behavior, Jason appears as neither wholly guilty nor totally innocent, being both the victim of circumstance and the agent of his own defeat. Furthermore, insofar as the Evil he comes to embody is rooted in the corruption, not only of his family, but of society at large, it clearly transcends the narrow limits of his shabby individuality.

The social dimension of the character is indeed crucial for a proper understanding of the third section and for a correct assessment of its significance within the novel. A number of critics, notably Olga Vickery and Cleanth Brooks,[25] have described the general movement of *The Sound and the Fury* as one of progressive expansion and opening, and have pointed to a gradual shift from private to public concerns. Michael Millgate, for his part, notes that the progression from the first to the third section indicates a growing awareness of the social and even economic issues involved in the action of the novel. There can be no question that Jason's monologue offers a broader perspective than the two previous ones, although his point of view is as narrowly subjective as that of his brothers (indeed more so than Benjy's). It calls the reader's attention beyond the Compson household, and by doing so it allows him to set the family drama in a social context and to relate it to all the subtle pressures and influences of a specific cultural environment.

Yet even more meaningful perhaps than the unfolding of the social scene in section 3 is the way in which society conditions and shapes Jason's very language and thought. None of the first three monologues is more deeply socialized, and none, as we have seen, is more thickly encrusted with ideological deposits. In this connection it should be noted too that Jason is the only one to speak the colloquial idiom of his region and the only one to seek a social identity. Both Benjy and Quentin are outsiders: the former is separated from the world by his idiocy, and the latter estranged from it through his neurotic obsessions. Jason's case is different, since he is at least trying to find his niche in society: ". . . I've got a position in this town" (234), he tells his niece, and throughout the novel we can see him making desperate efforts to put up a front, to keep the family name—what is left of it—intact in the eyes of public opinion. The irony is of course that he fails to do so. Jason does not enjoy the esteem of his fellow citizens, and the Jefferson community only tolerates him because of the respectable position once held by his family. So he too comes close to being an outsider, and he is at any rate too marginal, too much of an eccentric to be considered truly representative of his milieu.

Still, a Southerner he is, and although we should make allowance for the exaggerations and distortions of satire, there is no doubt that his portrait is to some extent a radioscopy of the Southern mind. But to what South does Jason belong, the old or the new, that of the Sartorises or that of the Snopeses? It has been argued, notably by George O'Donnell,[26] that in contrast to Quentin, the last defender of the aristocratic code, Jason stands for the crass materialism of the rising Snopeses. But it is certainly not enough to say that he is a Snopes. That he has much in common with Snopesism, as it is portrayed in Faulkner's later novels, no reader would think of denying. Jason abandons, or thinks he abandons, all allegiance to the values of the traditional South, and cynically congratulates himself on his lack of moral scruples (284); his greed, his dishonesty, his meanness rival anything Flem Snopes can offer. It is hardly surprising, then, that in a society in which Snopesism has become the common standard of behavior, Jason should be the only Compson to survive. But this is precisely what differentiates him from Flem: he just manages to survive, he does not make his fortune. According to Faulkner, Jason was the only member of his family able to stand up to the Snopeses on their own ground.[27] In point of fact, however, he is no match for Flem, and in *The Mansion* the latter has no more difficulty outwitting him than the other citizens of Jefferson.[28]

Jason lacks the patient craftiness and cold single-minded determination which pave the way to Flem's success. He is doubtless a very vocal exponent of the new mercantile non-ethic, but his bumbling ineptness in practical matters is a very poor illustration of Snopesism in action.[29] The reason is perhaps that his greed is of another order. The Snopeses are rapacious like beasts of prey; they are driven by the vulgar appetites and coarse ambitions of the rootless upstart, and their rise to money and power is as irresistible as a natural catastrophe. Jason, on the other hand, the last survivor of a degenerate bourgeois family, is caught in the paralyzing contradictions of his heritage; for him, life started with the searing experience of loss, and, do what he will, his blind hunger will never be quenched.

Jason should not be confused then with the rising class of the Snopeses anymore than he should be identified entirely with the class of his origins. Jason himself seems to feel uncertain as to where he belongs and shifts grounds according to mood and circumstance. Now he sides with the poor hill farmers (237), now he curses them (242) or denounces their improvidence (308–9); now he rails at his family's social pretensions, now he acts as the self-styled and self-appointed defender of the Compson name. Admittedly, Jason sees himself as a Bascomb, a member of the mercantile and uneducated lower middle-class family of his mother, rather than as an aristocratic Compson, yet in his status anxieties the haunting memory of the Compson past cannot be discounted. Jason feels déclassé, and it is this sense of social degradation that gives his resentment its sharp edge of bitterness. Jason is Faulkner's portrait of the addled petit bourgeois, and through him he has lent an eloquent voice to all the malcontents of the new South of the twenties: decayed aristocrats, grubbing small businessmen, hard-pressed dirt-farming rednecks, all those whom the hazards of the economic system had condemned to grovel in mediocrity and to boil with chronic frustration. Jason speaks for this mass of disgruntled Southern whites, and his discourse distils their grievances and complaints with sour precision.

Like most failures and misfits, Jason considers himself the victim of an unfair destiny which has robbed him of his due and pushed him out of his rightful place in society. It is quite remarkable that on the rare occasions when he switches from *I* to *we,* it is to voice a sullen sense of solidarity with his anonymous companions of misfortune:

> I dont see how a city no bigger than New York can hold enough people to take the money away from *us country suckers* (291-92. My italics).

But this furtive awareness of a victimization shared with others never leads Jason to a recognition of human interdependence. In characteristic American (and Southern) fashion, the feeling of helplessness in the face of inscrutable social and economic powers is overcompensated by a hysterical emphasis on the virtues of individual achievement:

> Besides, like I say I guess I dont need any man's help to get along I can stand on my own feet like I always have (256).

In their context, Jason's cocky assertions of autonomy (see also 258, 263, 307, 327) sound like ironic echoes of the legendary spirit of independence of the pioneers and frontiersmen from whom Jason is descended, and one might almost take them for a wry parody of Emersonian "self-reliance." What Jason's brand of individualism is worth we already know: it is nothing but the mask and alibi of his conformity.

Suspiciousness, intolerance, and prejudice round off the portrait, and it goes without saying that these features also belong to the typical petit bourgeois mentality. Xenophobia, anti-Semitism, racism, anti-intellectualism, misogyny: it is in these forms of aggressiveness, sanctioned and encouraged with varying degrees of hypocrisy by society at large, that the petit bourgeois's inarticulate resentment is eventually channeled and fixed. The political implications of this particular set of stereotyped attitudes and stock responses are obvious enough: Jason and his like are part of those strata of American society where the radical right has always recruited its most ardent supporters. Not that Jason is a conservative in the classical sense of the word; he has none of the latter's nostalgias for a bygone world, and he could not care less about tradition. But he comes pretty close to being what Richard Hofstadter has termed "the pseudo-conservative":[30] intent on keeping a good appearance in public, clinging self-righteously to the respectable image of himself in the roles of hard-working businessman, dutiful son and meritorious breadwinner of the Compson household, Jason conforms to conservative standards as far as his official selves are concerned. And he does not do so out of mere hypocrisy: there is evidence in his monologue that he deludes himself into taking his roles very seriously. Yet this brittle surface of conventionality is disrupted time and again by the violence of his deeper impulses. His is the split attitude of the pseudo-conservative: a rigid adherence to conformity contradicted by a virulent but largely unreasoned or even unconscious dissatisfaction with the established order of society. Anger, fear, restlessness, paranoid suspicion, status anxiety, and ethnic prejudice, there is none of the features listed by Hofstadter as characteristic of the pseudo-conservative syndrome that is not paralleled in Jason's monologue. Faulkner certainly had no sociological ambitions when he wrote *The Sound and the Fury,* but the unfailing sureness of touch with which he created Jason proves beyond any doubt that even at this still early stage of his career he was fully aware of the dialectical interrelatedness of individual and society. To a higher degree perhaps than any of his contemporaries, Faulkner possessed the historical and sociological imagination that succeeds in capturing the spirit of a time and a place. True, the embittered petit bourgeois mentality dramatized through Jason is not restricted to a single time and a single place. Yet if Jason is not just typical of the South of the early twentieth century, it is precisely because he is so distinctly Southern to begin with.

"There are too many Jasons in the South who can be successful, just as there are too many Quentins who are too sensitive to face reality":[31] this comment by the author confirms, if confirmation is needed, the representative character he attributed to these two figures, and it also points to their complementary function within the novel. Most Faulkner critics have interpreted this complementarity in symbolic terms and from a historical perspective: in Quentin's collapse they see the breakdown of the Southern aristocracy; in Jason they see the sinister prophet of Snopesism. Each of them is thus made to stand for one phase in the process of decay which Faulkner has dramatized through the downfall of the Compsons. This interpretation is quite valid as far as it goes, yet it requires careful qualification. One should beware, in particular, of overemphasizing the opposition between the two characters. What is most significant about them is not their antagonism but the almost organic nature of their complementarity. As I have repeatedly argued in the present chapter, Quentin and Jason are more deeply brothers than has been generally acknowledged, and the resemblances between them are so numerous and so disturbingly close that their monologues may be read as different versions of the same text or different performances of the same play. What the play is about is loss: loss of love through loss of self, loss of self through loss of love. Benjy, the dispossessed idiot on the threshold of the novel, embodies this condition of loss at its rawest and most elemental. In Quentin and Jason it assumes the far more elaborate forms of self-estrangement, and through their monologues Faulkner demonstrates with stunning insight how alienation *works* within the recesses of a mind. Both brothers lack the courage to undertake the perilous journey from innocence to experience and from self to other; neither passes the test of reality. Both remain moral morons. Theirs are essentially stories of failed initiations, stories of fatal self-delusion—catastrophes of innocence and tragicomedies of mistaken identities.

To conclude, one might say that alienation is rather psychosexual with Quentin and rather psychosocial with Jason. But even this would be yet another oversimplification, for private fantasies and public fables are shown to be complementary aspects of the same fiction-making in both sections, and Quentin's fantasying must be considered along with Jason's paranoid obsessions as symptoms of the same disease. Only the fates of the two brothers are really separate: one pays for alienation with his life; the other manages to survive. But Jason loses his soul in the process, and his survival is at best a grotesque travesty of Faulknerian "endurance."

7

An Easter without Resurrection?

And besides, the last word is not said—
probably shall never be said. Are not
our lives too short for that full utterance which through all our stammerings
is of course our only and abiding inten-
tion?

MARLOW IN *Lord Jim*

L'ineptie consiste à vouloir conclure.

GUSTAVE FLAUBERT

Having, on his own admission, failed to tell his story through the Compson brothers, Faulkner resolved, in the fourth and final section, to speak in his own voice.[1] Contrary to widely held assumptions, however, this new, "authorial" point of view is neither that of an all-seeing and all-knowing narrator nor that of a detached and strictly objective observer.[2] Faulkner's approach here is one found in many of his novels: free and flexible, keenly attentive to what is happening, while engaging at the same time in the process of interpretation. But if what is reported is not left totally unexplained, there is no full elucidation either. Meanings are suggested but never asserted. Faulkner's method is throughout conjectural, and its tentativeness is evidenced by the recurrence of comparative-conditional clauses (introduced by *as if* or *as though*) and words or phrases denoting uncertainty (*seemed, appeared, it might have been,* etc.). In this, section 4 differs notably from the preceding ones: in the first section, we are given facts without meaning; in the second and the third we find meanings divorced from facts; only the last section avoids the extremes of blank factualness and blind fantasying. The monologue from which it differs least is perhaps Quentin's, insofar as the latter is also a quest for meaning, albeit a doomed one; on the other hand, it is the very antithesis of Jason's: the paranoid Jason has ready explanations for everything, and, as we have seen, his explanations all narrow down to murderous prejudice. He is a model of interpretative terrorism, a telling exemplification of the imposture of "truth," and serves therefore as a foil to the narrator of the fourth section. Groping for plausible explanations through a maze of hypotheses, this narrator makes no claim to final truth. His position is in fact very close to the reader's: sharing in the reader's perplexities rather than answering his questions, he enjoys no other privileges than those of his intellectual and imaginative alertness.

Distance is the reader's major gain. No doubt the new perspective he is offered is not objective in absolute terms, but it is undeniably less subjective than that of the two previous sections and less confusing than Benjy's. No longer constrained to adopt the narrowly limited viewpoint of an idiot or the distorted vision of a neurotic, we can at last stand back and take in the whole scene.

Yet the opening of section 4 hardly mitigates the oppressive atmosphere of the previous ones. For being broader, the vision seems just as bleak as before:

> The day dawned bleak and chill, a moving wall of grey light out of the northeast which, instead of dissolving into moisture, seemed to

April Eighth, 1928

The day dawned bleak and chill, a moving wall of gray light out of the northeast which, instead of shrinking into moisture, seemed to disintegrate into minute and venomous particles, like dust. That needled laterally into the flesh, and precipitated not so much a moisture but a windless paroxysm of the penetrating dense that, where Dilsey emerged opened the door of her cabin and emerged, needled laterally into her flesh, and quite precipitated upon her so much a moisture as a substance partaking of the quality of thin stuck not quite congealed oil. She wore a stiff black straw hat perched upon her turban, and a maroon velvet cape with a border of mangy and anonymous fur upon a dress of purple silk, and she stood in the door for a while, her myriad and sunken face lifted to the weather, and one gaunt hand flat-soled as the belly of a fish, then she moved the cape aside and examined the bosom of her dress.

The gown fell gaunt from her shoulders, across her fallen breasts, then tightened upon her paunch and fell again, ballooning a little above the nether garments which she would remove layer by layer as the spring accomplished and the warm days, in color regal and moribund. She had been a big woman once, but now her bones rose like ruins or landmarks above the somnolent and impervious guts, and above that the collapsed face that gave the impression of the skull itself being in a travail of its own flesh, lifted into the driving day with an expression at once fatalistic and of a child's astonished disappointment, until she turned and entered the house again and closed the door.

disintegrate into minute and venomous particles, like dust that, when Dilsey opened the door of the cabin and emerged, needled laterally into her flesh, precipitating not so much a moisture as a substance partaking of the quality of thin, not quite congealed oil (330).

Suggesting the close of day rather than its beginning, the grim greyness of this limbo landscape reminds one of the twilight associated with the Quentin section. The traditional literary connotations of dawning are canceled: nothing here points to the promise of a world born afresh. Space is enclosed and constricted by "a moving wall of grey light"; humidity, hanging ominously in the air, threatens to crumble into an infinity of "minute and venomous particles, like dust," or assumes the repulsive quality of "congealed oil." Disquieting and desolate, and seemingly fraught with evil intent, the landscape here described would indeed not have been out of place in the second section. And not only does it lack the breadth and depth of living space; with no principle of order and cohesion to sustain it, it looks as though its disintegration were close at hand. It might almost stand as an emblem for the novel, materializing the mental and moral falling asunder of the Compsons, and its metaphorical significance is all the more plausible as the same suggestions of noncohesion occur in the portrait one finds a few pages later:

> . . . Luster entered, followed by a big man who appeared to have been shaped of some substance whose particles would not or did not cohere to one another or to the frame which supported it. His skin was dead looking and hairless; dropsical too, he moved with a shambling gate like a trained bear. His hair was pale and fine. It had been brushed smoothly down upon his brow like that of children in daguerrotypes. His eyes were clear, of the pale sweet blue of cornflowers, his thick mouth hung open, drooling a little (342).

Here comes Benjy, the idiot, and no reader can fail to recognize him in this lumpish, slobbering giant. His lack of motor coordination recalls his mental debility, his hairless skin and fat body indicate his castrated condition,[3] and his cornflower-blue eyes are symbolic reminders of the childish innocence buried within this ungainly mass of adult flesh.[4]

In much the same way the almost caricatural sketches of Jason and Mrs. Compson seem to be just what one would have expected. The physical resemblance between mother and son (underscored by the repetition of "cold") comes so to speak as a natural extension of their moral affinities:

> When she called for the first time Jason laid his knife and fork down and he and his mother appeared to wait across the table from one another, in identical attitudes; the one cold and shrewd, with close-thatched brown hair curled into two stubborn hooks, one on either side of his forehead like a bartender in caricature, and hazel eyes with black-ringed irises like marbles, the other cold and querulous, with perfectly white hair and eyes pouched and baffled and so dark as to appear to be all pupil or all iris (348).

The characters so portrayed make for a new sense of reality. Emerging from the confined, claustrophobic ambience of the three brothers' monologues into the common space of the visible, it is as if after *listening* to voices in the dark, we were suddenly allowed to *see* their owners in broad daylight and to relate each voice to a face and a body. The effect of the spectacle is startling, the more so as what we see strikes us as oddly familiar: the shock which the reader experiences in discovering Benjy or Jason is in fact a shock of recognition.[5]

Of the many changes taking place in the fourth section, this shift from *within* to *without* is the most readily perceptible. But what we have learned through living with the thoughts and obsessions of the three brothers comes at once to inform our new mode of perception and to condition our reading. The reading of the last section is necessarily the "richest," as it builds on all that precedes it, and everything in the text becomes instantly pregnant with significance. All readings of fiction may be said to move from the literal to the symbolic, for as a story develops it is bound to produce meanings which cross-refer and interrelate and combine into complex semantic clusters. In *The Sound and the Fury,* however, this process is deliberately emphasized through Faulkner's fictional strategy: in the first section he maintains the narrative at the most literal level by having the story told by an idiot; in the last, he achieves a maximum of symbolic reverberation by multiplying "objective correlatives" to the distress, disorder, and decay which he had so far been intent on revealing from within.

Easter Sunday begins ironically with a grey dawn, and this gloomy greyness continues almost unabated to the end. When Dilsey appears at her cabin door, she looks at the sky "with an expression at once fatalistic and of a child's astonished disappointment" (331).[6] As a further sinister omen, the air is soon filled with the shrill cries of jaybirds, which Southern folklore associates with hell:[7]

> A pair of jaybirds came up from nowhere, whirled up on the blast like gaudy scraps of cloth or paper and lodged in the mulberries, where they swung in raucous tilt and recover, screaming into the wind that ripped their harsh cries onward and away like scraps of paper or of cloth in turn. Then three more joined them and they swung and tilted in the wrung branches for a time, screaming (331-32).[8]

When Dilsey and her family start off for church, the rain has stopped, but the sun is "random and tentative" (362), and when it does manage to shine through, is so weak that it looks like "a pale scrap of cloth" (358). The countryside around them is desolate as far the eye can reach:

> A street turned off at right angles, descending, and became a dirt road. On either hand the land dropped more sharply; a broad flat dotted with small cabins whose weathered roofs were on a level with the crown of the road. They were set in small grassless plots littered with broken things, bricks, planks, crockery, things of a once utilitarian value. What growth there was consisted of rank weeds and the trees were mulberries and locusts and sycamores—trees that partook also of the foul desiccation which surrounded the houses; trees whose very burgeoning seemed to be the sad and stubborn remnant of September, as if even spring had passed them by . . . (362-63).

It is indeed a dismal landscape, a "waste land" forgotten by spring, and its barrenness, brokenness, and shabbiness are curiously reminiscent of the squalid suburb of New England where Quentin walked with the little Italian girl on the day of his suicide (cf. 161–65). And just as in Quentin's monologue, the suspicion arises that this world has been drained of its substance, that it is no more than a mirage poised on the edge of the abyss or a flimsy, deceptive décor masking nothingness:

> The road rose again, to a scene like a painted backdrop. Notched into a cut of red clay crowned with oaks the road appeared to stop short off, like a cut ribbon. Beside it a weathered church lifted its crazy steeple like a painted church, and the whole scene was flat and without perspective as a painted cardboard set upon the ultimate edge of the flat earth . . . (364).[9]

In the center of this unreal scenery stands the Compsons' house. As in other Faulkner novels, its fate is closely bound up with that of the family. The splitting up of the land and the gradual shrinking of the estate betoken the Compsons' economic and social decline, and point as well to the breakup and extinction of the family group itself, whose sole male survivor is Jason, a bachelor without progeny. As to the dilapidation of "the square, paintless house with its rotting portico" (372), it is yet another sign of the destructive work of time, and so even more specifically is the endless ticking of the clock, likened by the narrator to "the dry pulse of the decaying house itself" (355). Like Thomas Sutpen's mansion in *Absalom, Absalom!*, the Compsons' house, once the stately seat of the genos and the emblem of dynastic pride, has become a monument to decay and death.[10] The solidary destinies of the house and its inmates are neatly summed up in the "Appendix," where Faulkner refers to "the rotting family in the rotting house" (421).[11]

All these suggestions of disorder and decay should warn us against a hasty "positive" reading of the final section. The traditional symbols of rebirth are ironically reversed: dawn and spring are described in terms of desolation, and the irony is the more pointed as the action takes place on an Easter Sunday. At first glance, then, the tonality of the section is largely consonant with that of the preceding ones; moreover, the vision it reflects reminds one time and again of Quentin's monologue in section 2. The narrator's eye is certainly less distraught than Quentin's; it is the more remarkable that we are confronted again with the same imagery of destruction and exhaustion.

Are we to infer that Quentin's vision of despair possesses more general validity than we originally assumed? The conclusion seems warranted by the general "atmosphere" of the fourth section. There is one notable exception, however: the Easter service episode, whose function and significance we have not yet examined. On the other hand, the reader's spontaneous response to imagery and atmosphere is certainly no firm and reliable starting point for a full critical assessment. Yet, if one turns to structure, one apparently reaches very similar conclusions. Thus John V. Hagopian contends that "a structural analysis of the closing chapter of *The Sound and the Fury* does, in fact, reveal nihilism as the meaning of the whole."[12] Section 4 consists of four distinct narrative units. It begins with a prologue, going from dawn to about 9:30 A.M. and focusing successively on Dilsey (330–45), Jason (345–55), Benjy and Luster (355–58). As Hagopian shows, through the characters involved as well as through the themes adumbrated, the three scenes within the prologue foreshadow in order the three more extended narrative sequences on which the novel ends. The first of these sequences (from 9:30 A.M. to 1:30 P.M.) deals with Dilsey's departure for church, the Easter service, and her return home (358–76); the second sequence (chronologically parallel to the first) links up with section 3 and relates Jason's pursuit of Miss Quentin and the carnival man (376–92); the third and last sequence is centered upon Benjy's and Luster's trip to the cemetery, and ends with the incident near the monument to the Confederate Soldier (392–401). However brief, this outline of the section's narrative structure allows one to do away with one or two misconceptions, for it establishes at once irrefutably that Dilsey is not the focal figure throughout, and that the narrative of the Easter service does not occupy the whole section. Ignoring what should be evident to anyone, a number of critics have commented upon the fourth section as though Dilsey held the center of the stage from beginning to end, and as though its narrative contents could be reduced to the Easter service. Starting from false premises, they are inevitably led to false conclusions.

With a writer so deeply concerned with the architectonics of fiction, meaning cannot be dissociated from form, and in a novel like *The Sound and the Fury* the internal patterning of each section is surely as significant as the ordering of the four sections within the book.

Thus the counterpointing of the Easter service and of Jason's futile pursuit of his niece is obviously a deliberate procedure on the part of the novelist. As elsewhere, the montage of parallel actions allows Faulkner to weave a network of identities and differences. Their simultaneity, indicated at the outset by the morning bells tolling at Dilsey's departure (358) as well as at Jason's (376), is repeatedly recalled by references back and forth from one sequence to the other.[13] Through this temporal parallelism the contrasts are made the more conspicuous: the Negroes walk to the church in almost ritual procession, "with slow Sabbath deliberation" (364), while Jason is driving to the carnival (a profane travesty of a religious festival) with increasingly frantic haste. The first sequence is marked by a sense of peaceful social communication (illustrated by the exchange of greetings between Dilsey and her friends, 363), and, at church, by religious communion (367); the second emphasizes Jason's extreme isolation: alone in pursuit, alone in defeat. Similarly, Dilsey's humble piety, shared by the black community, is set over against Jason's sacrilegious pride as he defies divine power itself in his Satanic rage (382). Lastly, while the celebration of the Resurrection of Christ brings the promise of eternal life to the faithful, Jason's "passion" ends appropriately in a grotesque parody of death ("So this is how it'll end, and he believed he was about to die," 387).

The Easter service follows a slowly ascending curve culminating in Reverend Shegog's visionary sermon; Jason's tribulations, on the other hand, evoke a furious and farcical dive to disaster. The antithesis is worked out in the smallest details, and from a Christian point of view it is indeed tempting to read it as the opposition between Satan's wretched fall and the glorious Resurrection of Christ. Yet at this point it is important to remember that the Jason sequence comes *after* the paschal episode. True, in the last section Jason no longer appears as formidable as before, and the failure of his chase gives us for once the satisfaction of seeing the forces of evil beating a retreat. Everything suggests, however, that the rout is only temporary, and that Jason has lost nothing of his power to harm. And the very order of the episodes tips the balance in Jason's favor: the chase sequence reestablishes Jason in the leading role, even though it ends in his punishment, and so throws us back into the sordid, hate-filled atmosphere of the third section.

This regressive movement is pursued to the novel's close. From Jason the focus shifts to Benjy: coming full circle, the final pages carry us back to the beginning. Here again, as in the opening section, is Benjy with his guardian Luster. Once more, moaning and whimpering, he squats before his private "graveyard," the small mound of earth with its empty blue bottle and its withered stalk of jimson weed (393); once more, clinging to the fence, he watches the movements of the golfers (394). Even Caddy's ghost reappears, summoned by Luster's perverse whispering of her name to Benjy (394), and the latter immediately starts bellowing, only to be assuaged by Caddy's satin slipper, the last material trace of his lost sister, "yellow now, and cracked and soiled" (395).

As for the very last scene, Benjy and Luster's trip by horse and surrey to the town cemetery, it was likewise anticipated in the first section (cf. 9–13). Yet this time the funeral excursion does not follow its customary route. We first get a glimpse of Benjy almost restored to tranquillity, "his eyes serene and ineffable" (399), clutching his broken narcissus stalk.[14] Yet when, after reaching the Confederate statue in the town square, Luster turns the horse to the left instead of the accustomed right, Benjy once again begins to roar in agony (400). But then Jason looms up, back from Mottson and seemingly resurrected in all his avenging fury, to reestablish the order violated by Luster's swerve:

> With a backhanded blow he hurled Luster aside and caught the reins and sawed Queenie about and doubled the reins back and slashed her across the hips. He cut her again and again, into a plunging gallop, while Benjy's hoarse agony roared about them, and swung her about to the right of the monument. Then he struck Luster over the head with his fist (400).

Finding at last an opportunity to vent his pent-up anger and frustration, Jason brutalizes the old mare and lashes out at Luster. He even strikes Benjy, whose flower stalk is broken again. Yet for once his violence has apparently positive effects. Order is indeed reestablished, and in the last sentence of the novel, Benjy's world seems to have recovered its balance:

> The broken flower drooped over Ben's fist and his eyes were empty and blue and serene again as cornice and façade flowed smoothly once more from left to right; post and tree, window and doorway, and signboard, each in its ordered place (401).

Order is restored, but it is as empty as Benjy's idiotic stare or the petrified gaze of the Confederate Soldier (399). It brings to mind the endings of all the earlier sections: the smooth flow of things recalls the "smooth, bright shapes" (92) signaling Benjy's falling asleep, and in its utter meaninglessness the close of the novel also recalls the ultimate absurdity of Quentin's fussy funeral toilette in section 2 and the demented dream closing Jason's monologue in section 3. And what makes the scene so memorable is not so much the final glimpse of peace regained as the ironic effect of contrast resulting from its juxtaposition with Jason's outburst of violence. The title of the book is given here a further illustration, the most startling perhaps in its harsh stridence, and also the most literally accurate: with Benjy's wild howling—"just sound," as the author puts it—and Jason's unleashed rage, there is indeed nothing left of the Compson world but "sound and fury."

In terms of plot, this ending is no ending at all. The final scene with Jason and Benjy puts an arbitrary stop to the action; it does not bring the expected dénouement. No dramatic resolution, whether tragic or comic, is provided; the tensions built up in the course of the narration are left undiminished, and the novel's complexities and ambiguities are as baffling as ever. Thematically, however, the scene is a powerful and poignant echo of the violence and disorder we have been witnessing all along, a condensed representation of all that has been presented before. "The ending of *The Sound and the Fury*," as Beverly Gross notes, "is a significant and suggestive reflection on the novel as a whole. It concludes not an action, but the enactment of a process; the novel ends not with an ending, but with an unforgettable epitome of itself."[15]

To put it in Roland Barthes' terminology, one might say that as in so much of modern fiction the hermeneutic code fails here to work properly:[16] the reader's conventional expectations are flouted, the knots are not untied, the threads are not unraveled. Our bafflement at the novel's close is not unlike Benjy's sense of outrage and disorder. All we can do is to return to the beginning and attempt another reading of the book—with little hope ever to find out its supposed secret. Yet the impossibility—for author and reader alike—of reaching a safe conclusion does not imply the absence of all closure. *The Sound and the Fury* is open-ended as far as plot is concerned, and it is inconclusive in its meaning. But this does not prevent it from achieving an aesthetic integrity of its own.

Formal closure should not be confused with semantic closure, and in the present case the former even seems to have been achieved in some measure at the cost of the latter. In traditional fiction endings are pointers to a fixed rationale, outside the text, in the light of which its contradictions are eventually resolved; in *The Sound and the Fury* the ending refers us back to the text itself, that is, to a tissue, a web of words, in which meanings are held in dynamic suspension.

Hence my rejection of the nihilistic interpretation which Hagopian feels entitled to infer from his analysis of the novel's last section. For Hagopian it is clear that the novel provides a conclusion: each of the three narrative sequences of section 4 moves toward closure, but while in the first two sequences the closures remain tentative, the closure of the final episode with Benjy "shapes the ultimate meaning of the novel."[17] This meaning, Hagopian contends, is an authorial corroboration of Mr. Compson's nihilistic pronouncements in the second section: the latter's values finally prevail over Dilsey's, and "time is demonstrated to be indeed the *reducto absurdum* (sic) of all human experience."[18] Hagopian establishes irrefutably that the assumptions held by most religious-minded exegetes of the novel are contradicted by the structure of the last section. Yet, not content with proving these assumptions to be false, he succumbs in his turn to the temptation of reducing the book's significance to an unequivocal ideological statement. Another weakness of his argument is its excessive reliance on narrative structure, for even though structure *is* meaning, meaning does not arise from structure alone. The examination of the last section must therefore be taken further: it is not enough to isolate the broad units of the narrative, and to see how their ordering and patterning inflect significance; it is indispensable as well to scrutinize the finer mesh of the section's texture.

The shift in language and style is certainly one of the most arresting features of section 4. Free of the restrictions of the interior monologue, Faulkner now seems to speak in his own person, and a richer, denser, more ceremonious style comes to unfold. Previously held in check or fraught with ironic intent, Faulkner's rhetoric now bursts into full flower. Not that it dominates the whole section, but it infuses the prose of the narrative with new energies, and projects a very different light upon the various actors of the drama. Consider, for example, the portrait of Dilsey in the two opening pages:

> The gown fell gauntly from her shoulders, across her fallen breasts, then tightened upon her paunch and fell again, ballooning a little above the nether garments which she would remove layer by layer as the spring accomplished and the warm days, in colour regal and moribund. She had been a big woman once but now her skeleton rose, draped loosely in unpadded skin that tightened again upon a paunch almost dropsical, as though muscle and tissue had been courage or fortitude which the days or the years had consumed until only the indomitable skeleton was left rising like a ruin or a landmark above the somnolent and impervious guts, and above that the collapsed face that gave the impression of the bones themselves being outside the flesh, lifted into the driving day with an expression at once fatalistic and of a child's astonished disappointment, until she turned and entered the house again and closed the door (330-31).

This portrait is cruelly accurate in its particulars; it emphasizes Dilsey's deformity and decrepitude, and multiplies the signs of impending death: with her fallen breasts and her dropsical paunch,[19] the old black woman—a mere skeleton wrapped in a skin-bag—appears here as a grim memento mori. Yet, solemnized by the abstract magnificence of the epithets (most of which are ponderous polysyllabic Latinisms) and expanded by the suggestive power of the similes, the description goes well beyond the demands of realism, and far from degrading Dilsey to a macabre scarecrow, it raises her to tragic dignity. Dressed in "regal" color—a dress of purple silk and a maroon cape (330)[20]—she is lent from the outset an aura of majesty which belies the wretchedness of her ravaged, age-worn body. The servant, the descendant of slaves is turned into a sovereign figure. A queen of no visible kingdom, a queen dispossessed and "moribund," but one whose "indomitable" skeleton rises in the gray light of an inauspicious dawn as a challenge to death—a paradoxical symbol of that which transcends mortal flesh and triumphs over time, of that which "endures."[21] And similarly ennobled and embellished by the baroque "coruscations" of Faulkner's eloquence, Dilsey's tears become the essence of universal grief:

> Two tears slid down her fallen cheeks, in and out of the myriad coruscations of immolation and abnegation and time (368).

Benjy likewise appears in a different light. In Quentin's and Jason's monologues the figure of the idiot had gradually faded from the scene; now he comes right to the forefront again, not only in the closing scene but also at the beginning of the section and in the episode in the Negro church. What is perhaps most remarkable about Benjy in the final section is that his presence there is predominantly vocal: apart from the startling visual description we are given at his first appearance, he is more often heard than seen. His cries and whining—made haunting through the repetition of "crying," "wailing," "whimpering," "slobbering," "bellowing"—supply what might be called the basic soundtrack of the section. Never articulated as speech, scarcely human, Benjy's cries are the abject and pathetic expression of his nameless and unnameable suffering:

> Then Ben wailed again, hopeless and prolonged. It was nothing. Just sound. It might have been all time and injustice and sorrow become vocal for an instant by a conjunction of planets (359).
>
> But he bellowed slowly, abjectly, without tears; the grave hopeless sound of all voiceless misery under the sun (395).
>
> There was more than astonishment in it, it was horror; shock; agony eyeless, tongueless; just sound . . . (400).

These passages are reminders of Benjy's intense and inarticulate suffering, but in a sense they also suggest the writer's paradoxical gamble in the very act of creation. Indicative of a double deprivation—the absence of happiness and the absence of speech—Benjy's helpless cries express lack by lack, and in the text this state of extreme dispossession is forcibly emphasized by the recurrence of privative suffixes. Benjy's cries fail to say what he failed to preserve; they are the burning language of absence and the blind eloquence of the absurd. They are nothing: "just sound." In this nothing, though, there is everything: "all time and injustice and sorrow," "all voiceless misery under the sun." But is this conjunction of nothing and everything not to be found too in what seems to be at the very antipodes of the cry, that is, literature? And is not the voicing of the voiceless, the naming of the nameless also the deepest desire of the writer? Language at its most ambitious refers dialectically back to the inarticulateness of the cry: it is its negation in that it relies on the organizing and signifying powers of the word, while being also its completion insofar as it recaptures the immediate pathos of the cry. Not that all literature nurses this ambition, but *The Sound and the Fury* is surely a case in point, and may be considered Faulkner's most daring attempt to come as close as possible to that which is both revealed and silenced in the "eyeless" and "tongueless" agony of the cry. It was of course an impossible wager: to keep it was to lose it. For in the pregnant silence of the printed page the cry is no longer a cry; Benjy's whimperings and bellowings, by being named, are absorbed into the mute eloquence of written discourse, and appropriated by literature which turns them into symbols of its own impotence, of its own vanity.

The cry and the rhetoric: these are in a sense the polar extremes of the novel. From one it moves to the other, and the very ordonnance of the book may be said to reflect this movement of reappropriation. The first section, where we are supposed to listen to the idiot's inner voice, is in its extreme confusion the closest approximation to the "voiceless misery" of the cry; the last, where literature reasserts its claims and the writer reestablishes his authority, is seemingly the furthest from it. Yet Faulkner's rhetoric in the final section attempts to preserve something of the primal urgency of the cry, and in a way reverts to it, making it "vocal for an instant" by a conjunction of words. Moreover, this rhetoric obviously gains strength and persuasiveness from coming after Benjy's "sound," Quentin's *cri du coeur,* and Jason's "fury." Far from describing arabesques in the void, it traces them on soil already prepared. When Dilsey and Benjy reappear in the fourth section, they have already gathered so much weight and substance that their eventual metamorphosis into archetypes of endurance and suffering does not strike us as arbitrary allegorizing.[22]

From the concrete particulars of limited individual experience the last section moves toward the universality of the mythic and the archetypal. Thus Benjy, without ceasing to be a slobbering idiot, becomes a symbol of crucified innocence in the context of the Easter service at the Negro church; the man-child becomes an analogon of Christ. But the character in which the fusion of realism and symbolism is most successfully achieved is without any doubt Dilsey. Even though her function has often been mis-understood or overemphasized, there can be no question that she is the most memorable character in the last section. Technically, the point of view is not hers, and in dramatic terms her role is a limited one. Yet critics should not be blamed too roundly for attributing the last section to her; even Faulkner called it "the Dilsey section."[23] The one truly admirable character in the novel, she had a special place in the writer's affections: "Dilsey is one of my favorite characters, because she is brave, courageous, generous, gentle, honest. She is much more brave and honest and generous than me."[24] She is no less admirable as a literary creation. Her portrait is so sharply individualized and her figure so warm and earthy that the charge of excessive idealization is hardly relevant. As Cleanth Brooks has rightly noted, Dilsey is "no noble savage and no *schöne Seele*."[25] Nor should she be reduced to a racial stereotype. True, she seems to fit rather nicely in the tradition of the black mammy, and her literary lineage is readily traced back to Thomas Nelson Page.[26] However, the point is that her virtues, as they are presented in the novel, owe nothing to race.[27]

That she was meant to counterbalance the Compsons is obvious enough. Her words and actions offer throughout an eloquent con-trast to the behavior of her masters. In her role of faithful—though not submissive—servant, Dilsey represents the sole force for order and stability in the Compson household.[28] Not only does she see with tireless diligence and devotion to the family's material needs; she also tries, albeit with little success, to stave off the day of its disintegration. Taking on the functions and responsibilities traditionally assumed by the mother, she comes to replace the lamentable Mrs. Compson as keeper of the house. In the later sections, she appears as Benjy's last resort,[29] and she also defends Caddy and her daughter against Jason, the usurper of paternal authority.

In the face of the whining or heinous egoism of the Compsons, Dilsey embodies the generosity of total selflessness; in contrast to Quentin's tortured idealism and Jason's sordid pragmatism, she also represents the active wisdom of simple hearts. Without fostering the slightest illusion about her exploiters, expecting no gratitude for her devotion, Dilsey accepts the world as it is, while striving as best she can to make it somewhat more habitable. Unlike the Compsons, she does not abdicate before reality nor does she refuse time, which she alone is capable of gauging and interpreting correctly:

> On the wall above a cupboard, invisible save at night, by lamp light and even then evincing an enigmatic profundity because it had but one hand, a cabinet clock ticked, then with a preliminary sound as if it cleared its throat, struck five times.
> "Eight oclock," Dilsey said ... (342).

In his rage against time, Quentin tore off the hands of his watch. The Compsons' old kitchen clock has but one left and its chime is out of order. Yet Dilsey does not take offense at its "lying" and automatically corrects its errors. To her, time is no matter of obsession. Not that she adjusts to it out of mere habit. Her time is not simply a "natural" phenomenon, any more than her moral qualities are "natural" virtues. Faulkner describes her as a Christian, and no analysis of the character can afford to discount the deep religious convictions attributed to her. As Brooks again judiciously notes, "Dilsey does not believe in man; she believes in God."[30] Her capacity for endurance and power for loving are sustained and inspirited by the ardor of her faith. Hers is a seemingly naïve piety, a simple faith unencumbered by theological subtleties, but it gives her the courage to be and persevere which her masters lack, and provides her existence with a definite meaning and purpose. Dilsey envisions everything in the light of the threefold mystery of the Incarnation, Passion, and Resurrection of Christ. In Benjy she sees "de Lawd's chile" (396), one of the poor in spirit promised the Kingdom of God, and for her all human suffering is justified and redeemed in the divine sacrifice commemorated during Holy Week. Her attitude toward time proceeds quite logically from the tenets of her Christian faith. Whereas for Quentin, the incurable idealist, time is the hell of immanence, the *reductio ad absurdum* of all human endeavor, it is transfused with eternity for Dilsey. Not "a tale full of sound and fury signifying nothing," but the history of God's people. The Christ of her belief has not been "worn away by the minute clicking of little wheels" (94); his crucifixion was not a victory by time but a victory over time. Guaranteed in the past by the death and resurrection of the Son of God, and in the future by the promise of His return, bounded by the Passion and the Second Coming, time regains a meaning and a direction, and each man's existence becomes again the free and responsible adventure of an individual destiny. Dilsey's Christ-centered faith allows her to adhere fully to all of time's dimensions: her answer to the past is fidelity; the present she endures with patience and humility, and armed with the theologal virtue of hope, she is also able to face the future without alarm. While for Quentin there is an unbridgeable gap between the temporal and the timeless, Dilsey's eternity, instead of being an immobile splendor *above* the flux of time, is already present and at work *in* time, embodied in it just as the word was made flesh. Time, then, is no longer felt as endless and senseless repetition; nor is it experienced as an inexorable process of decay. It does have a pattern, since history has been informed from its beginnings by God's design. And it can be redeemed and vanquished, but, as T. S. Eliot puts it in the *Four Quartets,* "Only through time time is conquered."[31] Which is to say that the hour of its final defeat will be the hour of its fulfillment and reabsorption into eternity.

Firmly rooted in the eschatological doctrine of Christianity, Dilsey's concept of time is theo-logical, not chrono-logical. The assumptions on which it rests remain of course implicit, but it is in this orthodoxly Christian perspective that we are asked to interpret Dilsey's comment after Reverend Shegog's sermon: "I've seed de first en de last. . . . I seed de beginning, en now I sees de ending" (371; see also 375). Given the religious context of Easter where they occur, her words obviously refer to the beginning and end of time, to the Alpha and Omega of Christ. But it goes without saying that they apply as well to the downfall of the Compsons which Dilsey has been witnessing all along. The implication is certainly not that after all the Compsons may be saved, but what the oblique connection between the Passion Week and the family tragedy suggests is that for Dilsey the drama of the Compsons is above all one of redemption denied.

Yet what the story means to Dilsey is not necessarily what it means to us, nor what it means to the author. At this point the impossibility of any final interpretation becomes obvious again. For how are we to take the many references to Christianity included in the novel? And how do they relate to this story of decline and death? One may argue that Faulkner's use of them is ironical, that they point—derisively or nostalgically—to a vanishing myth and expose its total irrelevance as far as the Compsons are concerned. Or one may interpret them in terms of paradox, the more legitimately so, it seems, as paradox has been a major mode of Judeo-Christian thought and is indeed central to Christian faith itself. According to whether irony or paradox is taken to be the clue to Faulkner's intentions, diametrically opposed interpretations of the novel will suggest themselves to the reader. But the question is one of effects rather than intentions, and it is extremely difficult to settle, since paradox and irony alike work by way of inversion.

Inversion is one of Faulkner's favorite techniques. In *The Sound and the Fury* its procedures can be traced in many places, but nowhere perhaps are they as consistently and as intriguingly

used as in the episode of the Easter service.[32] With regard to the
rest of the novel (and more directly to the juxtaposed Jason sequence), the episode fulfills a contrasting function homologous
to that of Dilsey in relation to the other characters. And the contrast is so sharp and so unexpected that the reader is jolted into a
radically different mood. It is as if a spring of pure water suddenly
welled up in an arid desert, or as if the dismal clamor of the
accursed family were momentarily suspended to let us listen to
a gospel song. But the episode is no less surprising in the detail
of its composition and the movement of its development, both of
which owe a good deal of their impact to Faulkner's handling of
inversion. The sequence opens rather inauspiciously with the description of the desolate setting of Dilsey's walk to the church
(362–64): nothing yet heralds the upsurge of Easter joy. A sense
of expectancy is soon created, however, by the gathered congregation impatiently awaiting "dat big preacher" (362) from St. Louis.
But when he at last arrives, he turns out to be a shabby, monkey-
faced gnome:

> . . . when they saw the man who had preceded their minister enter
> the pulpit still ahead of him an indescribable sound went up, a sound
> of astonishment and disappointment.
> The visitor was undersized, in a shabby alpaca coat. He had a
> wizened black face like a small, aged monkey. And all the while that
> the choir sang again and while the six children rose and sang in thin,
> frightened, tuneless whispers, they watched the insignificant looking
> man sitting dwarfed and countrified by the minister's imposing bulk,
> with something like consternation (365-66).

The frustration, though, is turned into starry-eyed wonderment
when the preacher begins his sermon:

> His voice was level and cold. It sounded too big to have come from
> him and they listened at first through curiosity, as they would have
> to a monkey talking. They began to watch him as they would a man
> on a tight rope. They even forgot his insignificant appearance in the
> virtuosity with which he ran and poised and swooped upon the cold
> inflectionless wire of his voice, so that at last, when with a sort of
> swooping glide he came to rest again beside the reading desk with

one arm resting upon it at shoulder height and his monkey body as reft of all motion as a mummy or an emptied vessel, the congregation sighed as if it waked from a collective dream and moved a little in its seats (366).

Contrary to all expectations, belying the shabbiness and grotesqueness of his physical appearance, Reverend Shegog displays the mesmerizing talents of a brilliant orator. But there is more to come: a second, even more stunning metamorphosis occurs when the cold virtuosity of the "white" sermon suddenly bursts into the incantatory vehemence of "black" eloquence:

Then a voice said, "Brethren."
The preacher had not moved. His arm lay yet across the desk, and he still held that pose while the voice died in sonorous echoes between the walls. It was as different as day and dark from his former tone, with a sad, timbrous quality like an alto horn, sinking into their hearts and speaking there again when it had ceased in fading and cumulate echoes (367).

This is the moment of the decisive reversal: the preacher is no longer master of his rhetoric, nor is he anymore master of his voice. Instead of being the flexible instrument of his eloquence, the voice—having seemingly acquired a will of its own—now seizes his body and uses it as its tool. The tightrope artist has vanished; Shegog has become the docile servant of the Word:

He was like a worn small rock whelmed by the successive waves of his voice. With his body he seemed to feed the voice that, succubus like, had fleshed its teeth in him. And the congregation seemed to watch with its own eyes while the voice consumed him, until he was nothing and they were nothing and there was not even a voice but instead their hearts were speaking to one another in chanting measures beyond the need for words . . . (367).

The consuming voice not only reduces the preacher to a mere medium of the Easter message; it reaches out toward the congregation, and, delving into the innermost recesses of souls, unites them in a wordless chant of communion. The orderly discourse of cold reason, significantly associated with the facile tricks of "a white man" (366), has given way to the spontaneous language of the heart, which alone can break down the barriers of individual isolation; a language which moves paradoxically toward its own extinction, eventually resolving itself into "chanting measures beyond the need for words." All that "white" rhetoric could achieve was "a collective dream" (366); what is accomplished now is a truly collective experience, a welding of many into one. For the first time in the novel, separation and fragmentation are at least temporarily transcended; consciousness, instead of narrowing down to private fantasy and obsession, is expanded through the ritual reenactment of myth. In this unique instant of grace and ecstasy, all human misery is miraculously transfigured, all infirmities are forgotten, and the puny silhouette of the preacher rises before the faithful like a living replica of the crucified God:

> . . . his monkey face lifted and his whole attitude that of a serene, tortured crucifix that transcended its shabbiness and insignificance and made it of no moment (368).

We are now prepared to read, or perhaps rather listen to, the sermon itself. Once again inversion is at play, carrying us along in a seesaw movement of ups and downs, but the dominant mood is at present one of trust and exultation, any remaining doubts being swept away by the certainty of redemption: "I got de ricklickshun en de blood of de Lamb" (368). Yet the sermon begins on a plaintive note, faintly recalling Quentin's obsessions with time and death:

> Dey passed away in Egypt, de swinging chariots; de generations passed away. Wus a rich man: whar he now, O breddren? Wus a po man: whar he now, O sistuhn? (368-69).

There follows a breathless evocation of the persecuted childhood of Christ:

> "Breddren! Look at dem little chillen setting dar. Jesus wus like dat once. He mammy suffered de glory en de pangs. Sometime maybe she helt him at de nightfall, whilst de angels singin him to sleep; maybe she look out de do' en see de Roman po-lice passin" (369).

Jesus here becomes the paradigm for martyred innocence, and the relevance of this paradigm to present circumstances is poignantly emphasized by the implicit reference to Benjy, the innocent idiot, sitting amidst the Negro community, "rapt in his sweet blue gaze" (370).

The legendary and the actual, the past and the present are thus not only contrasted, but significantly linked. Myth infuses reality: projected into an immemorial past, Benjy as well as Dilsey are transformed into archetypal figures through their identification with Christ and the Madonna. Conversely, the remote events of the Passion are brought back to life again and quiver with pathetic immediacy in the compelling vision of the preacher:

> "I sees hit, breddren! I sees hit! Sees de blastin, blindin sight! I sees Calvary, wid de sacred trees, sees de thief en de murderer en de least of dese; I hears de boasting en de braggin: Ef you be Jesus, lif up yo tree en walk! I hears de wailin of women en de evenin lamentations; I hears de weepin en de cryin en de turnt-away face of God: dey done kilt Jesus; dey done kilt my Son!" (370).

With the death of Christ, the sermon reaches its nadir. The preacher now witnesses the seemingly absolute triumph of Evil, and his vision becomes one of utter chaos and destruction: "I sees de whelmin flood roll between; I sees de darkness en de death everlasting upon de generations" (370). Yet this note of despair (again reminiscent of the Quentin section) is not sustained, and immediately after everything is reversed by the miracle of the Resurrection. Shadows disperse, death is forever conquered in the glory of the Second Coming:

> I sees de resurrection en de light; sees de meek Jesus sayin Dey kilt Me dat ye shall live again; I died dat dem whut sees en believes shall never die. Breddren, O breddren! I sees de doom crack en hears de golden horns shoutin down de glory, en de arisen dead whut got de blood en de ricklickshun of de Lamb!" (370).

Although Reverend Shegog's Easter sermon only occupies a few pages in the novel, it looms there very large. And while it is true that it would carry even greater weight if Faulkner had chosen to place it at the novel's close, its impact is greater than a purely structural analysis of the fourth section would lead one to expect. Literary meanings and literary effects are differential, to be sure, but to assess them correctly it is not enough to see how they are "placed" within the text; it is also important to measure the amplitude of the differences, and the extent to which the Easter sermon differs from the rest of the novel is precisely what most Faulkner critics have failed to recognize. For its singularity is not only one of subject and theme, nor does it merely arise from a tonal switch. A radical reversal occurs, operating on all possible levels and altering the very fiber of the novel's texture. As the narrator's own preliminary comments suggest, another *voice* takes over, which is not that of any character, nor that of the narrator/author—a voice enigmatically self-generated and mysteriously compelling in its effects. Another language is heard, unprecedented in the novel, signaled at once by the cultural-ethnic shift from "white" to "black," the emotional shift from rational coldness to spiritual fervor, and lastly by the stylistic shift from the mechanical cadences of shallow rhetoric to the entrancing rhythms of inspired speech.

Not that this new language dispenses with formal devices: Shegog's sermon, so far from being an uncontrolled outpouring of emotion, is very firmly patterned and makes extensive use of rhetorical emphasis (questions and exclamations) as well as of such classical procedures as parallelism and incremental repetition (most conspicuous in the abundance of anaphoric constructions). The sermon is the ritual retelling of a mythic story fully known by all the members of the congregation: its narrative contents form a fixed sequence, and the mode of its transmission conforms likewise to a stable code. What needs to be stressed, too, is that the specific tradition to which this speech belongs is the folk tradition —well-established, particularly, in Afro-American culture—of the *oral* sermon.[33] Ritualized as it is, the preacher's eloquence is the eloquence of the spoken word, and Shegog's sermon reads indeed like the transcript of an oral performance. The effect is partly achieved through the faithful phonetic rendering of the Negro dialect. Yet Faulkner's greatest success is that he has also managed to capture the musical quality of the sermon: the "sad, timbrous quality like an alto horn, sinking into their hearts and speaking there again when it had ceased in fading and cumulate echoes" (367). More than anything else it is this musicality (i.e., that which, in his speech, belongs to another, nonverbal language) that ensures true communication between the speaker and the listeners, and among the audience itself. Myth and music—whose close affinities have been pointed out by Claude Lévi-Strauss[34]—cooperate in this Easter celebration to free all participants in the rite from "the need for words" and to unite them in a speechless and time-less communion.[35] What matters here is not so much the message conveyed as the collective ceremony of its utterance and its shar-ing, a ceremony allowing at once personal identity to be tran-scended and cultural identity to be confirmed.

Reverend Shegog's Easter sermon may be called a triumph of Faulkner's verbal virtuosity. It is noteworthy, however, that this triumph was achieved through a gesture of humility. For the novel-ist scrupulously refrained from improving on the tradition of the oral sermon as he found it. There is no literary embellishment, and there is hardly a personal touch one might attribute to the author. Shegog's sermon has been compared with records of ser-mons actually delivered: the difference between the latter and Faulkner's creation is barely noticeable.[36] Which is to say that, strictly speaking, it is no creation at all, but only evidence of Faulk-ner's extraordinary mimetic abilities. The writer here lays no claim to artistic originality, and his self-effacement is carried to such lengths that his own voice is no longer heard.[37] Instead we are *truly* listening to the anonymous voice of an unwritten tradition, grown out of ancient roots and periodically revivified by the rites of popular piety—a voice, that is, whose *authority* owes nothing to the talents of an *author*. This is what makes the sermon a unique moment in the novel: it marks the intrusion of the mythic into the fictional, the nonliterary into the literary, and by the same token it also signals the writer's willing renunciation of his authorial pride and of his prerogatives as a fiction-maker. It becomes very tempting, then, to see the preacher-figure as a double of the novelist himself: do not both surrender their identity as speakers/writers to become the vehicles of a mythic voice?

In the novel this voice is obviously a metaphor for religion: *religio,* what binds man to man, man to God, and in a sense the interrelated shifts pointed out so far are all subsumed by the crucial passage from profane to sacred. The voice that takes hold of the preacher induces a vision, and this moment of vision, fully shared in by the congregation, is in fact the only experience of spiritual enlightenment recorded in the whole book. To Dilsey, in particular, the preacher's words bring the encompassing revelation of eternity, the mystical and prophetic vision of "the beginning and the ending." In contrast to the blinded Compsons,[38] Dilsey and Reverend Shegog *see,* and their vision is apparently one that goes beyond the confines of time and flesh. It is a vision, too, that brings order and significance to their lives and gives them the strength to endure pain and loss. Is this to say that they embody Faulkner's vision, and that the Easter service at the Negro church provides the key to the novel's interpretation? For those who read *The Sound and the Fury* from theological premises, there is no doubt about the answer. Gabriel Vahanian[39] and Amos N. Wilder,[40] for example, compare the sermon in Faulkner's novel to the legend of the Grand Inquisitor in *The Brothers Karamazov* and to Father Mapple's sermon in *Moby Dick,* and do not hesitate to invest it with the same central hermeneutic function: ". . . it tells us the meaning of the various signs and symbols as on a geographical map; it tells us how to read the drama, how to interpret the characters of the plot that has been unfolding before us."[41]

From there to calling *The Sound and the Fury* a Christian
novel is a short step. It is a step too many, however, for although
there is much to suggest such an interpretation, there is little,
in the last resort, to validate it. Faulkner's work is misread as soon
as it is *arrested,* and criticism inevitably goes astray whenever it
seeks to reduce its intricate web of ambiguities to a single and
coherent pattern of meaning. *The Sound and the Fury* stubbornly
resists any attempt to dissolve its opaqueness into the reassuring
clarity of an ideological statement.

That Faulkner's fiction is heavily indebted to the Christian
tradition is beyond question, and the writer himself, in his interviews, freely acknowledged the debt.[42] But it is essential to relate
it to the specific context of the novelist's creation: to Faulkner
Christianity was first of all an inexhaustible fund of cultural references, a treasure of images and symbols, or to borrow one of his
own favorite words, an extremely useful collection of "tools."
How extensively he used these tools is confirmed at every turn in
his books. This, of course, does not settle the question of his relationship to Christianity. There is surely more than a mere craftsman's debt: myth is both the bad conscience and the utopia of
Western fiction, and for Faulkner as for many other modern
novelists, the Christian myth remains an ever-present paradigm,
an ordering scheme, a pattern of intelligibility toward which his
fiction never ceases to move as toward a lost horizon of truth, or
rather *through* which it is moving to produce its own myths.
Faulkner's quest and questioning remain to a very large extent
caught up in Christian modes of thought and expression, as can
be even more plainly seen in later works like *Go Down, Moses,
Requiem for a Nun,* and *A Fable.* Yet, deep and lasting though
it was, Faulkner's involvement with Christianity entailed no personal commitment to Christian faith, and none of his public pronouncements substantiates the claim that he considered himself
a Christian writer. Besides, even if Faulkner had been an avowed
believer, the relationship of his work to Christianity would still

be a problematical one, for insofar as it is literature, it necessarily displaces the myths on which it feeds. Aspiring to turn fictions into myths, it is fated to turn myths into fictions.

"A work of literature," Roland Barthes remarks, "or at least of the kind that is normally considered by the critics (and this itself may be a possible definition of 'good' literature) is neither ever quite meaningless (mysterious or 'inspired') nor ever quite clear; it is, so to speak, *suspended* meaning; it offers itself to the reader as a declared system of significances, but as a signified object it eludes his grasp. This kind of *dis-appointment* or *deception* . . . inherent in the meaning explains how it is that a work of literature has such power to ask questions of the world . . . without, however, supplying any answer."[43] Faulkner's fiction fully bears out Barthes's assumptions. The wealth of Christian allusions we find in a novel like *The Sound and the Fury* adds immeasurably to its semantic pregnancy, but in the last analysis Christian values are neither affirmed nor denied. Episodes like the Easter service and figures like Dilsey are impressive evidence of Faulkner's deep understanding of Christianity, and they seem to point to possibilities of experience which the ego-bound Compsons have irremediably lost. Yet, as Cleanth Brooks rightly notes, "Faulkner makes no claim for Dilsey's version of Christianity one way or the other. His presentation of it is moving and credible, but moving and credible only as an aspect of Dilsey's own mental and emotional life."[44] The reader's "disappointment" in this respect is all the greater as Faulkner's novel often *seems* to imply the existence of seizable significances: his ironies do suggest a radically negative vision, and his paradoxes bring us very close indeed to the spirit of Christianity. However, the point about Faulkner's ironies and paradoxes is that they are irreducibly *his*. Etymologically, irony implies dissembling, feigned ignorance, and paradox refers likewise to a hidden truth. If these classical definitions are retained, Faulkner's inversions are neither ironies nor paradoxes: they are not disguised affirmations but modes of questioning.

So the final leap is never made, nor should it be attempted by the reader. Shall we then agree with those critics to whom *The Sound and the Fury* is simply an ingenious montage of contrasting perspectives, a brilliant exercise in ambiguity? To pose and solve the question in these terms is again to miss the point. Those who insist on the novel's inconclusiveness and consider it a flaw are actually just as mistaken as those who refuse to acknowledge its indeterminacy: the former assume that a novel should have a determinable sense; the latter postulate that it has one. Both approaches ignore the specificity of literary discourse and disregard the very impetus of Faulkner's creation. For the contradictions informing it are never static antinomies; they generate a field of dynamic tension and are in fact what sets his books in motion. The tension is not solved, nor can it be, but this irresolution is not to be imputed to Faulkner's incapacity to make up his mind, and it will not do either to account for it by the assumption of some quixotic "quest for failure."[45] No more than to a Christian or a nihilistic statement *The Sound and the Fury* should be reduced to a neutral balancing of contrary views.

To Faulkner as a *writer* the choice was not between affirmation and denial, sense or nonsense so much as between literature and silence. As soon as words get written, meanings are produced, that is, both brought forth and exhibited, and the elaborately deceptive uses of language characteristic of literary discourse, far from canceling significance, may open up its infinite possibilities. It is true that modern writers such as Beckett or Robbe-Grillet have done their utmost to rarefy meaning, to bring literature as close as possible to the condition of silence. Faulkner, however, does not belong with these ascetics. His practice of fiction is more akin to Joyce's: it resembles it in its generosity, its openness, its inclusiveness, and the passionate eagerness of its quest. And like Joyce, Faulkner pursues his quest in the teeth of absurdity. "Prendre sens dans l'insensé"[46]—to make sense of and in the senseless, to take up

one's quarters where absurdity is at its thickest, is how Paul Eluard
defined the function of modern poetry. His definition also applies to
Faulkner's design, and nowhere perhaps is this design more in evidence than in the final section of *The Sound and the Fury*. The
novel's tensions are there raised to an almost unbearable pitch, and
the shrill irony of its ending leaves them forever unresolved. Yet si-
multaneously a countermovement develops, away from absurdity
toward some tentative ordering. Faulkner's rhetoric here is both at
its most ambitious and its most humble: at its most ambitious when
it gathers its energies to reassert the powers of language and the
authority of the writer; at its most humble when it effaces itself
behind the sacred eloquence of an Easter sermon and yields to the
authority of the myth. It is most significant, too, that in this section
Faulkner's inversions so often take on the colors of paradox. Given
their cultural context, these paradoxes seem to call for a Christian
interpretation, but one may wonder whether they do not all refer
back to the central paradox of the writer's own endeavor. For
Faulkner's creative process also tends to operate a radical inversion of signs; it too draws strength from its weakness, and glories
in its indigence. As we have seen, Reverend Shegog, the frail vessel
of the sovereign Word, may be taken for an analogon of the
novelist himself, reaching the point of inspired dispossession
where his individuality gives way to the "voice." And the mystical
vision granted to the preacher may likewise be said to metaphorize
the poetic vision sought after by the writer. What these analogies
seem to point to is the mirage of an ultimate reversal: that which
would restore the absolute presence of language to itself and thus
convert its emptiness into plenitude, its fragmentation into whole-
ness—fiction raised to mythos, speech raised to logos.[47] It is of
course an impossible dream: the quest is never completed, the reversal forever postponed. Yet in its very failure the novel succeeds. Even though the gap between text and meaning is always
there, the writing process manages to create an order of its own,
assigning each word and sentence to "its ordered place." It is an
order, or rather an ordering, generated out of the very vacuum of

language and the very emptiness of desire—an order in a sense as empty and contingent as Benjy's. With a difference, however: the patterned incompleteness of *The Sound and the Fury* waits for a reader and requires his active participation. Not that he can succeed where the author failed. But if his reading of the novel is not mindless consumption, he, too, will take part in the unending process of its production. Reading and rereading the book, he will write it again.

NOTES

1. Faulkner before Faulkner: Masks and Mirrors

1. *L'écriture et la différence* (Paris: Editions du Seuil, 1967), p. 44. My translation.

2. Faulkner's first published poem, "L'Après-Midi d'un Faune," appeared in *The New Republic* on August 6, 1919. It was soon followed by other pieces, most of which were published between 1919 and 1921 in *The Mississippian,* the newspaper of the University of Mississippi. Faulkner also dated a few unpublished poems during his stay at New Orleans in 1925, and by the time he left that city for Europe (July 7, 1925), four of his new poems had been published by *The Double Dealer.* The date of publication for his first book of poems, *The Marble Faun,* 1924, is misleading as to the time of its actual composition, since Faulkner dated it from the spring and early summer of 1919. Equally misleading is the date for *A Green Bough,* 1933: a first version of Faulkner's second book of verse was ready by 1925 under the title *A Greening Bough.* What complicates matters is that most of his poems were extensively revised before publication.

3. Preface to *The Marble Faun* (Boston: The Four Seas Company, 1924), p. 6. The book was reproduced photographically from the original edition by Random House in 1952.

4. See Harry Runyan, "Faulkner's Poetry," *Faulkner Studies,* III (Summer-Autumn 1954), 23–29; George P. Garrett, "An Examination of the Poetry of William Faulkner," *Princeton University Library Chronicle,* XVIII (Spring 1957), 124–35; Cleanth Brooks, "Faulkner as Poet," *The Southern Literary Journal,* I (December 1968), 5–19; H. Edward Richardson, *William Faulkner: The Journey to Self-Discovery* (Columbia: University of Missouri Press, 1969), pp. 47–60, 104–15.

5. The comparison is not unfair: Eliot was twenty-nine when he published *Prufrock and Other Observations;* Faulkner was twenty-seven when he published *The Marble Faun.* Moreover, Eliot's poems were also written much earlier than their publication date seems to suggest: "The Love Song of J. Alfred Prufrock," for example, was finished in 1911, when he was twenty-three.

6. "An Examination of the Poetry of William Faulkner," 125.

7. Richard P. Adams, *Faulkner: Myth and Motion* (Princeton, N. J.: Princeton University Press, 1968), p. 77.

8. *Uncollected Prose,* collected and edited by John P. Frayne, vol. I (London: Macmillan, 1970), p. 103.

9. "Verse Old and Nascent: A Pilgrimage," *The Double Dealer,* VII (April 1925), 129–31. Reprinted in *William Faulkner: Early Prose and Poetry,* edited by Carvel Collins (Boston: Little, Brown, and Co., 1962), pp. 114–18. Hereafter referred to as *EPP.*

10. "Books and Things," *The Mississippian* (November 10, 1920), 5. *EPP,* pp. 71–73.

11. *EPP,* p. 72.

12. *EPP,* p. 71.

13. "American Drama: Inhibitions," *The Mississippian* (March 17, 1922), 5; (March 24, 1922), 5. *EPP,* pp. 93–97.

14. *EPP,* p. 93.

15. "Books and Things: Joseph Hergesheimer," *The Mississippian* (December 15, 1922), 5. *EPP,* p. 101.

16. *EPP,* pp. 101–2.

17. *Lion in the Garden: Interviews with William Faulkner, 1926–1962,* ed. James B. Meriwether and Michael Millgate (New York: Random House, 1968), p. 253. Hereafter referred to as *LG.*

18. "American Drama: Eugene O'Neill," *The Mississippian* (February 3, 1922), 5. *EPP,* p. 86.

19. Preface to *The Marble Faun,* p. 7.

20. "American Drama: Inhibitions," *EPP,* p. 94.

21. See Joseph Blotner, *Faulkner: A Biography,* vol. 1 (New York: Random House, 1974), p. 140.

22. On *Marionettes,* see Noel Polk, "William Faulkner's *Marionettes,*" *Mississippi Quarterly,* XXVI (Summer 1973), 247–80. Reprinted in *A Faulkner Miscellany,* ed. James B. Meriwether (Jackson, Miss.: University Press of Mississippi, 1974), pp. 3–36.

23. On "The Hill," see H. Edward Richardson, *William Faulkner: The Journey to Self-Discovery,* pp. 99–103; Michel Gresset, "Faulkner's 'The Hill,'" *The Southern Literary Journal,* VI (Spring 1974), 3–18. My own comments are heavily indebted to these two essays, especially to Gresset's full and perceptive analysis of the sketch.

24. "The Hill," *EPP,* p. 91.

25. "Faulkner's 'The Hill,'" 12.

26. *Ibid.,* 13.

27. "The Hill," *EPP,* p. 91.

28. *EPP,* pp. 91–92.

29. *EPP,* p. 92.

30. *Labyrinths: Selected Stories & Other Writings,* trans. and ed. Donald A. Yates and James E. Irby (New York: New Directions, 1962), p. 182.

31. "Faulkner's 'The Hill,'" 14.

32. "Nympholepsy," *Mississippi Quarterly,* XXVI (Summer 1973), 403–9. Reprinted in *A Faulkner Miscellany,* pp. 149–55. The eight-page typescript belongs to the Henry W. and Albert A. Berg Collection of the New York Public Library.

33. *Ibid.,* 404.

34. *Ibid.,* 405.

35. *Ibid.*

36. *Ibid.,* 407.

37. *Ibid.*

38. Sexual encounters in Faulkner's fiction are frequently announced by the description of a male character lying in wait for a woman on the humid earth. Cf. "Then [George Farrar] lay down again, stretching, feeling the gracious earth through his clothing. . . ." (*Soldiers' Pay,* New York: Boni and Liveright, 1926, pp. 235–36) ; ". . . he felt soft damp earth through his trousers, upon his thighs" (*ibid.,* p. 238) ; "[Christmas] could feel the neversunned earth strike, slow and receptive, against him through his clothes: groin, hip, belly, breast, forearms. His arms were crossed, his forehead rested upon them, in his nostrils the damp rich odor of the dark and fecund earth" (*Light in August,* New York: Harrison Smith and Robert Haas, 1932, p. 215). The motif is clearly foreshadowed in "Nympholepsy": ". . . feeling the earth through his damp clothing, feeling twigs beneath his face and arm" (408).

39. "Everybody talked about Freud when I lived in New Orleans," said Faulkner in his 1956 interview with Jean Stein, "but I have never read him" (*LG,* p. 251).

40. Surprisingly enough, there is no reference to Frazer in Blotner's biography. Walter Brylowski, however, mentions private papers examined by Carvel Collins, which seem to establish that Faulkner read Sherwood Anderson's one volume edition of *The Golden Bough* while he was living in Anderson's apartment in 1925. See Brylowski, *Faulkner's Olympian Laugh* (Detroit, Mich.: Wayne State University Press, 1968), p. 84, note.

41. Faulkner had probably become acquainted with Joyce's work

before his stay in New Orleans. As early as 1924 he had been given a copy of *Ulysses,* and it seems safe to assume that at that time he had read at least parts of it. Faulkner's own statements on his indebtedness to Joyce have been contradictory. On this point, see Richard P. Adams, "The Literary Apprenticeship of William Faulkner," *Tulane Studies in English,* XII (1962), 138–39; Michael Millgate, *The Achievement of William Faulkner* (New York: Random House, 1966), pp. 14–15; Joseph Blotner, *Faulkner,* vol. I, p. 352.

42. All these pieces have been reprinted in *William Faulkner: New Orleans Sketches,* ed. Carvel Collins (New Brunswick, N. J.: Rutgers University Press, 1958). Hereafter referred to as *NOS.*

43. See Carvel Collins, Introduction to *NOS,* pp. xi-xxxiv.

44. Reported by William Faulkner, in "A Note on Sherwood Anderson," *Essays, Speeches and Public Letters by William Faulkner,* ed. James B. Meriwether (New York: Random House, 1966), p. 7. Originally published as "Sherwood Anderson: An Appreciation," *Atlantic,* CXCI (June 1953), 28.

45. See J. Blotner, *Faulkner,* vol. I, pp. 324–25, 369.

46. On this point, see Stanley Cooperman's excellent study, *World War I and the American Novel* (Baltimore, Md., and London: Johns Hopkins Press, 1967). Cooperman has some very perceptive comments on *Soldiers' Pay.*

47. On the question of influences, see Robert M. Slabey, *"Soldiers' Pay:* Faulkner's First Novel," *Revue des Langues Vivantes,* XXX (1964), 234–43; Michael Millgate, *The Achievement of William Faulkner,* pp. 61–67, and "Starting Out in the Twenties: Reflections on *Soldiers' Pay,"* *Mosaic,* VII (Fall 1973), 1–14. On Faulkner's specific debt to Beardsley, see Addison C. Bross, *"Soldiers' Pay* and the Art of Aubrey Beardsley," *American Quarterly,* XIX (Spring 1967), 3–23.

48. It is noteworthy that in *Soldiers' Pay* Faulkner draws rather heavily on his own verse, quoting several times from poems later collected in *A Green Bough.*

49. Michael Millgate, "Starting Out in the Twenties: Reflections on *Soldiers' Pay,"* 9.

50. See *A Green Bough* (New York: Harrison Smith and Robert Haas, 1933), pp. 7–11. The book was reproduced photographically from the original edition by Random House in 1952.

51. *Soldiers' Pay* (New York: Boni and Liveright, 1926), pp. 82–83. Hereafter referred to as *SP.*

52. *SP*, p. 295.

53. *SP*, p. 224.

54. *SP*, p. 225.

55. On the autobiographical aspect of the novel, see Michael Millgate, "Starting Out in the Twenties: Reflections on *Soldiers' Pay*," 13–14.

56. See J. Blotner, *Faulkner,* vol. I, pp. 192–97.

57. See Barbara Hand, "Faulkner's Widow Recounts Memories of College Weekends in Charlottesville," *Cavalier Daily,* 21 (April 1972), 4: "Mrs. Faulkner said that her husband used her as a model for one of his characters in his first novel, and that it 'hurt my feelings terribly.'"

58. *Faulkner in the University: Class Conferences at the University of Virginia, 1957–1958,* ed. Frederick L. Gwynn and Joseph L. Blotner (Charlottesville: University of Virginia Press, 1959), p. 257. Referred to hereafter as *FU.*

59. On the question of influences, see Michael Millgate, *The Achievement of William Faulkner,* pp. 68–75; Frederick L. Gwynn, "Faulkner's Prufrock—And Other Observations," *Journal of English and Germanic Philology,* LII (January 1953), 63–70; Robert M. Slabey, "Faulkner's *Mosquitoes* and Joyce's *Ulysses,*" *Revue des Langues Vivantes,* XXVIII (September–October 1962), 435–37; Joyce W. Warren, "Faulkner's 'Portrait of the Artist,'" *Mississippi Quarterly,* XIX (Summer 1966), 121–31; Phyllis Franklin, "The Influence of Joseph Hergesheimer upon *Mosquitoes,*" *Mississippi Quarterly,* XXII (Summer 1969), 207–13; H. Edward Richardson, *William Faulkner: The Journey to Self-Discovery,* pp. 134–38.

60. See Frederick L. Gwynn, "Faulkner's Prufrock—And Other Observations."

61. Blotner's biography provides the most complete account of Faulkner's models. See *Faulkner,* vol. I, pp. 514–22.

62. Hemingway parodied Anderson's style in *The Torrents of Spring* (1926). Faulkner did so in his introduction to *Sherwood Anderson & Other Famous Creoles,* a collection of caricatures by William Spratling, published in December 1926. The publication of the book was resented by Anderson and was probably the immediate cause of his break with Faulkner.

63. See Fairchild's reflections, in *Mosquitoes* (New York: Boni and Liveright, 1927), p. 231. Referred to hereafter as *Mos.*

64. *Mos,* p. 186.

65. *Mos.*, p. 210.

66. See *The Novels of William Faulkner: A Critical Interpretation* (Baton Rouge: Louisiana State University Press, 1959), pp. 8–14.

67. On this point, see Mary M. Dunlap, "Sex and the Artist in *Mosquitoes,*" *Mississippi Quarterly*, XXII (Summer 1969), 190–206.

68. See Floyd C. Watkins, *The Flesh and the Word* (Nashville, Tenn.: Vanderbilt University Press, 1971).

69. *Sanctuary* (New York: Cape and Smith, 1931), p. 13.

70. See Joyce W. Warren, "Faulkner's Portrait of the Artist," 121–31.

71. *Mos*, p. 339.

72. *Mos*, p. 154.

73. *A Portrait of the Artist as a Young Man,* ed. Chester G. Anderson (New York: The Viking Press, 1968), p. 217.

74. *Ibid.*, p. 172.

75. *Mos*, p. 339.

76. *A Portrait of the Artist as a Young Man,* p. 170.

77. *Mos*, p. 11.

78. *Mos*, p. 329.

79. On this point, see Kenneth William Hepburn, "Faulkner's *Mosquitoes*: A Poetic Turning Point," *Twentieth Century Literature*, XVII (January 1971), 19–27.

80. *Mos*, p. 11.

81. *Mos*, p. 322.

82. *Mos*, p. 339.

83. *Stephen Hero,* ed. Theodore Spencer (London: Jonathan Cape, 1956), p. 83.

84. *Ibid.*

85. See Thomas L. McHaney, "The Elmer Papers: Faulkner's Comic Portraits of the Artist," *Mississippi Quarterly*, XXVI (Summer 1973), 281–311. Reprinted in *A Faulkner Miscellany*, pp. 37–69.

86. *Mos*, p. 144.

87. See *Mos*, pp. 246–52.

88. "William Faulkner, Who Wrote 'Soldiers' Pay' Again Manifests Brilliancy, Promise and Foibles," New York *Evening Post*, June 11, 1927, Section III, 7. Reprinted in *A Reviewer's ABC* (New York: Meriden, 1958), pp. 197–200.

89. See *Flags in the Dust,* ed. Douglas Day (New York: Random House, 1973). The text of this version is based on a composite typescript that Faulkner retained with an earlier handwritten copy.

90. *LG*, p. 255.

91. On Faulkner's unfinished novel, "Father Abraham," see Joseph Blotner, *Faulkner,* vol. I, pp. 526–31.

92. Reported by William Faulkner, in "A Note on Sherwood Anderson," *Essays, Speeches and Public Letters,* p. 8.

93. "Books," in *Notes on Life and Letters* (London: Dent, Collected Edition, 1949), p. 6. The essay was first published in 1905.

94. *FU*, p. 285.

95. "Introduction," *Flags in the Dust*, p. x.

96. On *Sartoris* as a novel of manners, see Robert Scholes, "Myth and Manners in *Sartoris*," *The Georgia Review,* XVI (Spring 1962), 195–201.

97. Malcolm Cowley, *The Faulkner-Cowley File: Letters and Memories, 1944–1962* (New York: The Viking Press, 1966), p. 66.

98. On Faulkner's models for *Sartoris,* see Michael Millgate, *The Achievement of William Faulkner,* p. 25; Joseph Blotner, *Faulkner,* vol. I, pp. 532–38, 545–46.

99. Quoted by J. Blotner, in *Faulkner,* vol. I, pp. 531–32, from manuscript deposited at the Yale University Library.

100. *FU*, p. 23. See also p. 48 and "Ad Astra," *Collected Stories* (New York: Random House, 1950), pp. 407–29.

101. See *William Faulkner: The Yoknapatawpha Country* (New Haven, Conn.: Yale University Press, 1963), p. 103.

102. For a discussion of Bayard's literary sources, see Dieter Meindl, *Bewusstsein als Schicksal: Zu Struktur and Entwicklung von William Faulkners Generationsromanen* (Stuttgart: Metzler, 1974), pp. 90–106.

103. *Sartoris* (New York: Harcourt, Brace and Company, 1929), p. 161. Referred to hereafter as *Sar*.

104. *Sar,* p. 129.

105. Horace Benbow resembles Faulkner in many ways: he is of small stature; he is a tennis player and a pipe smoker, a friend of children and a devotee of Shakespeare and Keats, and like the author, he marries a divorcée. Moreover, the early versions of the novel contain samples of Horace's decadent poetry that are very like Faulkner's own early verse.

106. *Sar,* p. 1.

107. On the theme of mythmaking, see Olga W. Vickery, *The Novels of William Faulkner,* pp. 15–27.

108. *Sar,* p. 9.

2. Caddy, or The Quest for Eurydice

1. Faulkner's introduction survives in several partial and complete manuscript and typescript drafts. Two of them have been published: "William Faulkner: An Introduction for *The Sound and the Fury*," *The Southern Review*, N.S., VIII (October 1972), 705–10; "An Introduction to *The Sound and the Fury*," *Mississippi Quarterly*, XXVI (Summer 1973), 410–15. Both versions were edited by James B. Meriwether.

2. "An Introduction for *The Sound and the Fury*," *The Southern Review*, 708.

3. Faulkner's comments strongly suggest what modern French criticism has termed *intertextuality*. See Julia Kristeva, *Semeiotikè* (Paris: Editions du Seuil, 1969), p. 146: "Every text is the absorption and transformation of another text" (my translation).

4. "An Introduction for *The Sound and the Fury*," *The Southern Review*, 710.

5. *Ibid*. See also the introduction which Faulkner wrote for the Modern Library edition of *Sanctuary* in 1932: ". . . with one novel [Flags in the Dust] completed and consistently refused for two years, I had just written my guts into *The Sound and the Fury* though I was not aware until the book was published that I had done so, because I had done it for pleasure. I believed then that I would never be published again. I had stopped thinking of myself in publishing terms" (*Sanctuary*, New York: The Modern Library, 1932, vi).

6. "An Introduction for *The Sound and the Fury*," *The Southern Review*, 710.

7. See André Green, *Un Oeil en Trop: Le Complexe d'Oedipe dans la Tragédie* (Paris: Les Editions de Minuit, 1969), pp. 35–40.

8. In this connection it is interesting to note that Estelle Oldham, one of the models for Caddy, is compared to "a lovely vase" in one of Faulkner's letters. See J. Blotner, *Faulkner*, vol. I, p. 563.

9. "An Introduction for *The Sound and the Fury*," *The Southern Review*, 710.

10. *Ibid*., 709.

11. *Ibid*.

12. *Ibid*.

13. *Ibid*., 710.

14. *Ibid*., 709.

15. *Ibid*., 710.

16. *FU*, p. 61. See also *LG*, p. 146.

17. Quoted in James B. Meriwether, "Notes on the Textual His-

tory of *The Sound and the Fury*," *Papers of the Bibliographical Society of America,* LVI (Third Quarter, 1962), 289.

18. See *FU*, pp. 61, 77; *LG*, pp. 92, 146, 180.

19. *FU*, p. 61.

20. *Proust and Three Dialogues with Georges Duthuit* (London: John Calder, 1965), p. 125.

21. *LG*, pp. 146–47. See also p. 222.

22. The working title of the short story was "Twilight." See J. Blotner, *Faulkner,* vol. I, p. 566.

23. *LG*, p. 238.

24. *LG*, pp. 220–21.

25. *LG*, p. 180. Significant too is Faulkner's offer to provide an appendix to the novel for the Viking *Portable Faulkner* which Malcolm Cowley was editing in 1945. The many additions he made there to the original account of the Compson family (a number of which, incidentally, are inconsistent with the novel) are tangible evidence of his feeling that the story was "still not finished."

26. *LG*, p. 238.

27. *Der Mann Ohne Eigenschaften* (Hamburg: Rowohlt, 1952), p. 1640. My translation.

28. Donald M. Kartiganer, *"The Sound and the Fury* and Faulkner's Quest for Form," *English Literary History,* XXXVII (December 1970), 618.

29. "A Primitive Like an Orb," in *The Collected Poems* (New York: Alfred A. Knopf, 1951), p. 443.

30. "Le double et l'absent," *Critique,* XXIX (May 1973), 403–4. The idea that art is arrayed against loss and absence has also been developed by a number of British psychoanalysts. See Melanie Klein, "Infantile Anxiety-Situations Reflected in a Work of Art and in the Creative Impulse" and "Mourning and its Relation to Manic-Depressive States," in *Contributions to Psychoanalysis, 1921–1945* (London: The Hogarth Press, 1950). See also Hanna Segal, "A Psychoanalytical Approach to Aesthetics," *International Journal of Psychoanalysis,* XXXIII (1952), 196–207.

31. Reported by Maurice-Edgar Coindreau, in "Preface to *The Sound and the Fury,*" *The Time of William Faulkner* (Columbia: University of South Carolina Press, 1971), p. 41. The autobiographical source of the Damuddy episode is presumably the funeral of Faulkner's grandmother, Lelia Swift Butler, in 1907. Faulkner was then ten years old—approximately the same age as Quentin's at the time of Damuddy's death in the novel.

32. *The Time of Willam Faulkner*, p. 49.

33. "An Introduction for *The Sound and the Fury*," 710.

34. On this point, see "Fantasmes Originaires," in Jean Laplanche and J. B. Pontalis, *Vocabulaire de la Psychanalyse* (Paris: Presses Universitaires de France, 1967), pp. 157–59.

35. In this connection it is also interesting to note the phonic kinship of *muddy* and *Damuddy*.

36. "Fetishism" (1927), in *The Standard Edition of the Complete Psychological Works of Sigmund Freud*, ed. and trans. James Strachey (London: The Hogarth Press, 1964), vol. XXI, p. 154. All further references to Freud will be to this edition.

37. *Ibid.*, p. 155.

38. With regard to the Edenic connotations of the scene, it is noteworthy that in one of his interviews Faulkner confused Caddy's pear tree with an apple tree (see *FU*, p. 31). Some critics have pointed to further biblical connotations in the description of the scene in the novel: before Caddy climbs the tree, "a snake [crawls] out from under the house" (45), and a few moments later Dilsey says to her, "'You Satan . . . Come down from there'" (54).

39. *LG*, p. 244.

40. *FU*, p. 6.

41. See also what Faulkner told Maurice-Edgar Coindreau: ". . . the same thing happened to me that happens to many writers—I fell in love with one of my characters, Caddy. I loved her so much I couldn't decide to give her life just for the duration of a short story. She deserved more than that" (*The Time of William Faulkner*, p. 41). Faulkner's fascination with girls can be traced back to his earlier writings. Among the figures anticipating Caddy one might mention Juliet Bunden (in "Adolescence," an unpublished story written in 1922), Frankie (in an untitled and unpublished story seemingly written in 1924), Jo-Addie (in "Elmer," the uncompleted novel begun in 1925), the nameless girl who turns out to be "Little sister Death" (in "The Kid Learns," 1925), and Dulcie, the little heroine of Faulkner's tale, "The Wishing Tree" (1927). Most of the young female characters in his first three novels are also related to Caddy in some way or other, Patricia Robyn (*Mosquitoes*) being probably the one who bears the closest resemblance to her. The heroine of *The Sound and the Fury* is of course much more complex than any of these figures, and Faulkner's affective involvement with her has deep autobiographical sources. In creating her, he drew more than ever before on memories of his own childhood and adolescence. It seems safe to assume that Estelle Oldham,

whom he had come to know as a little boy and with whom he fell in love as a young teen-ager, served as a model for Caddy. But so did Sallie Murry, the tomboyish cousin to whom, as Joseph Blotner points out, Faulkner "had been almost as close as a sister" (*Faulkner,* vol. I, p. 568). And one might do well to remember that Estelle also served as a model for the devastating portrait of Cecily Saunders in *Soldiers' Pay.* Which is to say that Caddy, even though she rose out of the depths of Faulkner's private experience, is above all a literary creation.

42. Further name-confusions are induced by the presence in the novel of two Quentins (uncle and niece), two Jasons (father and son), and by the change of the idiot's name from Maury to Benjamin. To consider this a perverse game on Faulkner's part is clearly beside the point. As Joseph W. Reed suggests, the name-confusions may be seen as an index to inbreeding and degeneracy (see *Faulkner's Narrative,* New Haven, Conn.: Yale University Press, 1973, p. 76). At a deeper level, however, they refer to the author's central concern with the precarious status of the self. Name-confusion leads to identity confusion. True, Faulkner's characters generally preserve recognizable features, but the device tends to blur the boundaries between them. What is at stake here is the very concept of *character* and its function in the novel. In this connection it is worth noting that in their theoretical writings several among the most experimental of contemporary European novelists have precisely called attention to Faulkner's disconcerting use of names. Nathalie Sarraute comments upon it in *L'Ere du Soupçon* (Paris: Gallimard, 1956, p. 73), Michel Butor in *Répertoire* (Paris: Editions de Minuit, 1960, p. 252), Alain Robbe-Grillet in *Pour un Nouveau Roman* (Paris: Editions de Minuit, 1963, p. 28), and Ingeborg Bachmann makes it the main point of her essay on *The Sound and the Fury* ("Über 'Schall und Wahn'," in Gerd Haffmans, ed., *Über William Faulkner,* Zurich: Diogenes, 1973, pp. 127–29).

43. The importance of this image and of the scene it heralds is confirmed by a study of the manuscript. Originally section 2 started thus: "One minute she was standing there. The next Benjy was yelling and pulling at her. They went down the hall to the bathroom and stopped there, Caddy backed against the door. . . ." This page of the manuscript is reproduced in James B. Meriwether, *The Literary Career of William Faulkner: A Bibliographical Study* (Princeton, N. J.: Princeton University Library, 1961), illustration 11.

44. Pp. 69, 99, and *passim.* See also p. 88: "Her hair was like fire, and little points of fire were in her eyes. . . ."

45. See pp. 5, 8, 22, 48, 50, 51, 54, 58, 88. The reversible meta-

phor *girl* = *tree* can be traced back to Faulkner's earliest work: in *The Marble Faun* poplars are compared to "slender girls"; girls are likened to trees in *Marionettes*, his early play, as well as in *Soldiers' Pay* and *Mosquitoes*.

46. A similar ritual cleansing occurs in "There Was a Queen." See *Collected Stories* (New York: Random House, 1950), p. 741.

47. *Baudelaire* (Paris: Gallimard, 1947), p. 201. My translation.

48. The phrase is from Harry Modean Campbell and Ruel E. Foster, *William Faulkner: A Critical Appraisal* (Norman: University of Oklahoma Press, 1951), p. 54.

49. *La Ville,* 2nd edition (Paris: Mercure de France, 1920), p. 307.

50. For a full discussion of Caddy in psychological and moral terms see Catherine B. Baum, "'The Beautiful One': Caddy Compson as Heroine of *The Sound and the Fury*," *Modern Fiction Studies,* XIII (Spring 1967), 33–44; Eileen Gregory, "Caddy Compson's World," *Merrill Studies in The Sound and the Fury,* comp. James B. Meriwether (Columbus, Ohio: Charles E. Merrill, 1970), pp. 89–101.

51. *Notes and Reviews* (Cambridge, Mass.: Dunster House, 1921), p. 226.

3. Benjy, or The Agony of Dispossession

1. See Irena Kaluza's very helpful linguistic-stylistic study, *The Functioning of Sentence Structure in the Stream-of-Consciousness Technique of William Faulkner's "The Sound and the Fury"* (Krakow: Nakdalem Uniwersytetu Jagiellonskiego, 1967), reprinted by the Folcroft Press Inc. in 1970. According to I. Kaluza, directly reported dialogue represents 56% of the Benjy section, indirect quotations introduced by *he said* and the like 21%, and Benjy's stream-of-consciousness proper 23%. L. Moffitt Cecil likewise distinguishes between two levels of language: "Benjy's given rudimentary 'speech' and the more sophisticated dialogue which miraculously he recalls but cannot fully understand." See "A Rhetoric for Benjy," *The Southern Literary Journal,* III (Fall 1970), 32–46, especially 35–37.

2. For a study of Benjy's vocabulary, see L. Moffitt Cecil, "A Rhetoric for Benjy," 38–42. According to this critic, Faulkner allows the character a working vocabulary of some 500 words, including slightly over 200 nouns, 175 verbs or verbals, 61 adjectives, 37 adverbs, 25 prepositions, and 13 conjunctions.

3. I. Kaluza's study establishes that out of the 814 sentences of

the Benjy's idiolect, 686 are generated by basic syntactic patterns (84%), and that 462 of them (67%) consist of one-unit simple sentences.

4. Noam Chomsky, *Syntactic Structures* (The Hague: Mouton, 1957), p. 107.

5. I. Kaluza's study presents a very perceptive analysis of the linguistic devices used to convey this impression. See *The Functioning of Sentence Structure,* pp. 56–58.

6. "Beyond the Pleasure Principle" (1920), *Standard Edition,* vol. XVIII, p. 15.

7. *Ibid.*

8. *FU,* p. 64.

9. The theme of the brother-sister relationship is already outlined in Faulkner's unpublished early story "Adolescence" and in his uncompleted novel "Elmer"; it recurs in *Mosquitoes,* and yet again, with markedly incestuous undertones, in *Flags in the Dust/Sartoris.* It also figures prominently in later novels like *As I Lay Dying, Absalom, Absalom!,* and *The Hamlet.* A noteworthy point: there are sometimes several brothers; the sister is always unique.

10. *LG,* p. 146.

11. See Faulkner's statements on this point in *LG,* pp. 245–46.

12. Benjamin, the new name given to the idiot, means in Hebrew "child of the right hand," i.e., favorite child. According to Faulkner's testimony, however, it was not chosen with ironic intent. Confused with Joseph, the son sold into Egypt, Benjamin was rather intended to suggest abandonment and exile, as can be seen from Quentin's reflections in section 2 (211). See also *FU,* p. 18.

13. "An Introduction to *The Sound and the Fury,*" *Mississippi Quarterly,* XXVI (Summer 1973), 414.

14. *LG,* pp. 147–48.

15. Among the numerous discussions of Benjy's relationship to time, one of the best is Perrin Lowrey's "Concepts of Time in *The Sound and the Fury,*" in *English Institute Essays, 1952,* ed. Alan S. Downer (New York: Columbia University Press, 1954), pp. 57–82.

16. *A Fable* (New York: Random House, 1950), p. 296. See also "Appendix" in *The Sound and the Fury,* pp. 423–24, and *LG,* p. 246.

17. Besides being an identification motif, Luster's search for the lost quarter in the first section provides an ironical parallel to Benjy's quest and foreshadows Jason's chase after Miss Quentin (who has run off with his money) in section 3.

18. *FU,* p. 64.

19. See "The Interior Monologues of *The Sound and the Fury*," in *Merrill Studies in The Sound and the Fury*, comp. James B. Meriwether (Columbus, Ohio: Charles E. Merrill, 1970), pp. 59–79. The original version of this essay appeared in *English Institute Essays, 1952*, pp. 29–56.

20. See "Appendix," p. 423.

21. See "Faulkner and the Theme of Isolation," *Georgia Review*, XVIII (Spring 1964), 51. See also William A. Freedman, "The Technique of Isolation in *The Sound and the Fury*," *Mississippi Quarterly*, XV (Winter 1961–62), 21–26.

22. The gate is to Benjy what the door is to Quentin. Both are associated with Caddy and may be interpreted as sexual symbols.

23. The phrase drew comment in one of the first essays to be written on the novel: James Burnham's "Trying to Say," *The Symposium*, II (January 1931), 51–59.

24. See *FU*, pp. 4–5.

25. See "Appendix," p. 422, and the letter about *The Sound and the Fury* that Faulkner wrote to his literary agent Ben Wasson, and in which he stated that Benjy "tries to rape a young girl and is castrated" (undated letter in the Massey Collection at the University of Virginia, quoted in full by Michael Millgate, *The Achievement of William Faulkner*, pp. 93–94).

26. These image associations are echoed in the second monologue: Quentin links death and sleep (see 144, 215), and several times invokes hell-fire. Moreover, his suicide at the end of section 2 is symmetrical with Benjy's going to sleep at the close of section 1.

27. 17 narrative units are devoted to the day of Damuddy's death. See 19–22, 22–23, 23, 26–33, 38–39, 39, 40, 42–44, 45 (2 units), 46–47, 54–55, 75, 76, 89, 90, 91–92.

28. See *A Reader's Guide to William Faulkner* (New York: Farrar, Straus, 1964), pp. 103–4.

29. See *ibid.* For a fuller discussion, see Charles D. Peavy, "Faulkner's Use of Folklore in *The Sound and the Fury*," *Journal of American Folklore*, LXXIX (July-September 1966), 437–38.

30. *LG*, p. 245.

31. *FU*, p. 95.

32. On Faulkner's use of italics for indicating time-shifts, see James B. Meriwether, "The Textual History of *The Sound and the Fury*," in *Studies in The Sound and the Fury*, pp. 9–11. Faulkner rejected Ben Wasson's suggestion to replace italicization by wider spaces between lines, reminding his editor that he "purposely used italics for

both actual scenes and remembered scenes for the reason, not to indicate the different dates of happenings, but merely to permit the reader to anticipate a thought-transference, letting the recollection postulate its own date" (undated letter in Massey Collection). It is also noteworthy that Faulkner's own preference was for printing the Benjy section in inks of different colors.—The best guide for the chronology and scene-shifts in Benjy's and Quentin's sections is to be found in Edmond L. Volpe, *A Reader's Guide to William Faulkner,* pp. 353–77. See also George R. Stewart and Joseph M. Backus, "'Each in Its Ordered Place': Structure and Narrative in Benjy's Section of *The Sound and the Fury,"* *American Literature,* XXIX (January 1958), 440–56.

33. Some of the verbal clues are analyzed by Olga Vickery in *The Novels of William Faulkner,* pp. 33–34.

34. I am referring here to Roman Jakobson's definition of what he considers to be the two axes of language: the syntagmatic axis, based on the principle of contiguity, and the paradigmatic one, based on analogy. See "Two Aspects of Language and Two Types of Aphasic Disturbances," in *Fundamentals of Language,* ed. Jakobson and Morris Halle (The Hague: Mouton, 1956).

35. *William Faulkner: An Introduction and Interpretation* (New York: Barnes and Noble, 1963), p. 36.

36. See especially James M. Mellard's stimulating essay, "Caliban as Prospero: Benjy and *The Sound and the Fury,"* *Novel,* III (Spring 1970), 233–48. Mellard argues that Benjy's section is "a special handling of the narrative archetype of romance." Relating the character to the tradition of the fool as well as to pastoralism, he points out his close affinities with Shakespeare's Caliban: both are "natural men" and are used satirically to show up civilized corruption. Mellard's argument is convincing as far as it goes, but it overlooks the central ambiguity of Benjy's "innocence."

37. *LG,* p. 246.

38. *LG,* p. 146.

4. The Young Man, Desire, and Death

1. See I. Kaluza, *The Functioning of Sentence Structure,* p. 73.

2. As I. Kaluza's study shows, this rhetoric was very carefully worked out by Faulkner, and is the more efficient as it operates on all possible levels: syntactic, lexical, morphological, and phonemic. See *ibid.,* pp. 81–89.

3. *As I Lay Dying* (New York: Random House, 1964), p. 156. Originally published in 1930.

4. Close examination of *The Sound and the Fury* shows it to be *polyphonic* not only in its manifest structure, but in the very texture of each of its four parts. In all sections there is an interweaving and embedding of many voices. On the notion of polyphonic fiction, see Mikhail Bakhtin, *Problems of Dostoevski's Poetics* (Ann Arbor: Ardis, 1973). If Faulkner may be considered Dostoevski's American heir, it is because of the polyphonism—or, to use another term from Bakhtin, the *dialogism*—of his novels rather than because of a common thematics.

5. On this point, see Martha W. England, "Quentin's Story: Chronology and Explication," *College English,* XXII (January 1961), 228–35, and Jane Millgate's perceptive essay, "Quentin Compson as Poor Player: Verbal and Social Clichés in *The Sound and the Fury,*" *Revue des Langues Vivantes* (Bruxelles), XXXIV (1968), 40–49.

6. Shreve alludes ironically to Lochinvar, the hero of a ballad included in the fifth canto of Scott's *Marmion,* and makes an oblique reference to Byron's *Don Juan* (115); Spoade calls Quentin "the champion of dames" (207), and to Herbert Head he is a "half-baked Galahad" (136). The very name "Quentin" suggests gallantry and romance *(Quentin Durward),* and the irony is the more pointed here as the same name was borne by the first of the Compsons.

7. It is of course tempting to relate Quentin's role-playing to Faulkner's own impersonations (see my first chapter, pp. 6, 23–24, 32). The young man's penchant for romantic parts is one autobiographical trait among many.

8. "Time in Faulkner: *The Sound and the Fury,*" in *William Faulkner: Three Decades of Criticism,* ed. Frederick J. Hoffman and Olga W. Vickery (East Lansing: Michigan State University Press, 1960), p. 230.

9. *Go Down, Moses* (New York: Random House, 1942), pp. 130–31.

10. Read in Freudian terms, the equation *sex = dirt* might be considered an index of regression to the anal-sadistic stage of psychosexual development. The Natalie scene would then represent an abortive attempt to accede to genitality, and the hog wallow scene a return to pregenital sexuality. The traits associated with anal fixation are extremely numerous in the Quentin section: obsession with the pure/impure, sadistic impulses, compulsive orderliness and cleanliness, ablution rites, phobia of stains and soiled objects. In this respect as in others Quentin closely resembles his brother Jason: both are related to what Freud calls the "anal character" through their emphasis on order-

liness, their extreme obstinacy, and their strong sense of ownership (plain avarice with Jason, emotional possessiveness with Quentin). See S. Freud, "Character and Anal Erotism" (1908), *Standard Edition,* vol. IX, pp. 167–75.

11. The hog wallow scene points forward to Quentin's allusion to Euboelus (184), the swineherd who plunged with his herd into the chasm formed in the earth when Pluto emerged to rape Persephone. The sexual implications of the mythic reference are reinforced by the Rabelaisian and Shakespearean image of "the beast with two backs." Fusing these two references with a third one (the Gadarene swine described by Mark and Luke in the New Testament), Quentin resumes the image at the end of his monologue in the startling evocation of "swine untethered in pairs rushing coupled into the sea" (219)— a vision of apocalyptic sexuality, but also a significant prefiguration of Quentin's death in the Charles River.

12. On homeopathic, or imitative, magic, see James Frazer, *The Golden Bough,* abridged edition (London: Macmillan and Co. Ltd., 1963), pp. 16–49. The first critic to use the phrase with reference to Faulkner's fiction was Jean-Jacques Mayoux, in *Vivants Piliers: Le roman anglo-saxon et les symboles* (Paris: Julliard, 1960), p. 265.

13. *Light in August* (New York: Harrison Smith & Robert Haas, 1932), p. 174.

14. Here again one is reminded of the anal phase, during which the concepts of *dirt* and *property* polarize infantile behavior. Since this is also the time of separation from the mother, dirt, excrement—what is expelled from the body—becomes symbolically linked with the ambivalent feelings generated by the child's (re)expulsion from the mother's body. Caddy has become a "dirty girl" to Quentin insofar as she is no longer an extension of himself, i.e., his property. The dirt motif is thus directly related to the central experience of loss.

15. Faulkner himself pointed to the symbolism of the muddy drawers in his interview with Jean Stein. See *LG,* p. 245.

16. Rats often appear in scenes with sexual overtones. In the barn scene Quentin and Natalie hear a rat in the crib. The image of the rat is also associated with Caddy: after she has lost her virginity, her eyes are compared to "cornered rats" (185). In Faulkner's unfinished novel "Elmer" the same image occurs; it also figures in the closing section of *Mosquitoes* and in the rape scene in *Sanctuary.*

17. Lawrence E. Bowling was the first to call attention to this phobia of stains in "Faulkner and the Theme of Innocence," *Kenyon Review,* XX (Summer 1958), 466–87, especially 469–70. References

to stained objects abound in section 2. Apart from those already mentioned, consider "a red smear on the dial" (99), "a man in his stained hat" (110), and "a soiled pink garter" (115), where the connection between Quentin's phobia and his sexual obsessions is particularly evident. Dirt and stain imagery is a recurrent feature in Faulkner's novels, most conspicuous in the sexual nightmare of *Sanctuary*.

18. Suspecting Quentin's taste of the clean and pure, Herbert Head thinks he can buy his friendship with a brand-new fifty dollar bill: ". . . look at it it's just out of convent look not a blemish not even been creased yet see here" (135-36). One notes the image of the convent, linking physical cleanliness with the notion of chastity.

19. "One cannot 'plan' to kill oneself. One can make preparations for it and act in anticipation of the final gesture which still belongs to the normal category of things to be done, but this gesture is not made with a view to death, it does not envision death, it does not hold it in its grasp. Hence the love of minute detail, the patient and manic attention to trifling matters often evinced by someone about to die. Other people are surprised and say: 'When you want to die, you don't think of so many things.' But in fact one doesn't *want* to die, death cannot be an object of volition, it is impossible to want to die, and so the will, stopped short on the uncertain threshold of what it cannot accomplish, resorts with its calculating wisdom to grappling with everything it can still seize hold of in the neighborhood of its limits." Maurice Blanchot, *L'Espace Littéraire* (Paris: Gallimard, 1955), p. 105. My translation.

20. Quentin thus reverts to the position of the infant within the oedipal triangle. In this respect it should be noted that Caddy later gives her brother's name to her own daughter: symbolically, Quentin II is both the fruit of the imaginary incest and Quentin's homologue as Caddy's child.

21. A number of critics assume that there is a "suicide pact" between Quentin and his sister. The assumption has been questioned by Charles D. Peavy in "A Note on the 'Suicide Pact' in *The Sound and the Fury*," *English Language Notes*, V (March 1968), 207-9. There is no final proof in these matters, but Quentin is obviously not meant to be taken as a reliable narrator of his past, and in his monologue it is often difficult to distinguish fact from fancy.

22. Quentin's erotic interest in his sister's body is evidenced by many of his reminiscences, and is most obvious in his (probably half-imaginary) account of the knife scene (188-90).

23. See Ernest Jones, *Hamlet and Oedipus* (New York: Norton, 1949). Critics have often noted the affinities between Quentin and

Shakespeare's hero. See, for example, Cleanth Brooks, "Primitivism in *The Sound and the Fury*," *English Institute Essays, 1952,* pp. 13–14. See also William R. Taylor, *Cavalier and Yankee* (New York: Doubleday Anchor Books, 1963), pp. 137–40. As Taylor points out, Quentin is one among many "Southern Hamlets": "The introverted gentleman has a long history in Southern fiction which runs the gamut from Poe's neurasthenic Roderick Usher to Faulkner's Quentin Compson III and includes along the way contributions by Simms, Harriet Beecher Stowe and practically all the talents large and small that have examined Southern life" (p. 138).

24. Bland's symbolic function is further emphasized by imagery assimilating him to a royal personage (112, 130, 149), and it is interesting to note that his mother is likewise compared to a queen. No doubt irony plays its part in these similes, but to Quentin this regal couple is also a mythicized image of the parental couple. Moreover, through the superimposition of the husband-wife relationship on the son-mother relationship one can see the incest motif emerge once again. The ambiguous intimacy between Mrs. Bland and her son, her wide-eyed admiration for his amorous exploits, her ecstatic marveling at his handsomeness (130–31) are in themselves suggestive of near-incestuous relations.

25. In the confrontation scenes between Quentin and his sister's lovers the contrast between his impotence and their manliness is underscored by the ironic use of phallic symbols: Ames' revolver, Head's cigar. One recalls that Ames offers to lend Quentin his revolver, and Head offers him a cigar, both of which are refused. His attitude confirms the denial of sexuality in which his impotence originates. It seems safe to assume that this symbolism was intentional: similar phallic imagery is to be found in Faulkner's uncompleted early novel "Elmer," whose immature hero to some extent prefigures Quentin. The contrast between Quentin and his rivals is further suggested on the symbolic level through their respective relations to the elements of water and fire. For Quentin water means both death and desire, and one of the last memories in his monologue is significantly a remote childhood memory about the nights when he would get up to go to the bathroom, "seeking water" (215). Ames and Bland, his surrogate, on the other hand, possess what Quentin at once desires and dreads; they have both gained mastery over the female element: Bland is an accomplished oarsman; as to Ames, Caddy tells Quentin that "he's crossed all the oceans all around the world" (187). At the same time these two figures are related to fire (a traditional symbol of male potency): Bland

through his association with the sun, Ames through his remarkable marksmanship and through his association with bronze and asbestos.

26. See Michael Millgate, *The Achievement of William Faulkner,* p. 95: "Faulkner's alterations achieve certain improvements in phrasing and elaborate the insistence on time, but perhaps the most interesting of the new elements are the references to Mr. Compson. Throughout the section, as revised in the carbon typescript and the published book, Quentin's mind runs on his father almost as much as it does on Caddy." Mr. Compson's reflections upon time in the opening of the second section (93) as well as his speculations about virginity (143) are missing from the manuscript. It is most significant, too, that while many of the references to "Father said" were added upon revision, Faulkner removed "said" from Quentin's final (imagined) conversation with Mr. Compson (219–22). In the manuscript, Faulkner followed the normal pattern of reported speech ("He said . . . and I said . . . ") ; in the published version, the only clues to change of speaker are the pronouns which are run into the prose without any punctuation mark. Moreover, to suggest the shrinking of Quentin's self, Faulkner substituted "i" for "I." On this point, see Faulkner's comments in *FU,* p. 18.

27. It is important to bear in mind, though, that the conversations reported by Quentin are to some degree imaginary. When Faulkner was asked if Quentin had talked of incest to his father, he answered that he never did. See *FU,* pp. 262–63.

28. *FU,* p. 3.

29. *FU,* p. 3.

30. One might even argue that there is to some extent an ironical permutation of roles: the weak but affectionate Mr. Compson becomes a parodic mother figure; Mrs. Compson acts at times as a father substitute, especially in her harshly repressive attitude toward Benjy and Caddy. A similar inversion can be seen in Quentin and Caddy: Quentin is the weakling; Caddy has inherited the reckless courage of the original Compsons. In their childhood games, Quentin remembers, "she never was a queen or a fairy she was always a king or a giant or a general" (215). The inversion of parental/sexual roles occurs in other Faulkner novels, notably *As I Lay Dying* (Anse-Addie) and *The Wild Palms* (Harry-Charlotte).

31. The possibility of a merger between the oedipal father image and an ancestral figure is corroborated by clinical experience. See, for example, the case analyzed by Erik H. Erikson in *Identity: Youth and Crisis* (New York: Norton & Company, 1968), pp. 61–62.

32. On Lacan's concept of the *Name-of-the-Father*, see his *Ecrits* (Paris: Seuil, 1966), pp. 812–13 and *passim*.

33. The drama of (non-) recognition is dealt with more openly in *Absalom, Absalom!*, where Charles Bon vainly waits to be recognized by Thomas Sutpen, his father.

34. I am referring again to two of Lacan's concepts. The imaginary, the symbolic, the real are to Lacan the three essential registers of the psychoanalytic field. The first is marked by the prevalence of a narcissistic relation to the image of a similar being, as evidenced by the "mirror stage" in the early development of the child. The second refers to the symbolic systems structuring interhuman relationships, especially language.

35. The phrase is from Guy Rosolato, "Du Père," in *Essais sur le Symbolique* (Paris: Gallimard, 1969), p. 49. My translation.

36. *Ibid.*, p. 48. My translation.

37. Quentin's desire to avoid oedipal involvement is also attested by the fantasy of being his father's father, i.e., unfathered: *"Say it to Father will you I will am my fathers Progenitive I invented him created I him Say it to him it will not be for he will say I was not and then you and I since philoprogenitive"* (152). In Faulkner's fiction being fatherless is considered alternately a positive privilege and a fatal flaw. It means total self-possession for Lucas Beauchamp, "who fathered himself, intact and complete" (*Go Down, Moses,* p. 118) ; for Joe Christmas, the protagonist of *Light in August*, it is a source of anguish and alienation. Incidentally, the fantasy of self-generation is also that of the writer—both son and father to his work.

38. In sociohistorical terms, this obsession with incest may reflect the panic of a declining social class which struggles for survival but refuses any influx of outside blood. It is interesting to note that incest is a common theme in French drama during the last years of the Ancien Régime and in the work of Barbey d'Aurevilly, another chronicler of a decaying society. It is also worth consideration that in the South which Faulkner knew cases of incest between father and daughter, brother and sister appear to have been relatively frequent. Andrew Lytle, another Southern novelist, writes in this respect: "For many years it has seemed to me that incest was a constant upon the Southern scene. There was plenty of circumstantial evidence. The boys' and girls' rooms seemed too obviously separated. I remember in old houses the back stairs with solid paneling to hide ankles and lower legs as the girls came down. Call it prudery, but what is prudery? The fear of incest, if

incest it was, was perhaps not overt, but I knew of whore houses where too many of the girls had been ravished by fathers and brothers. Even if these were extreme instances—I had no way to know how general they may have been—still they were indicative" ("The Working Novelist and the Mythmaking Process," in *Myth and Mythmaking,* ed. Henry A. Murray, Boston: Beacon Press, 1968, p. 147).

39. Quentin's dream is analogous to Jewel Bundren's in *As I Lay Dying:* both wish to remove the object of love (Quentin's sister, Jewel's mother) from the "loud world" and secure sole possession. Horace Benbow's attitude toward his sister in *Sartoris* and Harry Wilbourne's toward his mistress in *The Wild Palms* point to the same desire.

40. See Sigmund Freud, "Mourning and Melancholia" (1917), *Standard Edition,* vol. XIV, pp. 243–58.

41. Quentin's "mourning" in a sense reduplicates the psychic processes involved in the writing of the novel (see my second chapter). Both processes are responses to loss and aim at a restoration of the lost object. But while Quentin's mourning develops into melancholia and ends in death, Faulkner's is converted into a creative act.

It should be noted, too, that there are references, literal or oblique, to mourning throughout the book. The most ironical, perhaps, is found in section 3, when Jason recalls his mother going "around the house in a black dress and a veil . . . crying and saying her little daughter was dead" (286), after she has seen one of the boys from town kissing Caddy. Equally remarkable is the mythic reversal of the motif in the Easter celebration of the final section, where the sorrow and despair over death eventually yield to the joyful certitude of resurrection.

42. The hypothesis of an identification with the lost sister would account in some measure for Quentin's feminine features and for the latent homosexuality which seems to characterize his relationship to Shreve ("Calling Shreve my husband," 96).

43. Quentin's wish to erase Ames out of existence, significantly linked with his revulsion from sex and his horror of procreation, reveals itself most startlingly in this fantasied *coitus interruptus:* "If I could have been his mother lying with open body, lifted laughing, holding his father with my hand refraining, seeing, watching him die before he lived" (98). There are strong suggestions here of the primal scene, and it is most remarkable that Quentin identifies with the mother figure and her desire—a negative desire, refusing maternity, refusing the child's birth before its conception: it is Quentin's own relation to his mother, or rather her relation to him, that is projected onto the fantasy scene.

44. Freud notes that in the condition of melancholia the superego is transformed into "a pure culture of the death instinct." See "The Dependent Relationships of the Ego" (1923), *Standard Edition*, vol. XIX, p. 53.

45. See *Sartoris*, p. 257 / *Flags in the Dust*, p. 243: "And then Belle again, enveloping him like a rich and fatal drug, like a motionless and cloying sea in which he watched himself drown"; *The Wild Palms* (New York: Random House, 1939), pp. 44–45: ". . . he seemed to be drowning, volition and all, in the yellow stare." See also my comments on Faulkner's early sketch "Nympholepsy" in Chapter 1.

46. The symbolic equivalence *death = wedding* also appears in the implicit assimilation of the marriage announcement to a bier (*"It lay on the table a candle burning at each corner upon the envelope tied in a soiled pink garter two artificial flowers,"* 115) and in Quentin's reflections about the trunks assembled for Caddy's trip to French Lick, the Indiana resort town where she was to look for a husband (*"Bringing empty trunks down the attic stairs they sounded like coffins French Lick. Found not death at the salt lick,"* 117).

47. The fusion of Eros and Death is very strongly suggested in the evocation which Faulkner gives of Quentin's suicidal drive in his Appendix to the novel: ". . . who loved death above all, who loved only death, loved and lived in a deliberate and almost perverted anticipation of death as a lover loves and deliberately refrains from the waiting willing friendly tender incredible body of his beloved, until he can no longer bear not the refraining but the restraint and so flings, hurls himself, relinquishing, drowning" (411).

5. Of Time and the Unreal

1. Among the discussions of time by American critics, the most rewarding are those of Peter Swiggart, "Moral and Temporal Order in *The Sound and the Fury*," *Sewanee Review*, LXI (Spring 1953), 221–37; Perrin Lowrey, "Concepts of Time in *The Sound and the Fury*," in Alan S. Downer, ed., *English Institute Essays, 1952* (New York: Columbia University Press, 1954), pp. 57–82; Douglas Messerli, "The Problem of Time in *The Sound and the Fury*," *The Southern Literary Journal*, VI (Spring 1974), 19–41. On the problem of time in Faulkner's fiction, see also Olga W. Vickery, "The Contours of Time," in *The Novels of William Faulkner*, pp. 226–36; Margaret Church, "William Faulkner: Myth and Duration," in *Time and Reality: Studies in Contemporary Fiction* (Chapel Hill: University of North Carolina

Press, 1963), pp. 227–50; Karl E. Zink, "Flux and the Frozen Moment: The Imagery of Stasis in Faulkner's Prose," *PMLA,* LXXI (June 1956), 285–301.

2. "A propos de 'Le Bruit et la Fureur': La temporalité chez Faulkner," *Nouvelle Revue Française,* LII (June 1939), 1057–61, and LIII (July 1939), 147–51. Reprinted in *Situations I* (Paris: Gallimard, 1947), pp. 70–81. American translations: "On *The Sound and the Fury:* Time in the Work of Faulkner," in Jean-Paul Sartre, *Literary and Philosophical Essays,* trans. Annette Michelson (London: Rider & Co., 1955), pp. 79–87; "Time in Faulkner: *The Sound and the Fury,"* trans. Martine Darmon, in *William Faulkner: Three Decades of Criticism,* pp. 225–32.—Taking their cue from Sartre's essay, French critics have shown persistent interest in Faulkner's concept of time. See especially Jean Pouillon, "Temps et Destinée chez Faulkner," in *Temps et Roman* (Paris: Gallimard, 1946), pp. 238–60; Jean-Jacques Mayoux, "William Faulkner: Le temps et la destinée," in *Vivants Piliers: Le roman anglo-saxon et les symboles* (Paris: Julliard, 1960), pp. 229–49; Michel Gresset, "Temps et destin chez Faulkner," *Preuves,* 155 (January 1964), 44–49. Of these essays only Pouillon's has been translated into English: "Time and Destiny in Faulkner," in Robert Penn Warren, ed., *Faulkner: A Collection of Critical Essays* (Englewood Cliffs, N. J.: Prentice-Hall, 1966), pp. 79–86.

3. See Henry J. Underwood, "Sartre on *The Sound and the Fury:* Some Errors," *Modern Fiction Studies,* XII (Winter 1966–67), 477–79.

4. The word "shadow" occurs repeatedly in the first section. In the second it becomes one of the key words, the most frequently used (53 occurrences) after "water" (61 occurrences).

5. The anthropological significance of the double was first studied by James Frazer, notably in *The Golden Bough.* Freud pointed out its psychoanalytical implications in his essay on "the uncanny" (1919). For more extended discussions of the motif, see Otto Rank, *Beyond Psychology* (New York: Dover Publications, 1958) and Carl G. Jung, *Psychology and Alchemy* (New York: Pantheon Books, 1953); *The Archetypes and the Collective Unconscious* (London: Routledge & Kegan Paul, 1959).

6. In Quentin's monologue shadow and darkness are associated on several occasions with woman and sex. See, for example: ". . . walking along in the shadows and whispering with their soft girlvoices lingering in the shadowy places" (183). See also the description of Caddy's encounter with Dalton Ames, in which the fusion of shadows

suggests sexual union of the bodies: "their shadows one shadow her head rose it was above his on the sky higher their two heads" (192); "her shadow high against his shadow one shadow" (192); "leaning down her shadow the blur of her face leaning down from his high shadow" (193).

7. "[The shadow] personifies everything that the subject refuses to acknowledge about himself and yet it is always thrusting itself upon him directly or indirectly—for instance, inferior traits of character and other incompatible tendencies." Carl G. Jung, *The Archetypes and the Collective Unconscious*, pp. 284-85.

8. When questioned on the significance of the shadow motif in Quentin's section, Faulkner answered: "That wasn't a deliberate symbolism. I would say that that shadow that stayed on his mind so much was foreknowledge of his own death . . ." (*FU*, p. 2). In this respect one should note Faulkner's implicit reference to the fears about shadows in popular beliefs. To lose one's shadow or to walk on it have been considered evil omens in many cultures, and Quentin recalls the Negro superstition about "a drowned man's shadow" (111), as he stands on the bridge and looks at his shadow in the water below him.—For further comments on the shadow motif, see Kathryn Gibbs Gibbons, "Quentin's Shadow," *Literature and Psychology*, XII (Winter 1962), 16-24; Louise Dauner, "Quentin and the Walking Shadow: The Dilemma of Nature and Culture," *Arizona Quarterly*, XXI (Summer 1965), 159-71.

9. The jeweler is himself a rather intriguing figure. There is something faintly demonic about him, and the brief sketch we are given of him has many symbolic connotations. Functionally, insofar as he is expected to answer Quentin's questions, he reminds one of Mr. Compson, the *father*. Metonymically, through his profession and environment, and above all through his "rushing" eye (103), he is turned into a symbol of *time*, and "the metal tube screwed into his face" (102) relates him more specifically to mechanical time. It is interesting to note that Quentin's description of him is focused exclusively on his *eye*, as though he were a Cyclops amidst his infernal smithy. In myths and folklore, the unique eye has been traditionally associated with either subhuman or superhuman vision, divine or demonic knowledge. It is precisely because of his presumed knowledge of time that Quentin pays a visit to the jeweler. Yet the latter's eye is also "blurred" (103): Father Time will not reveal his secret.

10. "Time in Faulkner: *The Sound and the Fury*," *Three Decades of Criticism*, p. 228.

11. *Ibid.,* pp. 226–27.

12. I prefer this more literal but also more suggestive translation of "enforcement" to "suspension," the term by which it has been rendered in *Three Decades of Criticism.*

13. On this point, see Karl E. Zink, "Flux and the Frozen Moment: The Imagery of Stasis in Faulkner's Prose," 285–301.

14. The first critic to call attention to this motif was Melvin Backman, in *Faulkner: The Major Years* (Bloomington & London: Indiana University Press, 1966), pp. 24–26. As Backman points out, the same triad appears in the opening pages of *Sanctuary.*

15. *A la recherche du temps perdu,* III (Paris: Pléiade, 1954), p. 872. My translation.

16. See Lawrence Thompson, "Mirror Analogues in *The Sound and the Fury,*" *English Institute Essays, 1952,* pp. 83–106. Thompson argues persuasively that, beyond the literal mirror references, the mirror metaphor may be used to define the whole thematic structure of the novel.

17. Here again there is a significant parallel between sections 1 and 2. At the close of section 1, after being undressed by Luster, Benjy looks at himself and begins to cry (90); at the close of section 2, Quentin looks at himself in the mirror, noticing his black eye and the bloodstain on his vest. In both scenes there are references to physical injury, and both scenes point ironically back to Caddy. In Benjy's case, the implied reference to his castration sends us back to its cause: the attempted rape of the Burgess girl, whom Benjy mistook for his sister; Quentin's black eye and bloodied vest recall his fight with Bland, whom he mistook for his sister's first lover.

18. "Mélange" (1939), in *Oeuvres,* vol. I (Paris: Pléiade, 1957), p. 332. My translation.

19. There are many references to broken things in section 2, notably in the scene with the little Italian girl (161–65).

20. On the motif of obliquity, see John W. Hunt, *William Faulkner: Art in Theological Tension* (Syracuse, N. Y.: Syracuse University Press, 1965), pp. 62–64.

21. It is worth recalling that the first page of the manuscript of *The Sound and the Fury* bears the title *Twilight.* However, it is impossible to determine whether this title was intended for the short story that Faulkner originally planned to write or for the first section or for the complete novel. The symbolism of twilight fits Benjy's monologue as well as it does Quentin's and insofar as it evokes the notion of decline it equally well epitomizes the story of the Compson family. The twi-

light motif appears very early in Faulkner's work, notably in "The Hill," and is also found in later novels like *As I Lay Dying, Light in August,* and *Absalom, Absalom!.*

22. Quentin's predicament is not unlike Harry Wilbourne's in *The Wild Palms.* For the latter, however, grief becomes a deliberate choice of life against death: "*Yes,* he thought, *between grief and nothing I will take grief*" (p. 324).

23. Faulkner himself suggests that "when he wants the old fish to live, it may represent his unconscious desire for endurance, both for himself and for his people" (*FU,* p. 18).

24. See *Soldiers' Pay,* p. 57: "If a man could be freed for a moment from the forces of gravity [he] would be a god, the lord of life, causing the high gods to tremble on their thrones: he would thunder at the very gates of infinity like a mailed knight." The theme of flight can be traced back to Faulkner's early prose and poetry, and reappears in a number of his stories and novels from *Soldiers' Pay* through *Pylon* to *A Fable.* Flying stands most often for nonacceptance of human finitude, the heroic quest for "glory" through a meteoric death.

25. Bland's rowing is significantly associated with his mother's presence. Quentin describes them "moving side by side across Massachusetts on parallel courses like a couple of planets" (112), and refers to "the wet oars winking him along in bright winks and female palms" (138). Bland's godlike ascent is conditioned by his ideal relationship to his mother.

26. A similar dissociation occurs in "Carcassonne," a short story presumably written in 1926 and originally published in *These Thirteen* (New York: Jonathan Cape and Harrison Smith, 1931), pp. 352–58. It also presents the monologue of a dying or dead young man. His body lies "on the rippled floor, tumbling peacefully to the wavering echoes of the tides" (p. 358), while he rides a horse *"with eyes like blue electricity and a mane like tangled fire, galloping up the hill and right off into the high heaven of the world"* (p. 358).

27. On Quentin as a Romantic hero, see Robert M. Slabey, "The 'Romanticism' of *The Sound and the Fury,*" *Mississippi Quarterly,* XVI (Summer 1963), 146–59

28. On Faulkner's references to Keats's ode, see especially Joan S. Korenman, "Faulkner's Grecian Urn,' *The Southern Literary Journal,* VII (Fall 1974), 3–23.

29. On Quentin as a poet, see François Pitavy's fine essay, "Quentin Compson, ou le regard du poète," *Sud, n° 14/15 (1975),* 62–80.

30. In 1955 he told Jean Stein: "Ishmael is the witness in *Moby Dick* as I am Quentin in *The Sound and the Fury*." Quoted by Joseph Blotner in *Faulkner,* vol. II, p. 1522.

31. On the autobiographical aspects of the character, see Jackson J. Benson, "Quentin Compson: Self-Portrait of a Young Artist's Emotions," *Twentieth Century Literature,* XVII (July 1971), 143–59.

32. The strongest case for Quentin as a "moral agent" is made by Mark Spilka in "Quentin Compson's Universal Grief," *Contemporary Literature,* XI (Autumn 1970), 451–69. My own analysis does not bear out Spilka's contention that "Quentin's attraction to death is an attraction to timeless verities," and that "he grieves on universal bones."

6. Jason, or The Poison of Resentment

1. See James M. Mellard's illuminating essay on "Faulkner's Jason and the Tradition of Oral Narrative," *Journal of Popular Culture,* II (Fall 1968), 195–210.

2. Significantly enough, "you" already occurs in the second sentence of Jason's speech. Most often his "you" is an all-inclusive "you," referring at once to Jason himself as receiver of his own message, to an implied audience of people sharing his cultural values, and—outside the time-space of the novel—to the reader. While in the first two sections most of the elements of the speech event are problematical, they are all strongly marked in the third—evidence that we are moving closer to normal communication patterns.

3. In contrast to sections 1 and 2, in which time-shifts are very frequent (especially in Quentin's monologue), section 3 contains only one major flashback: Jason's reminiscence of his father's funeral and of the yet earlier scene when Mr. Compson brought home Caddy's infant child (243–50).

4. George Washington Harris' Sut Lovingood was one of Faulkner's favorite characters in fiction: ". . . I like Sut Lovingood from a book written by George Harris about 1840 or '50 in the Tennessee mountains. He had no illusions about himself, did the best he could; at certain times he was a coward and knew it and wasn't ashamed; he never blamed his misfortunes on anyone and never cursed God for them" (Interview with Jean Stein, in *LG,* p. 251). It is worth noting that the traits which Faulkner admired in Harris' character are precisely those opposing him to the self-deluded and self-pitying Jason: Sut Lovingood knows he is a rogue, and judges himself as harshly as the sordid world in which he moves.

5. See Robert C. Elliot, "The Satirist Satirized: Studies of the Great

Misanthropes," in *The Power of Satire: Magic, Ritual, Art* (Princeton, N. J.: Princeton University Press, 1960), pp. 130–222.

6. See James M. Mellard, "Type and Archetype: Jason Compson as 'Satirist'," *Genre*, VI (June 1971), 173–88.

7. See Robert C. Elliot, "The Satirist Satirized," pp. 130–222.

8. "Interviews in Japan, 1955," in *LG*, p. 149.

9. *The Tragic Mask: A Study of Faulkner's Heroes* (Chapel Hill: The University of North Carolina Press, 1963), p. 144.

10. *The Rhetoric of Fiction* (Chicago & London: The University of Chicago Press, 1961), p. 307.

11. James Dahl, "A Faulkner Reminiscence: Conversations with Mrs. Maud Falkner," *Journal of Modern Literature*, III (April 1974), 1028.

12. The suspicion that Jason may be to some extent self-caricature is strengthened by what we know of Faulkner's many-sided personality through Joseph Blotner's biography. Faulkner was at times irascible and arrogant, and could be stunningly rude.

13. Between Mrs. Compson and Addie Bundren, Jason and Jewel there are striking similarities. Though Addie is much more sympathetically drawn than Mrs. Compson, she is also a self-centered mother, and her influence on her children is also largely negative. Jewel, on the other hand, while being capable of abnegation and heroism, resembles Jason in his uncontrollable rage and in his estrangement from the rest of the family.

14. On Jason's indebtedness to his father's philosophy, see Duncan Aswell's perceptive essay, "The Recollection and the Blood: Jason's Role in *The Sound and the Fury*," *Mississippi Quarterly*, XXI (Summer 1968), 211–18. It is noteworthy too that Mr. Compson (as quoted by Quentin) occasionally makes reflections which would not be out of place in Jason's speech: "pennies has healed more scars than jesus" (221).

15. See *William Faulkner: The Yoknapatawpha Country*, p. 339.

16. This incident relates Jason's childhood to Popeye's in *Sanctuary:* Popeye cuts up two live lovebirds and a kitten. See *Sanctuary*, p. 301. Jason's action is of course less gruesome: he is a Popeye with inhibitions.

17. In the first two sections there are many indications about Jason that presage what he will become as an adult. He is a fat and greedy child; he is a loner and never misses a chance to tattle on his siblings; he is always seen with his hands in his pockets, and chooses to play treasurer when his playmates launch into kite-making.

18. See Faulkner's comment: ". . . to him all the rest of the town and the world and the human race too except himself were Compsons, inexplicable yet quite predictable in that they were in no sense whatever to be trusted" ("Appendix," 421).

19. John L. Longley was the first critic to identify Jason as paranoid. See *The Tragic Mask*, p. 222. For further comments on this subject, see Charles D. Peavy, "Jason Compson's Paranoid Pseudocommunity," *Hartford Studies in Literature*, II (1970), 151–56.

20. At times Jason even seems to derive a masochistic pleasure from his humiliations, especially during his frustrated pursuit of Miss Quentin. When the sheriff refuses to help him catch his niece, "he [repeats] his story, harshly recapitulant, seeming to get an actual pleasure out of his outrage and impotence" (378).

21. In Faulkner cosmetic habits are often an index to sexual promiscuity. See, for example, the emphasis on Temple Drake's outrageously scarlet lips in *Sanctuary*.

22. John L. Longley, *The Tragic Mask*, p. 147.

23. For Jason's indebtedness to the formulaic manner, see James M. Mellard, "Faulkner's Jason and the Tradition of Oral Narrative."

24. "The Recollection and the Blood: Jason's Role in *The Sound and the Fury*," 216.

25. See *The Novels of William Faulkner*, pp. 30–31, and *William Faulkner: The Yoknapatawpha Country*, pp. 325–26.

26. "Faulkner's Mythology," *Kenyon Review*, I (Summer 1939), 285-99. Reprinted in *William Faulkner: Three Decades of Criticism*, pp. 82–93.

27. See "Appendix," 420, and Faulkner's letter to Malcolm Cowley in *The Faulkner-Cowley File* (New York: The Viking Press, 1966), p. 25.

28. See *The Mansion* (New York: Random House, 1959), pp. 322–27, 330, 332, 334.

29. Irving Howe notes in this respect that "like those quasi-intellectuals who abandon old allegiances to become the spokesmen of a rising new class, Jason formulates the values of Snopesism with a cleverness and vengeance which no Snopes could express." *William Faulkner: A Critical Study*, second edition (New York: Vintage Books, 1962), p. 50.

30. See "The Pseudo-Conservative Revolt—1954," in *The Paranoid Style in American Politics and Other Essays* (New York: Vintage Books, 1967), pp. 41–65. Hofstadter borrowed the phrase from *The*

Authoritarian Personality, published in 1950 by Theodore W. Adorno and his associates.

31. *FU,* p. 17.

7. An Easter without Resurrection?

1. See *LG,* pp. 147 and 245.

2. On this point, see Margaret Blanchard, "The Rhetoric of Communion: Voice in *The Sound and the Fury,*" *American Literature,* XLI (January 1970), 555–65.

3. There is some evidence that Faulkner has drawn on scientific observations. The physical portrait of Benjy very closely resembles the picture of the cretin drawn by Louis Berman, an American physiologist,, in *The Glands Regulating Personality* (1921). On this point, see Mick Gidley, "Another Psychologist, a Physiologist and William Faulkner," *Ariel,* II (October 1971), 83.

4. The association of cornflower-blue eyes with innocence already appears in the portrait of Benjy's prototype in "The Kingdom of God," the early story published in the *Times-Picayune* of April 25, 1925. On the similarities between the two characters, see Charles D. Peavy, "An Early Casting of Benjy: Faulkner's 'The Kingdom of God'," *Studies in Short Fiction,* III (Spring 1966), 347–48.

5. A similar device is used in *As I Lay Dying,* where the description of Dewey Dell by Moseley and Macgowan at the close of the novel lends physical substance to a character so far "heard" from within.

6. The mixture of surprise and resignation with which Dilsey reacts to the bad weather is paralleled by the placid astonishment expressed by Anse Bundren when it is beginning to rain on the morning of his departure for Jefferson. See *As I Lay Dying,* p. 72.

7. That Faulkner knew about the meaning of jaybirds in folklore is attested a few pages later, when Luster throws a rock at the birds, shouting "Git on back to hell, whar you belong at" (335). On this point, see Charles D. Peavy, "Faulkner's Use of Folklore in *The Sound and the Fury,*" 442–43.

8. The simile occurs several times in Faulkner's early work, notably in *The Marble Faun* (p. 24) and "Nympholepsy" (405).

9. The description of the Negro church is foreshadowed in the closing pages of *Soldiers' Pay:* ". . . at last, crouching among a clump of trees beside the road, they saw the shabby church with its canting travesty of a spire" (p. 319).

10. Building houses is a recurrent motif in Faulkner's fiction, but it can be traced in the writings of many other American novelists. As Richard Poirier notes, there is "something like an obsession in American literature with plans and efforts to build houses, to appropriate space to one's desires, perhaps to inaugurate therein a dynasty that shapes time to the dimensions of personal and familial history" (*A World Elsewhere: The Place of Style in American Literature*, New York: Oxford University Press, 1966, p. 17). On this point, see also Allen Guttman, "Images of Value and a Sense of the Past," in *The Conservative Tradition in America* (New York: Oxford University Press, 1967), pp. 47–77.

11. In *The Mansion* we are told that a few years after the events related in *The Sound and the Fury* Benjy set fire to the house and burned to death in it. These facts are not consistent with the information provided in the "Appendix." Benjy's death and the destruction of the house by fire are obviously afterthoughts, probably suggested to Faulkner by the similarities between the Compson story and that of the Sutpens.

12. "Nihilism in Faulkner's *The Sound and the Fury*," *Modern Fiction Studies*, XIII (Spring 1967), 46.

13. On leaving Jefferson, Jason thinks that "every damn one of them will be at church" (381); Dilsey, back in the house, "[enters] a pervading reek of camphor" in Mrs. Compson's room (373), while Jason misses the camphor that would relieve his headache (391). Lastly, at one o'clock, Dilsey tells Luster and Benjy that Jason will not be home for dinner (392); the latter, at the same moment, is leaving Mottson where people are "turning peacefully into houses and Sunday dinners" (392).

14. The symbolism of the narcissus has been diversely construed. According to Faulkner himself, the choice of that flower was not intentional: "The narcissus was given to Benjy to distract his attention. It was simply a flower which happened to be handy that 5th of April. It was not deliberate" (*LG*, p. 246). Relating the flower to the mythological figure of Narcissus, several critics regard it as a symbol of the egocentricity of all the Compsons (see, for example, Lawrence Thompson, *William Faulkner*, pp. 48–49). Others refer it to biblical and Christian symbolism. Thus Lawrence E. Bowling points out that "the narcissus has also a Christian tradition, for it is the flower which in the Bible is called 'the rose' and is identified with Jesus (Isaiah 35:1, Song of Songs 2:1). Thus Benjy's narcissus, like Benjy himself, symbolizes not only the world's selfishness but also its need for love. The association

of Benjy's narcissus with the Savior is made more specific and significant
by the fact that the flower has been broken twice, the two breaks sym-
bolizing the two crucifixions: the first by the ancient world and the second
by the modern world" ("Faulkner and the Theme of Innocence," 485–
86). Beside this biblical interpretation, a Freudian reading might be
considered. Given the importance of the castration motif, it seems
permissible to interpret the flowers associated with Benjy as images of
his mutilated manhood. I have already hinted at the sexual symbolism
of jimson weed; the narcissus may be another inverted phallic symbol,
and this hypothesis is the more plausible as it belongs in the category
of *broken* things, references to which are particularly numerous in
sections I and 2, that is, in those where castration is at stake. It appears, moreover, that all of Benjy's objects and playthings represent
and compensate losses, whether they are phallic substitutes like the
flowers or, in D. W. Winnicot's phrase, "transitional objects" (i.e.,
substitutes for the mother's breast) like the cushion. The most obviously symbolic of these objects is the soiled satin slipper: a reminder
of Caddy and her wedding, but also a classic sexual fetish—which
sends us back again to the pervasive issue of castration.

15. "Form and Fulfillment in *The Sound and the Fury*," *Modern
Language Quarterly*, XXIX (December 1968), 449.

16. According to Roland Barthes, all narrative texts result from
the interweaving of five codes. The hermeneutic code, or "voice of
truth," refers to the unraveling of the plot. See *S/Z* (Paris: Seuil,
1970).

17. "Nihilism in *The Sound and the Fury*," 47.

18. *Ibid.*, 55.

19. The paradoxical association of obesity with gauntness found
here recurs in the portrait of Hightower in *Light in August* (see p.
82).

20. Faulkner here seems to play deliberately with color symbolism.
Purple and maroon are royal colors, but in the Christian tradition
purple is also a liturgic color (associated with Advent, Lent, and Good
Friday) and the color of martyrdom. The terrestrial symbolism of purple, with its suggestions of sacrificial suffering, mourning, and peni-
tence is contrasted with the celestial symbolism of blue. When Dilsey
later reemerges from her cabin, she is dressed in blue gingham (332).
Blue is the color of the Virgin, and, in the novel, the symbol of Benjy's
innocence. In this connection, it is worth recalling that in the episode
of the Easter service the symbolic equation of Dilsey with the Virgin
and of Benjy with Christ is repeatedly suggested (369–71).

21. In this the portrait of Dilsey announces the tribute that Faulkner was later to pay to her and to her kin: "They endured" ("Appendix," 427).

22. The transformation of these two characters into archetypes has been noted by Peter Swiggart in *The Art of Faulkner's Novels* (Austin: University of Texas Press, 1962), pp. 106–7. To Swiggart, however, the rhetoric of the final section serves purely parodic purposes, which seems to me a highly questionable view.

23. See *The Faulkner-Cowley File*, p. 31.

24. *LG*, pp. 244–45. An early casting of Dilsey is to be found in "The Devil Beats His Wife," a story which Faulkner began after his return from Europe in December 1925, but never completed. A number of critics assume that Dilsey has been modeled on Caroline Barr, the "mammy" of the Faulkner family to whose memory *Go Down, Moses* was to be dedicated thirteen years later. The resemblances, however, are rather tenuous. Molly, Lucas Beauchamp's wife in *Go Down, Moses*, comes much closer to being a portrait of Caroline Barr.

25. *William Faulkner: The Yoknapatawpha Country*, p. 343.

26. See George E. Kent's sharply critical assessment of Faulkner's "mammies" in "The Black Woman in Faulkner's Works, with the Exclusion of Dilsey," Part II, *Phylon*, XXXVI (March 1975), 55–67.

27. This is not to say that there is no significant contrast between whites and blacks. Some of Quentin's observations aptly summarize the latter's function in the novel: ". . . a nigger is not a person so much as a form of behaviour; a sort of obverse reflection of the white people he lives among" (106); or: "They come into white people's lives like that in sudden sharp black trickles that isolate white facts for an instant in unarguable truth like under a microscope" (211). Dilsey and, to a lesser degree, her husband, her children, and grandchildren testify to the virtues which Ike McCaslin attributes to blacks in *Go Down, Moses:* endurance, pity, tolerance, fidelity, love of children (see *Go Down, Moses*, p. 295). It should be noted, however, that in the younger generation of the Gibsons these virtues seem to be less developed than among their elders, as can be seen, for example, from Luster's occasional cruelty toward Benjy. And there is nothing to suggest that the Negroes are morally superior to the whites because they belong to a different race. Dilsey, with her customary clear-sightedness, tells her grandson Luster that he is just as fallible as his white masters: "Lemme tell you somethin, nigger boy, you got jes as much Compson devilment in you es any of em" (344). Faulkner's treatment of blacks in *The Sound and the Fury*, albeit not totally free of stereotypes, is

never tritely sentimental, and testifies to a tact and intelligence not always found among white Southern novelists. Let us add that if the contrast between the white family and the black community allows him to introduce an oblique comment upon the downfall of the Compsons, racial relationships are not central in *The Sound and the Fury* as they are in *Light in August, Absalom, Absalom!, Go Down, Moses,* and *Intruder in the Dust.*

28. In his interviews Faulkner stressed the principle of cohesion represented by Dilsey in the Compson household. See *FU,* p. 5, and *LG,* p. 126.

29. Dilsey's solicitude for Benjy is already emphasized in the first section. She is the only one to remember his thirty-third birthday and to celebrate it with a cake she buys with her own money. It is interesting to note that the manuscript of the novel includes no reference to Benjy's birthday—an indication that in revising the section Faulkner felt the need to provide further illustration of Dilsey's kindness and so to prepare the reader for the full revelation of her personality in section 4. See Emily K. Izsak, "The Manuscript of *The Sound and the Fury:* The Revisions in the First Section," *Studies in Bibliography,* Bibliographical Society, University of Virginia, XX (1967), 189–202.

30. *William Faulkner: The Yoknapatawpha Country,* p. 343.

31. *Collected Poems, 1909–1962* (New York: Harcourt, Brace & World, 1963), p. 178.

32. See Victor Strandberg, "Faulkner's Poor Parson and the Technique of Inversion," *Sewanee Review,* LXXIII (Spring 1965), 181–90.

33. On Faulkner's indebtedness to the tradition of the oral sermon, see Bruce A. Rosenberg's useful study, "The Oral Quality of Reverend Shegog's Sermon in William Faulkner's *The Sound and the Fury,*" *Literatur in Wissenschaft und Unterricht,* II (1969), 73–88.

34. See "Ouverture," in *Le Cru et le Cuit* (Paris: Plon, 1964), pp. 9–40, especially pp. 23–26, 34–38.

35. Claude Lévi-Strauss notes that music and mythology are both "time-killing machines." See *ibid.,* p. 24.

36. See Bruce A. Rosenberg, "The Oral Quality of Reverend Shegog's Sermon."

37. Bruce A. Rosenberg points out that "one would be hard pressed to identify [the sermon] as a literary creation" (*ibid.,* 82).

38. Note the many references to empty eyes or troubled vision: the "blurred" eye of the jeweler (103), Caddy's eyes "like the eyes in the statues blank and unseeing and serene" (202), Benjy's vacant

gaze (399), not to mention the empty eyes of the Confederate soldier (399). The picture of the eye on page 388 also points to the importance of the motif of seeing/not seeing.

39. See *Wait Without Idols* (New York: George Braziller, 1964), pp. 93–116.

40. See "Faulkner and Vestigial Moralities," in *Theology and Modern Literature* (Cambridge, Mass.: Harvard University Press, 1958), pp. 113–31.

41. Vahanian, *Wait Without Idols,* p. 111.

42. See *FU,* pp. 86, 117; *LG,* pp. 246–47.

43. "Criticism as Language," *Times Literary Supplement,* September 27, 1963, 739–40.

44. *William Faulkner: The Yoknapatawpha Country,* p. 348.

45. See Walter J. Slatoff, *Quest for Failure: A Study of William Faulkner* (Ithaca, N. Y.: Cornell University Press, 1960), pp. 149–58. Similar approaches to Faulkner's fiction can be found in Robert M. Adams, *Strains of Discord: Studies in Literary Openness* (Ithaca, N. Y.: Cornell University Press, 1958), and in James Guetti, *The Limits of Metaphor: A Study of Melville, Conrad, and Faulkner* (Ithaca, N. Y.: Cornell University Press, 1967).

46. Paul Eluard, *Poésie Ininterrompue* (Paris: Gallimard, 1946), p. 32.

47. The dream of presence and plenitude as well as the priority granted to the spoken word over the written, relate Faulkner's work to the mainstream of Western philosophy, and more specifically to what Jacques Derrida calls (and denounces as) "the metaphysics of presence," i.e., the assumption that, however inaccessible to individual experience, absolute plenitude exists, and the concomitant belief that, whatever the inadequacies of language, the latter is virtually capable of working toward the transparency of pure speech and full meaning. In this respect Faulkner never outgrew the romantic idealism of his youth—a position reflected time and again in his work, but often belied by his practice of writing.

SELECTIVE BIBLIOGRAPHY

A. COMMENTS BY WILLIAM FAULKNER

1. Introductions:

Meriwether, James B., ed. "William Faulkner: An Introduction for *The Sound and the Fury.*" *The Southern Review,* N.S., VIII (October 1972), 705–10. Text written in 1933 for a new edition of the novel then planned by Random House. Faulkner's account of his creative experience is a unique document which anyone interested in *The Sound and the Fury* should consult.

————, ed. "An Introduction to *The Sound and the Fury.*" *Mississippi Quarterly,* XXVI (Summer 1973), 410–15. Reprinted in *A Faulkner Miscellany,* ed. James B. Meriwether (Jackson, Miss.: University Press of Mississippi, 1974), pp. 156–61. A longer and different version of the 1933 introduction, including comments upon the predicament of the Southern writer missing from the version published in *The Southern Review.*

2. The "Compson Appendix":

Faulkner, William. "Appendix: Compson, 1699–1945." Written in the fall of 1945 and first published in the Viking *Portable Faulkner* edited by Malcolm Cowley in the spring of 1946; republished in a slightly different version in the Modern Library double volume of *The Sound and the Fury* and *As I Lay Dying* as a foreword to the novel to replace a proposed introduction which Faulkner refused to supply; republished at the end of the 1966 Random House edition with minor editorial changes. In discussing the novel, it is important to remember that the "Compson Appendix" is no organic part of it.

Cowley, Malcolm. *The Faulkner-Cowley File: Letters and Memories, 1944–1962.* New York: The Viking Press, 1966. Includes Faulkner's correspondence with Cowley on the "Compson Appendix."

Meriwether, James B., ed. "A Prefatory Note by Faulkner for the Compson Appendix." *American Literature,* XLIII (May 1971), 281–84. The draft of a brief introduction to the "Compson Appendix," written in 1946, with a commentary by the editor upon its date and significance.

3. Interviews:

Gwynn, Frederick L., and Joseph L. Blotner. *Faulkner in the University: Class Conferences at the University of Virginia, 1957–1958.* Charlottesville: University of Virginia Press, 1959. Includes numerous comments on the novel.

Meriwether, James B., and Michael Millgate, eds. *Lion in the Garden: Interviews with William Faulkner 1926–1962.* New York: Random House, 1968. See especially his interviews in Japan (pp. 146–49, 169–70) and his well-known interview with Jean Stein (pp. 244–46).

Fant, Joseph L., and Robert Ashley, eds. *Faulkner at West Point.* New York: Random House, 1964. Includes some comments on the novel.

B. CHECKLISTS AND SURVEYS OF CRITICISM

Bassett, John. *William Faulkner: An Annotated Checklist of Criticism.* New York: David Lewis, 1972, pp. 32–52. Bassett provides the most comprehensive listing of Faulkner criticism to date. As far as American criticism of *The Sound and the Fury* is concerned, there are very few omissions, but the listing of studies in foreign language is partial and inconsistent (no mention is made of the only book-length study of the novel, published in Germany in 1969). The annotations are occasionally inaccurate or misleading; their utility is further impaired by the scarcity of evaluative comment.

Meriwether, James B. "William Faulkner." In Bryer, Jackson R., ed., *Fifteen Modern American Authors.* Durham, N. C.: Duke University Press, 1969, pp. 175–210. The most valuable essay on the state of Faulkner scholarship and criticism at the end of the sixties. Includes a brief but judicious survey of criticism on *The Sound and the Fury* up to 1968.

For criticism since 1963, see the annual surveys published in *American Literary Scholarship* (Durham, N. C.: Duke University Press). The bibliographical essays on Faulkner have been by Richard P. Adams (for 1963 and 1964), Robert R. Wiggins (1965–67), Olga W. Vickery (1968), Michael Millgate (1969–72), and James B. Meriwether since 1973.

C. SCHOLARLY AND CRITICAL STUDIES

The following bibliography lists most criticism on the novel up to 1974. Early reviews and doctoral dissertations are not listed.

Absalom, H. P. "Order and Disorder in *The Sound and the Fury.*" *Durham University Journal,* LVIII (December 1965), 30–39. Focuses on the first section, with emphasis on Faulkner's uses of time.

Adams, Richard P. *Faulkner: Myth and Motion.* Princeton, N. J.: Princeton University Press, 1968, pp. 215–48. A well-informed and fairly stimulating study, integrating earlier criticism and making significant use of Faulkner's own comments. Adams concentrates on the novelist's use of the "mythic method" (parallels with Christ, the Grail legend, the Persephone story); he is wise enough to realize that the mythic analogies only provide structural patterns, but fails to show how they work in the novel.

Adams, Robert M. "Poetry in the Novel; or Faulkner Esemplastic." *Virginia Quarterly,* XXXIX (Summer 1953), 419–34. A sympathetic early study, stressing the power and boldness of Faulkner's "poetic" vision.

Aiken, Conrad. "William Faulkner: The Novel as Form." *Atlantic Monthly,* CLXIV (November 1939), 650–54. Included in *A Reviewer's ABC,* New York: Meridian Books, 1958, pp. 200–7. Repr. in Hoffman, Frederick J., and Olga W. Vickery, eds., *William Faulkner: Three Decades of Criticism,* East Lansing: Michigan State University Press, 1960, pp. 135–42, and in Warren, Robert Penn, ed., *Faulkner: A Collection of Critical Essays,* Englewood Cliffs, N. J.: Prentice-Hall, 1966, pp. 46–52. A brilliant and perceptive early essay on Faulkner's technique and art, including some shrewd observations on *The Sound and the Fury.* Aiken calls it "a novelist's novel—a whole textbook on the craft of fiction in itself, comparable in its way to *What Maisie Knew* or *The Golden Bowl.*"

Alexandrescu, Sorin. *William Faulkner.* Bucharest, Rumania: Editura pentru Literatura Universala, 1969. More concerned with the general structural laws governing Faulkner's work than with the specific patterns of individual novels.

Anderson, Charles. "Faulkner's Moral Center." *Etudes Anglaises,* VII (January 1954), 48–58. Relates Faulkner to the moralists of ancient Rome and interprets the collapse of the Compson family as "a failure of *virtus.*"

Aswell, Duncan. "The Recollection and the Blood: Jason's Role in *The Sound and the Fury.*" *Mississippi Quarterly,* XXI (Summer

1968), 211–18. A very perceptive essay, pointing out similarities between Jason and his brothers, and considering his monologue as an ironic commentary on the novel's major themes.

Auer, Michael J. "Caddy, Benjy, and the Acts of the Apostles: A Note on *The Sound and the Fury.*" *Studies in the Novel,* VI (Winter 1974), 475–76. Claims the Acts of the Apostles 8:26–40 to be the source for the name "Candace," and relates Benjy to the Ethiopian eunuch mentioned in the passage.

Bachmann, Ingeborg. "Über 'Schall und Wahn'." In Haffmans, Gerd, ed. *Über William Faulkner,* Zurich: Diogenes, 1973, pp. 127–29. Original reflections by a prominent contemporary German writer. Relates Faulkner's confusing use of names to his concept of reality, and views it as a major aspect of his modernity.

Backman, Melvin. "Sickness and Primitivism: A Dominant Pattern in William Faulkner's Work." *Accent,* XIV (Winter 1954), 61–73. Sees a significant contrast between sick heroes (Quentin) and healthy primitives (Benjy, Dilsey). An interesting oversimplification.

———. "Faulkner's Sick Heroes: Bayard Sartoris and Quentin Compson." *Modern Fiction Studies,* II (Autumn 1956), 95–108. Traces parallels between the two characters.

———. *Faulkner: The Major Years. A Critical Study.* Bloomington: Indiana University Press, 1966, pp. 13–40. A sensible general study. Has discerning comments upon symbolic motifs, but neglects important matters such as the problem of time.

Bass, Eben. "Meaningful Images in *The Sound and the Fury.*" *Modern Language Notes,* LXXVI (December 1961), 728–31. A brief note on imagery, too brief to be of much use.

Bassan, Maurice. "Benjy at the Monument." *English Language Notes,* II (September 1964), 46–50. Develops the hypothesis that the courthouse square is a symbolic clock-face, on which Benjy moves counter-clockwise because he is not in time, and that when the surrey turns left, putting him into time, he is horrified.

Baum, Catherine B. "'The Beautiful One': Caddy Compson as Heroine of *The Sound and the Fury.*" *Modern Fiction Studies,* XIII (Spring 1967), 33–44. The first full discussion of Caddy. Does justice to the complexity of the character, yet distorts its significance through unwarranted dependence on the "Compson Appendix."

Bedell, George C. *Kierkegaard and Faulkner: Modalities of Existence.* Baton Rouge: Louisiana State University Press, 1972, pp. 22–23, 134–37, 184–90, 195–206, 244–55, and *passim.* Provides isolated insights into Quentin's despair and Dilsey's faith, and comments aptly on Jason's relation to time and money, but reading Faulkner through Kierkegaard raises a number of methodological questions which the book as a whole fails to solve.

Beja, Morris. "William Faulkner: A Flash, a Glare." In *Epiphany in the Modern Novel*, Seattle: University of Washington Press, 1971, pp. 182–210, especially 182–89, 192–93. Makes the point that Faulkner's epiphanies always involve the recollection or recapture of the past.

Benson, Jackson J. "Quentin Compson: Self-Portrait of a Young Artist's Emotions." *Twentieth Century Literature*, XVII (July 1971), 143–59. Investigates the close relationship of Quentin to his creator and argues that Faulkner uses the character "to expiate the emotional excesses of his own frustration and depression." Some of Benson's points are questionable, but his analysis avoids biographical fallacy.

————. "Quentin's Responsibility for Caddy's Downfall." *Notes on Mississippi Writers*, V (Fall 1972), 63–64. Contends—not very convincingly—that Quentin is guiltless of Caddy's doom.

Blanchard, Margaret. "The Rhetoric of Communion: Voice in *The Sound and the Fury*." *American Literature*, XLI (January 1970), 555–65. An intelligent discussion of the narrative perspective and tonality in the fourth section, suggesting that the point of view adopted is in fact the reader's.

Bleikasten, André. "Noces Noires, Noces Blanches: Le jeu du désir et de la mort dans le monologue de Quentin Compson." *Recherches Anglaises et Nord-Américaines* (Strasbourg), VI (1973), 142–69. An earlier version of the fourth chapter of the present study.

Blöcker, Günter. "William Faulkner." In *Die Neuen Wirklichkeiten*, Berlin: Argon Verlag, 1957, pp. 112–23. Partly translated by Jacqueline Merriam in Warren, Robert Penn, ed., *Faulkner: A Collection of Critical Essays*, Englewood Cliffs, N. J.: Prentice-Hall, 1966, pp. 122–26. A provocative approach, though Blöcker overemphasizes the mythic and tends to romanticize Faulkner into an untutored genius.

Blotner, Joseph. *Faulkner: A Biography*, vol. I. New York: Random House, 1974, pp. 566–79, 588–90, 602–3, 626–28, 636–39, 666–68, 810–13, 1196–98, and *passim*. Relates the novel to the biographical context and provides extremely useful information on the circumstances of its composition and publication.

Booth, Wayne C. *The Rhetoric of Fiction*. Chicago and London: The University of Chicago Press, 1961, pp. 112–13, 152, 160, 198, 274, 306–8. Incidental remarks on Faulkner's handling of point of view and an interesting commentary on the reader's response to Jason's section.

Bowling, Lawrence E. "Faulkner: Technique of *The Sound and the Fury.*" *Kenyon Review,* X (Autumn 1948), 552–66. Repr. in Hoffman, Frederick J., and Olga W. Vickery, eds., *William Faulkner: Two Decades of Criticism,* East Lansing: Michigan State College Press, 1951, pp. 165–79. An early general discussion of Faulkner's narrative technique and a justification of its thematic appropriateness.

————. "Faulkner and the Theme of Innocence." *Kenyon Review,* XX (Summer 1958), 466–87. Describes the novel as an exploration of the concept of innocence from the conflicting views of puritanism (innocence as freedom from sin and guilt) and humanism (innocence as ignorance). Offers some valid insights into one of the major themes, but Caddy's character is misrepresented and the Christian interpretation which the author infers from his analysis is hardly convincing.

————. "William Faulkner: The Importance of Love." *Dalhousie Review,* XLIII (Winter 1963–64), 474–82. Sees the absence of love as the major cause of the family disintegration. Cf. Carvel Collins (1957).

————. "Faulkner and the Theme of Isolation." *Georgia Review,* XVIII (Spring 1964), 50–66. A thematic study focusing on Faulkner's symbols and imagery. Defines the novel as "the portrait of the break-up of a culture, the death of a civilization which has lost its ideals and its moral perspective." Cf. William A. Freedman (1962).

————. "Faulkner: The Theme of Pride in *The Sound and the Fury.*" *Modern Fiction Studies,* XI (Summer 1965), 129–39. The expectations raised by the title are not quite fulfilled, but the essay supplies a relevant analysis of the imagery of the second section, and aptly points out the symbolic import of certain episodes of Quentin's last day.

Broderick, John C. "Faulkner's *The Sound and the Fury.*" *Explicator,* XIX (November 1960), Item 12. Refutes Earle Labor (1959) on hysterectomy.

Brogunier, Joseph. "A Housman Source in *The Sound and the Fury.*" *Modern Fiction Studies,* XVIII (Summer 1972), 220–25. "The True Lover" of *A Shropshire Lad* as a source for the knife-scene in the Quentin section.

Brooks, Cleanth. "Primitivism in *The Sound and the Fury.*" In Downer, Alan S., ed., *English Institute Essays 1952,* New York: Columbia

University Press, 1954, pp. 5–28. A vigorous refutation of the mistaken notion of Faulkner's primitivism.

————. "Faulkner's Vision of Good and Evil." *Massachusetts Review*, III (Summer 1962), 692–712. Included in *The Hidden God: Studies in Hemingway, Faulkner, Yeats, Eliot, and Warren*, New Haven, Conn.: Yale University Press, 1963, pp. 22–43. On men, women, and their relationship to innocence.

————. "Man, Time, and Eternity." In *William Faulkner: The Yoknapatawpha Country*. New Haven, Conn., and London: Yale University Press, 1963, pp. 325–48. Fairly comprehensive in its approach and extremely perceptive in its analysis, Brooks's general study is one of the very best to have appeared. Especially valuable on theme and character.

Broughton, Panthea Reid. *William Faulkner: The Abstract and the Actual*. Baton Rouge: Louisiana State University Press, 1974, pp. 27–28, 90–91, 92–93, 112–16, 116–17, 188–91. Argues that the Compsons fail to come to terms with life because of their rigid insistence on order. Miss Broughton's study sheds no new light on the novel, but reacts healthily against sentimental misconceptions about Benjy.

Brown, Calvin S. "Dilsey: From Faulkner to Homer." In Zyla, W. T., and W. M. Aycock, eds., *William Faulkner: Prevailing Verities and World Literature—Proceedings of the Comparative Literature Symposium*, vol. 6, Lubbock: Texas Tech. University, 1973, pp. 57–75. Argues that Dilsey should be interpreted as a servant figure, and not as a racial stereotype.

Brylowski, Walter. "The Dark Vision." In *Faulkner's Olympian Laugh: Myth in the Novels*, Detroit, Mich.: Wayne State University Press, 1968, pp. 59–85. Traces mythical allusions and analogies, discusses Faulkner's structural use of the Christian myth, and contrasts Quentin's "mythic mode of thought" with Benjy's pre-mythic mode and Jason's rational-empirical mode (?). The informing myth is taken to be that of "the god of love crucified" rather than that of the Fall. Brylowski's discussion goes beyond the simplicities of earlier mythic readings, yet his application of Cassirer's theories is at times procrustean.

Burnham, James. "Trying to Say." *The Symposium*, II (January 1931), 51–59. A hardly known early essay-review which discusses the novel with sympathetic understanding and makes some nice points on Faulkner's "feeling for inarticulateness."

Campbell, Harry Modean. "Experiment and Achievement: *As I Lay*

Dying and *The Sound and the Fury." Sewanee Review,* LI (April 1943), 305–20. An early discussion, viewing *The Sound and the Fury* as a not quite successful attempt to combine the action of traditional fiction with the "mental drama" of the post-Joycean modern novel. Tries to be fair to Faulkner, yet shows little understanding for the nature of his achievement.

————, and Ruel E. Foster. *William Faulkner: A Critical Appraisal.* Norman: University of Oklahoma Press, 1951, pp. 50–60, 125–30. Analyzes some of Faulkner's imagery in the light of Freud's *Interpretation of Dreams.* Quentin's inner conflict is construed as a tension between Christian myth and "the myth of cosmic pessimism." Occasionally suggestive, but very sketchy.

Cecil, L. Moffitt. "A Rhetoric for Benjy." *The Southern Literary Journal,* III (Fall 1970), 32–46. Distinguishes two levels of language in the first section: Benjy's own "speech" and the remembered speech of other characters in the novel.

Chase, Richard. *The American Novel and Its Tradition.* Garden City, N. Y.: Doubleday Anchor Books, 1957, pp. 219–36. Relates the book to the traditions of American and European fiction. *The Sound and the Fury* is defined as the most "novelistic" of Faulkner's work, the one in which the native element of romance is most successfully integrated.

Clerc, Charles. "Faulkner's *The Sound and the Fury." Explicator,* XXIV (November 1965), Item 29. Relates the associations between Quentin and St. Francis to the allusive complexity of the sister-water-death imagery in the second section.

Cobau, William W. "Jason Compson and the Costs of Speculation." *Mississippi Quarterly,* XXII (Summer 1969), 257–61. Argues that despite inaccuracies and improbabilities Faulkner has made skillful use of the general principles of cotton speculation to dramatize significant aspects of Jason's character.

Coffee, Jessie, "Faulkner's *The Sound and the Fury." Explicator,* XXIV (October 1965), Item 21. The "Nancy" mentioned in the novel is an animal, not the black woman that appears in "That Evening Sun" and in *Requiem for a Nun.*

Coindreau, Maurice-Edgar. "Preface to *The Sound and the Fury."* Trans. George M. Reeves. *Mississippi Quarterly,* XIX (Summer 1966) 107–15 (originally published in French in 1938). Included in *The Time of William Faulkner: A French View of Modern American Fiction,* ed. and trans. George M. Reeves, Columbia: University of South Carolina Press, 1971, pp. 41–50. A still suggestive introduction to the novel by Faulkner's most prominent French translator.

Collins, Carvel. "The Interior Monologues of *The Sound and the Fury.*" In Downer, Alan S., ed., *English Institute Essays 1952,* New York: Columbia University Press, 1954, pp. 29–56. First revised edition in Malin, Irving, ed., *Psychoanalysis and American Fiction,* New York: Dutton, 1965, pp. 223–42; second revised edition in Meriwether, James B., comp., *The Merrill Studies in The Sound and the Fury,* Columbus, Ohio: Charles E. Merrill, 1970, pp. 59–79. An influential and controversial essay, stressing Faulkner's debt to Shakespeare and to Joyce, and suggesting the possibility of an indebtedness to Freud's theory of psychic agencies.

————. "The Pairing of *The Sound and the Fury* and *As I Lay Dying.*" *Princeton University Library Chronicle,* XVIII (Spring 1957), 114–23. Points out thematic and structural parallels between the two novels, and defines their common subject as "the general effect of lack of love in a family." According to Collins, *The Sound and the Fury* is closely patterned on the Passion Week, and all three Compson brothers are to be seen as inverted Christ figures. Another influential essay, which has opened up new possibilities of interpretation; unfortunately, it has also encouraged a number of silly symbolic readings.

————. "Faulkner's *The Sound and the Fury.*" *Explicator,* XVII (December 1958), Item 19. A comparison between Quentin Compson and Quentin Durward: "each valued honor in an age which had abandoned it."

————. "Miss Quentin's Paternity Again." *Texas Studies in Literature and Language,* II (Autumn 1960), 253–60. Disposes of the extravagant assumptions held by a number of critics about Miss Quentin's paternity, and demonstrates conclusively that the identity of the girl's father must remain a mystery.

————. "William Faulkner: *The Sound and the Fury.*" In Stegner, Wallace, ed., *The American Novel from James Fenimore Cooper to William Faulkner,* New York: Basic Books, 1965, pp. 219–28. Recapitulates some of the arguments developed in Collins' earlier essays.

Cook, Albert S. "Plot as Discovery." In *The Meaning of Fiction,* Detroit, Mich.: Wayne State University Press, 1960, pp. 232–41. Praises Faulkner's ability to develop his characters in relation to their past.

Cowan, James C. "Dream-Work in the Quentin Section of *The*

Sound and the Fury." Literature and Psychology, XXIV, n° 3 (1974) 91–98. A Freudian reading of some of Quentin's reveries.

Cowan, Michael H., ed. *Twentieth Century Interpretations of The Sound and the Fury.* Englewood Cliffs, N. J.: Prentice-Hall, Inc., 1968. Excerpts from Faulkner interviews and from essays and book chapters by Evelyn Scott, Maurice Edgar Coindreau, Irving Howe, Olga W. Vickery, Perrin Lowrey, Cleanth Brooks, Carvel Collins, Louise Dauner, Robert M. Slabey, John W. Hunt, Walter J. Slatoff, and Hyatt H. Waggoner. Edmond L. Volpe's chronology of scenes and guide to scene-shifts are appended. The utility of this anthology is impaired by the drastic condensation of all the essays included. Cowan's introduction is well-informed and competent.

Cross, Barbara M. *"The Sound and the Fury:* The Pattern of Sacrifice." *Arizona Quarterly,* XVI (Spring 1960), 5–16, Relates the novel's symbolism to the ritual gestures and the cosmic time of the myth world inventoried in *The Golden Bough.* The essay offers some interesting suggestions, but the analogies drawn are often strained and never related to the specific context of the novel.

Dauner, Louise. "Quentin and the Walking Shadow: The Dilemma of Nature and Culture." *Arizona Quarterly,* XXI (Summer 1965), 159–71. A Jungian analysis of shadow imagery in the Quentin section, with emphasis on the theme of the double.

Davis, William V. *"The Sound and the Fury:* A Note on Benjy's Name." *Studies in the Novel,* IV (Spring 1972), 60–61. Benjy's name is doubly appropriate because its biblical origins suggest two apt meanings: "Son of Sorrow" and "Son of the South."

————. "Death Ritual: Further Christian Allusions in *The Sound and the Fury." Notes on Mississippi Writers,* VI (Spring 1973), 27–32. Two mildly interesting suggestions on Christian symbolism in the second section.

Dickerson, Mary Jane. " 'The Magician's Wand': Faulkner's Compson Appendix." *The Mississippi Quarterly,* XXVIII (Summer 1975), 317–37. A careful and suggestive examination of the Appendix, exploring its thematic connections with the fiction Faulkner wrote between 1929 and 1945, and tracing its influence on later writings.

Dove, George N. "Shadow and Paradox: Imagery in *The Sound and the Fury."* In Burton, Thomas G., ed., *Essays in Memory of Christine Burleson in Language and Literature by Former Colleagues and Students,* Johnson City: Research and Advisory Council, East Tennessee State University, 1969, pp. 89–95. Adds little to previous criticism on the subject.

Edel, Leon. *The Psychological Novel 1900–1950.* Philadelphia: Lippincott, 1955, pp. 33–34, 147–53, and *passim.* Emphasizes Faulkner's concern with time and makes stimulating comparisons with other stream-of-consciousness novelists.

_____. "How to Read *The Sound and the Fury?*" In Burnshaw, Stanley, ed., *Varieties of Literary Experience: Eighteen Essays in World Literature,* New York: New York University Press, 1962, pp. 241–57. Included in *The Modern Psychological Novel,* New York: Grosset & Dunlap, 1964, pp. 162–76. A sound and sensible general essay, emphasizing the originality of Faulkner's fictional procedures and insisting on the necessity of "a new way of reading."

England, Martha Winburn. "Teaching *The Sound and the Fury.*" *College English,* XVIII (January 1957), 221–24. Reflections on the difficulties of teaching the novel, followed by a chronology of events in the first section.

_____. "Quentin's Story: Chronology and Explication." *College English,* XXII (January 1961), 228–35. A brief and at times perceptive discussion of Quentin's section, followed by a detailed chronology of the events recorded in his monologue.

Fasel, Ida. "Spatial Form and Spatial Time." *Western Humanities Review,* XVI (Summer 1962), 223–34. Approaches the novel in the light of Bergson's distinction between time and *durée.*

_____. "A 'Conversation' between Faulkner and Eliot." *Mississippi Quarterly,* XX (Fall 1967), 195–206. Examines the thematic, structural, and technical similarities between *The Sound and the Fury* and *The Waste Land,* and points to specific debts in imagery and phrasing.

Frederickson, Michael A. "A Note on 'The Idiot Boy' as a Probable Source for *The Sound and the Fury.*" *Minnesota Review,* VI (Winter 1966), 368–70. Wordsworth's ballad as a possible influence.

Freedman, William A. "The Technique of Isolation in *The Sound and the Fury.*" *Mississippi Quarterly,* XV (Winter 1961–62), 21–26. Discusses symbols of confinement and isolation, and examines their function in the novel's thematic structure. Cf. Bowling (1964).

Fridy, W. " 'Ichthus': An Exercise in Synthetic Suggestion." *South Atlantic Bulletin,* XXXIX (May 1974), 95–101. Christian connotations of the fish symbol in the scene of Quentin's encounter with the three boys.

Garmon, Gerald M. "Faulkner's *The Sound and the Fury.*" *Explicator,* XXV (September 1966), Item 2. Speculates on the symbolic significance of the sparrows in the second section.

_____. "Mirror Imagery in *The Sound and the Fury.*" *Notes on Mississippi Writers,* II (Spring 1969), 13–24. A brief discussion of the meaning of mirrors for Benjy and Quentin.

Gatlin, Jesse C., Jr. "Of Time and Character in *The Sound and the Fury.*" *Humanities Association Bulletin,* XVII (Autumn 1966), 27–35. Breaks little fresh ground.

Geffen, Arthur. "Profane Time, Sacred Time, and Confederate Time in *The Sound and the Fury.*" *Studies in American Fiction,* II (Autumn 1974), 175–97. Discusses the novel in the light of Mircea Eliade's concepts of sacred and profane time; suggests symbolic connections between critical events in the Compson story and significant dates in Confederate history.

Geismar, Maxwell. *Writers in Crisis: The American Novel 1925–1940.* Boston: Houghton Mifflin, 1942, pp. 154–59, and *passim.* Despite Geismar's gross misconceptions about Faulkner, his discussion of *The Sound and the Fury* has its merits and rightly stresses the importance of childhood in the novel's thematic pattern.

Gibbons, Kathryn Gibbs. "Quentin's Shadow." *Literature and Psychology,* XII (Winter 1962), 16–24. Another Jungian reading of the shadow symbol in Quentin's section. Cf. L. Dauner (1965).

Gibson, William M. "Faulkner's *The Sound and the Fury.*" *Explicator,* XXII (January 1964), Item 33. Comparisons with Dante's *Inferno* and *The Scarlet Letter.*

Gold, Joseph. "Faulkner's *The Sound and the Fury.*" *Explicator,* XIX (February 1961), Item 29. On Luster and his role in the final scene.

Grant, William E. "Benjy's Branch: Symbolic Method in Part I of *The Sound and the Fury.*" *Texas Studies in Literature and Language,* XIII (Winter 1972), 705–10. Comments upon Christian symbolism in the first section and its relationship to the other sections, with special emphasis on the motif of ritual cleansing.

Graves, T. W., Jr. "A Portrait of Benjy." *William and Mary Review,* II (Winter 1964), 53–57. A slight sketch rather than a portrait.

Greer, Dorothy D. "Dilsey and Lucas: Faulkner's Use of the Negro as a Gauge of Moral Character." *Emporia State Research Studies,* XI (September 1962), 43–61. Discusses Dilsey as the moral norm of the novel.

Gregory, Eileen. "Caddy Compson's World." In Meriwether, James B., comp., *The Merrill Studies in The Sound and the Fury,* Columbus: Charles E. Merrill, 1970, pp. 89–101. Takes issue with earlier assessments of the character. A judicious rehabilitation and beyond question the best essay on Caddy to have appeared.

Gresset, Michel. "Psychological Aspects of Evil in *The Sound and the Fury.*" *Mississippi Quarterly,* XIX (Summer 1966), 143–53. Revised for inclusion in *The Merrill Studies in The Sound and the Fury,* pp. 114–24. Describes *The Sound and the Fury* as "a novel about an ordeal," unfolding itself upon three levels: individual (identity test), cultural (social integration), metaphysical. A provocative essay.

Griffin, Robert. "Ethical Point of View in *The Sound and the Fury.*" In Langford, Richard E., ed., *Essays in Modern American Literature,* De Land, Fla.: Stetson University Press, 1963, pp. 55–64. Argues that each section refers back to a distinct moral point of view: amorality (sect.1), hypermorality (sect.2), hypocrisy (sect.3), moral realism (sect.4).

Gross, Beverly. "Form and Fulfillment in *The Sound and the Fury.*" *Modern Language Quarterly,* XXIX (December 1968), 439–49. A close and judicious examination of the novel's ending, arguing that the resolution it offers is a poetic epitome of the whole book.

Guetti, James. *The Limits of Metaphor: A Study of Melville, Conrad, and Faulkner.* Ithaca, N. Y.: Cornell University Press, 1967, pp. 148–53. Stresses Faulkner's supposed concern with structural confusion and "imaginative failure." A brilliant study based on questionable assumptions. For a similar approach, see W. Slatoff (1960).

Gunter, Richard. "Style and Language in *The Sound and the Fury.*" *Mississippi Quarterly,* XII (Summer 1969), 264–79. Included in *The Merrill Studies in The Sound and the Fury,* pp. 140–56. An appreciative essay-review of Irena Kaluza's book. Also personal comments upon Jason.

Gwynn, Frederick L. "Faulkner's Raskolnikov." *Modern Fiction Studies,* IV (Summer 1958), 169–72. A comparison between Quentin and the hero of *Crime and Punishment.* Cf. J. Weisgerber (1965).

Hagopian, John V. "Nihilism in Faulkner's *The Sound and the Fury.*" *Modern Fiction Studies,* XIII (Spring 1967), 45–55. Included in *The Merrill Studies in The Sound and the Fury,* pp. 102–13. A rigorous structural analysis of the last section; Hagopian's conclusions, however, are highly questionable.

Hardy, John Edward. "William Faulkner: The Legend behind the Legend." In *Man in the Modern Novel,* Seattle: University of Washington Press, 1964, pp. 149–55, and *passim.* Another discussion of Christian symbolism. Sees Miss Quentin as one of the novel's Christ figures.

Harris, Wendell V. "Faulkner's *The Sound and the Fury.*" *Explicator,*

XXI (March 1963), Item 54. Traces analogies between the Compson children and their parents.

―――――. "Of Time and the Novel." *Bucknell Review,* XVI (March 1968), 114–29. Observations on the rendering of subjective time through stream-of-consciousness techniques.

Hathaway, Baxter, "The Meanings of Faulkner's Structures." *English Record,* XV (December 1964), 22–27. Refers occasionally to Faulkner's contrapuntal structures, but no serious analysis is provided.

Hoffman, Frederick J. *William Faulkner.* New York: Twayne Publishers, 1961, pp. 49–60. A well-informed and competent introduction, praising Faulkner's ingenuity and calling attention to the many-sidedness of his achievement.

Hornback, Vernon T., Jr. "The Uses of Time in Faulkner's *The Sound and the Fury.*" *Papers on English Language and Literature,* I (Winter 1965), 50–58. Sensible, yet adds little to earlier discussions of the subject.

Howe, Irving. *William Faulkner: A Critical Study.* Second edition, revised and expanded (first edition in 1952). New York: Vintage Books, 1962, pp. 46–52, 157–74. An alert and well-written general study. Howe finds Quentin too much of a clinical case and quibbles with some of Faulkner's symbols, but on the whole his treatment of the novel is sympathetic.

Howell, Elmo. "A Note on Faulkner's Negro Characters." *Mississippi Quarterly,* XI (Fall 1958), 201–3. On Old Job as a moral touchstone to Jason.

Howell, John M. "Hemingway and Fitzgerald in Sound and Fury." *Papers on Language and Literature,* II (Summer 1966), 234–42. Puts forward the interesting suggestion that Faulkner parodied " the romantic despair and cynicism" of Hemingway and Fitzgerald.

Hughes, Richard. Preface to *The Sound and the Fury.* London: Chatto and Windus, 1931. A brief laudatory introduction by the British novelist who had already written the preface to *Soldiers' Pay.*

Humphrey, Robert. "Form and Function of Stream of Consciousness in William Faulkner's *The Sound and the Fury.*" *University of Kansas City Review,* XIX (Autumn 1952), 34–40. Revised for *Stream of Consciousness in the Modern Novel,* Berkeley: University of California Press, 1954, pp. 17–21, 64–70, 104–11. Relates Faulkner to the development of stream-of-consciousness fiction, arguing that his originality lies in a successful combination of interior monologue and more traditional devices such as plot.

Hunt, John W. *"The Sound and the Fury:* The Locus and Status of

Meaning." In *William Faulkner: Art in Theological Tension,* Syracuse, N. Y.: Syracuse University Press, 1965, pp. 35–99. The longest study in English. Hunt's analysis is thoughtful and perceptive; despite its theological assumptions, his approach to the novel avoids the pitfalls of religious reductionism, even though his insistence on "positive" meaning may be questioned.

Iser, Wolfgang. "Perception, Temporality, and Action as Modes of Subjectivity. William Faulkner: *The Sound and the Fury.*" In *The Implied Reader: Patterns of Communication in Prose Fiction from Bunyan to Beckett,* Baltimore, Md., and London: Johns Hopkins University Press, 1974, pp. 136–52. A rewarding study of Benjy, Quentin, and Jason as reduced forms of the self, with illuminating references to Merleau-Ponty's *Phenomenology of Perception.*

Izsak, Emily K. "The Manuscript of *The Sound and the Fury:* The Revisions in the First Section." *Studies in Bibliography,* XX (1967), 189–202. A scholarly study of Faulkner's revisions and additions in the first section.

Kaluza, Irena. *The Functioning of Sentence Structure in the Stream-of-Consciousness Technique of William Faulkner's "The Sound and the Fury": A Study in Linguistic Stylistics.* Krakow: Nakladem Uniwersytetu Jagiellonskiego, 1967. Reprinted by Folcroft Library Editions in 1970. A full and careful linguistic analysis of the first three sections. Extremely useful, especially on sections 1 and 2.

Kartiganer, Donald M. "*The Sound and the Fury* and Faulkner's Quest for Form." *English Literary History,* XXXVII (December 1970), 613–39. Investigates Faulkner's technique of fragmentation and argues that the novel is "about the very agony of seeing and creating encompassing order." A fresh and provocative study, with legitimate emphasis on the close interdependence of moral concerns and aesthetic preoccupations in Faulkner's fiction.

Kenner, Hugh. "The Last Novelist." In *A Homemade World: The American Modernist Writers,* New York: Alfred A. Knopf, 1975, pp. 194–221. An essay in Kenner's highly idiosyncratic manner. Contains some stimulating observations on Faulkner's "Art Nouveau beginnings" and on his affinities with *Symbolisme.*

Kerr, Elizabeth M. *Yoknapatawpha: Faulkner's "Little Postage Stamp of Native Soil."* New York: Fordham University Press, 1969. Incidental comments on the cultural and historical background of the novel.

Klotz, Marvin. "The Triumph Over Time: Narrative Form in William Faulkner and William Styron." *Mississippi Quarterly,* XVII (Winter

1963–64), 9–20. Finds Styron's narrative method more traditional than Faulkner's.

Korenman, Joan S. "Faulkner's Grecian Urn." *The Southern Literary Journal,* VII (Fall 1974), 3–23, especially 9–12. A pertinent essay on Faulkner's use of Keats's ode. Argues that Quentin's ideal lies in Keatsian stasis.

Labor, Earle G. "Faulkner's *The Sound and the Fury.*" *Explicator,* XVII (January 1959), Item 30. Suggests that in the "knife scene" Quentin considers hysterectomy, not incest. Preposterous.

Le Breton, Maurice. "Technique et Psychologie chez William Faulkner." *Etudes Anglaises,* I (September 1937), 418–38. An interesting early appraisal in French. Le Breton sympathizes with Faulkner's aims and methods, but considers *The Sound and the Fury* "a dangerous experiment."

————. "Temps et Personne chez William Faulkner." *Journal de Psychologie,* XLIV (January-June 1951), 344–54. Scrutinizes the relationship between time and identity, and makes suggestive comparisons with Virginia Woolf's novels.

Lee, Edwy B. "A Note on the Ordonnance of *The Sound and the Fury.*" *Faulkner Studies,* III (Summer-Autumn 1954), 37–39. Opposes narrative structure (in present) and dream structure (in past). Very cursory.

Litz, Walton. "William Faulkner's Moral Vision." *Southwest Review,* XXXVII (Summer 1952), 200–9. Discusses the novel in terms of vision and blindness, and stresses the conflict between fate and freedom.

Longley, John L. "Faulkner Villains." In *The Tragic Mask: A Study of Faulkner's Heroes,* Chapel Hill: University of North Carolina Press, 1963, pp. 144–50. A judicious discussion of Jason.

————. " 'Who Never Had a Sister': A Reading of *The Sound and the Fury.*" *Mosaic,* VII (Fall 1973), 35–53. A sensible general essay focusing on the major characters.

Lowrey, Perrin H. "Concepts of Time in *The Sound and the Fury.*" In Downer, Alan S., ed., *English Institute Essays, 1952,* New York: Columbia University Press, 1954, pp. 57–82. A seminal essay on Faulkner's uses of time, disposing of the notion of a unique time concept in the novel.

Malin, Irving. *William Faulkner: An Interpretation.* Stanford, Calif.: Stanford University Press, 1957. Emphasizes the importance of the father-son relationship, but provides no significant insight into the novel.

Materassi, Mario. "Il primo grande romanzo di Faulkner: *The Sound and the Fury.*" *Convivium,* XXXV (May-June 1967), 303–24. Reprinted in *I Romanzi di Faulkner,* Rome: Edizioni di Storia e Letteratura, 1968, pp. 93–120. A well-informed and thorough study, commenting upon the novel's themes as well as on its symbols and narrative devices.

McHaney, Thomas L. "Robinson Jeffers' 'Tamar' and *The Sound and the Fury.*" *Mississippi Quarterly,* XXII (Summer 1969), 261–63. Thematic and verbal similarities between the Quentin-Caddy relationship and the story of incest in Jeffers's poem.

Mellard, James M. "Faulkner's Jason and the Tradition of Oral Narrative." *Journal of Popular Culture,* II (Fall 1968), 195–210. Demonstrates convincingly that in Jason's speech Faulkner has used the traditional procedures of oral narrative.

_____. "Jason Compson: Humor, Hostility and the Rhetoric of Aggression." *Southern Humanities Review,* III (Summer 1969), 259–67. Analyzes the respective functions of "humor," "wit," and "the comic" in Jason's "rhetoric of aggression," and points to the ways in which they serve Faulkner's satiric purpose.

_____. "Caliban as Prospero: Benjy and *The Sound and the Fury.*" *Novel,* III (Spring 1970), 233–48. Relates the first section to the archetype of romance and to the tradition of pastoral satire, and suggests parallels with *The Tempest.*

_____. "The Sound and the Fury: Quentin Compson and Faulkner's 'Tragedy of Passion'." *Studies in the Novel,* II (Spring 1970), 61–75. Contends that the second section meets the requirements of the "tragedy of passion" archetype as defined in Northrop Frye's *Fools of Time.*

_____. "Type and Archetype: Jason Compson as 'Satirist'." *Genre,* IV (June 1971), 173–88. Examines how the ambivalences of Jason's character can be related to the formal demands of satire.

Meriwether, James B. "Notes on the Textual History of *The Sound and the Fury.*" *Papers of the Bibliographical Society of America,* LVI (Third Quarter, 1962), 285–316. Republished in revised form as "The Textual History of *The Sound and the Fury,*" in *The Merrill Studies in The Sound and the Fury,* pp. 1–32. A scrupulous investigation of Faulkner's writing of the novel and of the latter's publishing history. Corrects a number of mistakes and contains extremely useful information which anyone interested in *The Sound and the Fury* should be familiar with.

_____, comp. *Merrill Studies in The Sound and the Fury.* Columbus,

Ohio: Charles E. Merrill Publishing Company, 1970. Contains the full text of eight previously published essays (some of them revised) by James B. Meriwether, Walter Brylowski, Carvel Collins, John V. Hagopian, Michel Gresset, Michael Millgate, Richard Gunter and one original essay on "Caddy Compson's World" by Eileen Gregory. A valuable anthology.

Messerli, Douglas. "The Problem of Time in *The Sound and the Fury:* A Critical Reassessment and Reinterpretation." *The Southern Literary Journal,* VI (Spring 1974), 19–41. Takes issue with earlier analyses and attempts to reinterpret the problem of time in the light of Eugène Minkowski's "lived time" phenomenology. Sees Dilsey as the embodiment of Faulkner's moral order and Caddy as "life itself without human order." A cogent reassessment and a reasonable reinterpretation.

Millgate, Jane. "Quentin Compson as Poor Player: Verbal and Social Clichés in *The Sound and the Fury.*" *Revue des Langues Vivantes* (Bruxelles), XXXIV (1968), 40–49. Emphasizes the importance of role-playing in the Compson family as revealed by ritualized behavior and cliché-ridden rhetoric. A refreshing and intelligent essay on a neglected aspect of the novel.

Millgate, Michael. *The Achievement of William Faulkner.* New York: Random House, 1966, pp. 86–103. Despite its relative brevity, Millgate's study of the novel remains one of the most useful yet written. It is rich in insights, and derives additional value from its use of manuscript and typescript evidence.

————. "William Faulkner: The Problem of Point of View." In LaFrance, Marston, ed., *Patterns of Commitment in American Literature,* Toronto: University of Toronto Press, 1967, pp. 181–92. Included in *The Merrill Studies in The Sound and the Fury,* pp. 125–39. Discusses Faulkner's handling of point of view in the novel and relates it interestingly to the narrative techniques used in his later fiction.

————. "Faulkner and Lanier: A Note on the Name Jason." *Mississippi Quarterly,* XXV (Summer 1972), 349–350. Discusses Faulkner's possible awareness of a passage about a cotton-speculating Jason in Sidney Lanier's poem "Corn."

Miner, Ward L. "Faulkner and Christ's Crucifixion." *Neuphilologische Mitteilungen,* LVII (1956), 260–69. A commentary on Christian symbolism.

Moloney, Michael F. "The Enigma of Time: Proust, Virginia Woolf, and Faulkner." *Thought* XXXII (Spring 1957), 69–85. An un-qualified restatement of Sartre's position, assuming that "the bleakness of Faulkner's time philosophy is inescapable."

Morillo, Marvin. "Faulkner's *The Sound and the Fury.*" *Explicator*, XXIV (February 1966), Item 50. Argues that Shreve's reference to "Byron's wish" points to the English poet's incestuous relation with his half-sister. Cf. P. Swiggart (1963).

Mueller, William R. "The Theme of Suffering: William Faulkner's *The Sound and the Fury.*" In *The Prophetic Voice in Modern Fiction*, New York: Association Press, 1959, pp. 110–35. Examines the theme of suffering in the light of the Bible; claims that Dilsey "may serve as the incarnate embodiment of Faulkner's faith in man." Another reading in Christian terms.

Murray, Edward. *The Cinematic Imagination: Writers and the Motion Pictures.* New York: Frederick Ungar, 1972, pp. 154–58, 160–63. Brief comments on the cinematic quality of Faulkner's techniques and on Martin Ritt's shoddy movie version of *The Sound and the Fury* (1959).

Naples, Diane C. "Eliot's 'Tradition' and *The Sound and the Fury.*" *Modern Fiction Studies*, XX (Summer 1974), 214–17. A catalogue of mythic references and mythic analogies, many of which seem highly implausible. Just as questionable is the author's assumption that Faulkner uses the "mythic method" as T. S. Eliot did.

O'Connor, William Van. "*The Sound and the Fury* and the Impressionist Novel." *Northern Review*, VI (June-July 1953), 17–22. Slightly revised for *The Tangled Fire of William Faulkner*, Minneapolis: University of Minnesota Press, 1954, pp. 37–45. A brief general study, useful in its time.

——. "Hawthorne and Faulkner: Some Common Ground." *Virginia Quarterly Review*, XXXIII (Winter 1957), 105–23. Points to common themes such as incest and family decline.

O'Faolain, Sean. "William Faulkner, or More Genius Than Talent." In *The Vanishing Hero: Studies in Novelists of the Twenties*, London: Eyre & Spottiswoode, 1956, pp. 99–134, especially 119–24. Thinks that *The Sound and the Fury* is "so unreadable, in that complete sense of the word *read* which implies to understand, that it might be safely wagered that nobody on earth ever has read or ever will read the novel except Faulkner himself." A memorable case of critical blindness.

O'Nan, Martha. "William Faulkner's Benjy: Hysteria." In *The Role of Mind in Hugo, Faulkner, Beckett and Grass,* New York: Philosophical Library, 1969, pp. 13–22. Irrelevant pseudo-psychiatric speculations on Benjy.

Page, Sally R. "The Ideal of Motherhood: *The Sound and the Fury.*" In *Faulkner's Women: Characterization and Meaning,* De Land, Fla.: Everett/Edwards, Inc., 1972, pp. 45–70. Oversimplifies the role of women and misreads the whole novel through excessive emphasis on the theme of motherhood.

Pate, F. Willard. "Benjy's Names in the Compson Household." *Furman Studies,* XV (May 1968), 37–38. Argues that the names used by other characters in referring to Benjy serve as an index to the way they treat him.

Peavy, Charles D. "The Eyes of Innocence: Faulkner's 'The Kingdom of God'." *Papers on Language and Literature,* II (Spring 1966), 178–182. Points out parallels between Benjy and the idiot in the early sketch.

————. "An Early Casting of Benjy: Faulkner's 'The Kingdom of God'." *Studies in Short Fiction,* III (Spring 1966), 347–48. Makes the same point as "The Eyes of Innocence."

————. "Faulkner's Use of Folklore in *The Sound and the Fury.*" *Journal of American Folklore,* LXXIX (July-September 1966), 437–47. Comments interestingly on Faulkner's use of popular beliefs and superstitions, and on the symbolic suggestions they add to his imagery. Especially useful on the flower symbolism.

————. "A Note on the Suicide Pact' in *The Sound and the Fury.*" *English Language Notes,* V (March 1968), 207–9. Questions the existence of a "suicide pact" between Quentin and Caddy.

————. " 'Did You Ever Have a Sister?'—Holden, Quentin and Sexual Innocence." *Florida Quarterly,* I (Winter 1968), 82–95. A comparison between Quentin and the young protagonist of *Catcher in the Rye.*

————. "Jason Compson's Paranoid Pseudocommunity," *Hartford Studies in Literature,* II (1970), 151–56. An investigation of Jason's neurosis based on Norman Cameron's concept of "paranoid pseudocommunity."

————. " 'If I Just Had a Mother': Faulkner's Quentin Compson." *Literature and Psychology,* XXIII, n°3 (1973), 114–21. Makes a number of interesting points on Quentin's neurosis.

Pelham, Edgar. *The Art of the Novel.* New York: Macmillan, 1933, pp. 347–52. One of the few sympathetic appraisals to appear in the thirties.

Peper, Jürgen. *Bewusstseinslagen des Erzählens und Erzählte Wirk-lichkeiten.* Leiden: E. J. Brill, 1966, pp. 125–44 and *passim.* Discusses Faulkner's rendering of "inner perception" in the monologues.

Pitavy, François. "Quentin Compson, ou le regard du poète." *Sud* (Marseille), n° 14/15 (1975), 62–80. A sensitive study of Quentin as a failed poet.

Powell, Sumner C. "William Faulkner Celebrates Easter, 1928." *Perspective,* II (Summer 1949), 195–218. An early discussion of symbolic imagery, with emphasis on Christian parallels.

Pratt, J. Norwood. "Faulkner's *The Sound and the Fury.*" *Explicator,* XXIII (January 1965), Item 37. Rather gratuitous speculations on the sparrow which Quentin watches from his window, proceeding from the assumption that it symbolizes Caddy and death.

Ramsey, Roger. "Faulkner's *The Sound and the Fury.*" *Explicator,* XXX (April 1972), Item 70. Relates Benjy's capacity for "smelling" death to his memory of the rotting corpse of Nancy, the mare.

Reed, Joseph W. *Faulkner's Narrative.* New Haven, Conn., and London: Yale University Press, 1973, pp. 74–83. Provides no thorough and methodical discussion of the novel *as* narrative, but offers provocative observations on the reader's response to the four sections of the book. Argues—not quite convincingly—that the Jason section arouses the most complex response.

Richardson, Kenneth E. *Force and Faith in the Novels of William Faulkner.* The Hague: Mouton, 1967, pp. 24–29, 70–73, 100–3, and *passim.* Stresses the responsibilities of the Compson parents in the family drama, and contrasts their life-denying attitudes with Dilsey's capacity for love.

Rodrigues, Esabio L. "Time and Technique in *The Sound and the Fury.*" *Literary Criterion* (Mysore, India), VI (Summer 1965), 61–67. Dwells on Faulkner's "creative fury" and minimizes his concern with form. Totally beside the point.

Rosenberg, Bruce A. "The Oral Quality of Reverend Shegog's Sermon in William Faulkner's *The Sound and the Fury.*" *Literatur in Wissenschaft und Unterricht,* II (1969), 73–88. A very useful study of Faulkner's indebtedness to the tradition of the oral sermon.

Ruiz Ruiz, José M. "El sentido de la vida y de la muerte en *The Sound and the Fury,* de William Faulkner." *Filologia Moderna* (Madrid), XIII (1973), 117–38. Concentrates on religious symbolism, but adds little of interest to previous discussions of the subject.

Ryan, Marjorie. "The Shakespearean Symbolism in *The Sound and the*

Fury." *Faulkner Studies,* II (Autumn 1953), 40–44. Relates Quentin to the passage in *Macbeth* from which the book takes its title.

Sandstrom, Glenn. "Identity Diffusion: Joe Christmas and Quentin Compson." *American Quarterly,* XIX (Summer 1967), 207–23. Analyzes Quentin's neurotic personality in the light of Eric Erikson's theory of identity.

Sartre, Jean-Paul. "A propos de 'Le Bruit et la Fureur': La temporalité chez Faulkner." *La Nouvelle Revue Française,* LII (June 1939), 1057–61; LIII (July 1939), 147–51. Included in *Situations I,* Paris: Gallimard, 1947, pp. 70–81. Translated by Martine Darmon, in Hoffman, Frederick J., and Olga W. Vickery, eds., *William Faulkner: Three Decades of Criticism,* East Lansing: Michigan State University Press, 1960, pp. 225–32. Another translation is Annette Michelson's in *Literary and Philosophical Essays,* London: Rider and Co., 1955, pp. 79–87. The latter is reprinted in Warren, Robert Penn, ed., *Faulkner: A Collection of Critical Essays,* Englewood Cliffs, N. J.: Prentice-Hall, 1966, pp. 87–93. Though it is mistaken in its premises and its conclusions, Sartre's seminal essay remains one of the most provocative ever written on this novel.

Scott, Evelyn. *On William Faulkner's "The Sound and the Fury."* New York: Jonathan Cape and Harrison Smith, 1929. Partly reprinted in Cowan, Michael H., ed., *Twentieth Century Interpretations of The Sound and the Fury,* pp. 25–29. An enthusiastic essay by a fellow novelist who had read the galley proofs. Published as a pamphlet at the same time as the novel, it called *The Sound and the Fury* a tragedy with "all the spacious proportions of Greek art" and hailed it as "an important contribution to the permanent literature of fiction." Evelyn Scott was not quite alone in her enthusiasm (there were more sympathetic reviewers than has generally been assumed), but she was alone in seeing Faulkner's novel as "a reassertion of humanity in defeat." Her essay thus announced the humanistic interpretations that came to prevail in the forties and to which most critics still subscribe today.

Slabey, Robert M. "The 'Romanticism' of *The Sound and the Fury.*" *Mississippi Quarterly,* XVI (Summer 1963), 146–59. Points to Romantic traits in Quentin's character.

Slatoff, Walter J. *Quest for Failure: A Study of William Faulkner.* Ithaca, N. Y.: Cornell University Press, 1960, pp. 149–58, 254–55, and *passim.* Traces unresolved ambiguities, incomplete patterns, and suspended significances; explains the novel's inconclusiveness in terms of Faulkner's supposed "quest for failure." An interesting approach, even though the underlying thesis seems very questionable.

Spilka, Mark. "Quentin Compson's Universal Grief." *Contemporary Literature*, XI (Autumn 1970), 451–69. Interprets Quentin's drama as a quest for timeless values.

Stewart, George R., and Joseph M. Backus. " 'Each in Its Ordered Place': Structure and Narrative in Benjy's Section of *The Sound and the Fury.*" *American Literature*, XXIX (January 1958), 440–56. An elaborate attempt to unravel the chronological intricacies of section 1 (including two tables and a map of the Compson property), marred by ludicrous speculations on Miss Quentin's father and by naïve misconceptions about Faulkner's methods and purposes.

Strandberg, Victor. "Faulkner's Poor Parson and the Technique of Inversion." *Sewanee Review*, LXXIII (Spring 1965), 181–90. A fine essay, particularly illuminating on the Easter service episode in the closing section.

Straumann, Heinrich. *Faulkner.* Frankfurt am Main, Bonn: Athenäum Verlag, 1968, pp. 79–119. A sensitive, intelligent, and thoroughly informed general essay in German.

Swiggart, Peter. "Moral and Temporal Order in *The Sound and the Fury.*" *Sewanee Review*, LXI (Spring 1953), 221–37. Takes issue with Sartre's interpretation of time in *The Sound and the Fury*, but fails to supply a wholly consistent interpretation of his own.

————. *The Art of Faulkner's Novels.* Austin: University of Texas Press, 1962, pp. 38–40, 61–70, 87–107. A comprehensive study, dealing with theme, narrative technique, and symbolic patterns. Still useful, especially for its close analysis of imagery.

————. "Faulkner's *The Sound and the Fury.*" *Explicator*, XXII (December 1963), Item 31. Locates the source of Shreve's reference to Byron's "wish" in the sixth canto (stanza 27) of *Don Juan*.

Thompson, Lawrence R. "Mirror Analogues in *The Sound and the Fury.*" In Downer, Alan S., ed., *English Institute Essays, 1952*, New York: Columbia University Press, 1954, pp. 83–106. Reprinted in *William Faulkner: Three Decades of Criticism*, pp. 211–25, and in *Faulkner: A Collection of Critical Essays*, pp. 109–21. An influential essay, arguing persuasively that the mirror analogue can be extended to the novel's thematic structure.

————. *William Faulkner: An Introduction and Interpretation.* New York: Barnes and Noble, 1963, pp. 29–52. A sane and substantial general study focusing on Faulkner's use of thematic counterpoints.

Thornton, Weldon. "A Note on the Source of Faulkner's Jason." *Studies in the Novel,* I (Fall 1969), 370–72. Identifies Jason in II Maccabees as a possible source for the naming of Jason Compson.

Tilley, Winthrop. "The Idiot Boy in Mississippi: Faulkner's *The Sound and the Fury." American Journal of Mental Deficiency,* LIX (January 1955), 374–77. Irrelevant objections to the credibility of Benjy as a character.

Ulich, Michaela. *Perspektive und Erzählstruktur in William Faulkners Romanen.* Heidelberg: Carl Winter, 1972, pp. 23–44. One of the most searching and most original analyses of narrative point of view and narrative structure. Contending that the interior monologues present subjective worlds rather than subjective perspectives on the world, M. Ulich sees in the drastic reduction of narrative distance a salient feature of Faulkner's technique.

Underwood, Henry J., Jr. "Sartre on *The Sound and the Fury:* Some Errors." *Modern Fiction Studies,* XII (Winter 1966–67), 477–79. On Sartre's misquotations and misinterpretations.

Vahanian, Gabriel. "William Faulkner: Rendezvous with Existence." In *Wait Without Idols,* New York: George Braziller, 1964, pp. 93–116. A Christian reading of the novel. Focuses on Dilsey and on the Easter service, and argues that *The Sound and the Fury* "affirms the possibility of a new beginning."

Vickery, Olga W. *"The Sound and the Fury:* A Study in Perspective." *PMLA,* LXIX (December 1954), 1017–37. Slightly revised for *The Novels of William Faulkner: A Critical Interpretation,* Baton Rouge: Louisiana State University Press, 1959 and 1964, pp. 28–49. A sensitive and closely argued study of the novel, analyzing the thematic and structural interrelations between its parts with greater rigor than any previous discussion of the book. Though it was written in the early fifties, Olga Vickery's essay has preserved all its relevance.

Volpe, Edmond L. *A Reader's Guide to William Faulkner.* New York: Farrar, Straus, 1964, pp. 87–126, 353–77. A full and sound general study. Extremely helpful chronologies of scenes and guides to scene-shifts are appended.

Waggoner, Hyatt H. "'Form, Solidity, Color'." In *William Faulkner: From Jefferson to the World,* Lexington: University of Kentucky Press, 1959, pp. 34–61. Emphasizes Christian elements, but cautiously refrains from imposing a Christian interpretation on the novel.

Wagner, Linda Welshimer. "Jason Compson: The Demands of

Honor." *Sewanee Review,* LXXIX (October–December 1971), 554–75. An overzealous attempt at rehabilitating Jason.

Wall, Carey. *"The Sound and the Fury:* The Emotional Center." *Midwest Quarterly,* XI (Summer 1970), 371–87. Defines the Compsons' experience in terms of spiritual pain, and traces its phases from relative peace through tenseness and frenzy to emotional exhaustion. A stimulating essay.

Walters, Paul S. "Theory and Practice in Faulkner: *The Sound and the Fury." English Studies in Africa,* X (March 1967), 22–39. Mostly a recapitulation of earlier criticism.

Watkins, Floyd C. "The Word and the Deed in Faulkner's Great Novels." In *The Flesh and the Word,* Nashville, Tenn.: Vanderbilt University Press, 1971, pp. 181–202. Inquires into the relationship between language and reality in *The Sound and the Fury, As I Lay Dying,* and *Sanctuary.*

Weber, Robert Wilhelm. *Die Aussage der Form: Zur Textur und Struktur des Bewusstseinromans. Dargestellt an William Faulkners "The Sound and the Fury."* Heidelberg: Carl Winter, 1969. A very thorough book-length study of the overall structure as well as of the lexical, syntactic, and rhetorical texture of the novel.

Weinstein, Arnold L. "Vision as Feeling: Bernanos and Faulkner." In *Vision and Response in Modern Fiction.* Ithaca, N. Y., and London: Cornell University Press, 1974, pp. 91–153, especially 111–35. Stresses the power and originality of Faulkner's "affective technique," and the emotive involvement which his novel demands from the reader.

Weisgerber, Jean. "Faulkner et Dostoevski: *The Sound and the Fury." Revue de Littérature Comparée,* XXXIX (1965), 406–21. See translation in *Faulkner and Dostoevsky,* pp. 179–92.

————. "Faulkner's Monomaniacs: Their Indebtedness to Raskolnikov." *Comparative Literature Studies,* V (June 1968), 181–93. Points out resemblances between Quentin and Dostoevski's hero. Cf. F. L. Gwynn (1958).

————. *Faulkner and Dostoevsky: Influence and Confluence.* Athens, Ohio: Ohio University Press, 1974, pp. 179–92. Contends that "among the sources of *The Sound and the Fury* we must reserve a high place for *Crime and Punishment* and an honorable mention for *The Brothers Karamazov."* The evidence adduced is substantial but hardly conclusive.

Whicher, Stephen E. "The Compsons' Nancies: A Note on *The Sound and the Fury* and 'That Evening Sun'." *American Literature,* XXVI (May 1954), 253–55. Establishes that the "Nancy" mentioned by the Compson children is not the Negro woman from the short story but the corpse of a mare.

Wilder, Amos N. "Faulkner and the Vestigial Moralities." In *Theology and Modern Literature,* Cambridge, Mass.: Harvard University Press, 1958, pp. 113–31. Included in Barth, J. Robert, ed., *Religious Perspectives in Faulkner's Fiction: Yoknapatawpha and Beyond,* Notre Dame, Ind.: University of Notre Dame Press, 1972, pp. 91–102. *The Sound and the Fury* viewed as a critique of fossilized religion and as an affirmation of authentic faith. Overemphasizes the significance of Dilsey and the last section as most theologically oriented interpretations do.

Young, James D. "Quentin's Maundy Thursday." *Tulane Studies in English,* X (1960), 143–51. Converts the gulls and sparrows of the second section into doves to make them symbols of the Holy Ghost! An extreme case of irrelevant symbol-mongering.

INDEX

270 INDEX

Characters and characterization, 8, 18, 19–21, 29, 34, 36–39, 56, 66, 67–68, 95–96, 142–43, 146–48, 178–79, 188–89, 191–92
Chase, Richard, 250
Chateaubriand, François-René de, 142
Childhood, 53, 75, 96–97, 115, 151, 152, 254
Chomsky, Noam, 219
Christ, 95, 166, 183, 184, 191, 193, 194, 197, 198
Christianity, 192–94, 197–98, 201–3
Church, Margaret, 229
Claudel, Paul, 65, 121
Clerc, Charles, 250
Cobau, William W., 250
Coffee, Jessie, 250
Coindreau, Maurice-Edgar, 53, 215, 216, 250
Collins, Carvel, 79, 149, 209, 210, 251
"Compson Appendix," 110, 116, 142, 163, 215, 219, 229, 236, 238, 240, 243–44, 252
Conrad, Joseph, 16, 34, 44, 45
Cook, Albert S., 251
Cooperman, Stanley, 210
Cowan, James C., 251
Cowan, Michael H., 252
Cowley, Malcolm, 35, 213, 215, 236, 243
Crime and Punishment (Dostoevski), 255, 267
Cru et le cuit, Le (Lévi-Strauss), 241

Dahl, James, 235
Dante Alighieri, 29, 254
Davis, William V., 252
Day, Douglas, 34, 212
Death, 14, 21–22, 39, 54–55, 84–85, 92, 101–3, 112, 117–20, 137, 140–42, 188, 224, 229
Death of Ivan Ilyich, The (Tolstoi), 141
"Dependent Relationships of the Ego, The" (Freud), 229
Derrida, Jacques, 4, 242
Desire, 14, 46–47, 51, 56, 60, 80, 83, 92, 107–9, 229
"Devil Beats His Wife, The," 240
Dickens, Charles, 147

Dickerson, Mary Jane, 252
Don Juan (Byron), 222
Dos Passos, John, 128
Dostoevski, Feodor Mikhailovich, 44, 45, 150, 222, 267
Double, 9, 13, 24, 36, 124, 201, 230
Dove, George N., 252
Dunlap, Mary M., 212

Early Prose and Poetry (Faulkner), 208, 209
Ecrits (Lacan), 227
Edel, Leon, 253
Eliade, Mircea, 254
Eliot, Thomas Stearns, 6, 7, 18, 25, 193, 207, 253, 261
Elliot, Robert C., 234, 235
"Elmer," 32, 38, 212, 216, 219, 223, 225
Eluard, Paul, 205, 242
England, Martha W., 222, 253
Enormous Room, The (Cummings), 17
Erikson, Erik H., 226, 264
Espace littéraire, L' (Blanchot), 224
Essais sur le symbolique (Rosolato), 227
Essays, Speeches and Public Letters (Faulkner), 210, 213
Evil, 53, 91, 98, 99, 148, 167–68, 198

Fable, A, 17, 76, 202, 219, 233
Failure, 48–50, 110, 205–6
Falkner, Maud, 149, 235
Falkner, William Clark, 35
Family: brother-sister relationship, 74–75, 77–78, 91, 97, 150, 219; father-son relationship, 109–14, 151, 226, 227; mother-child relationship, 78, 96–97, 151, 192, 225; parental roles, 112, 226. See also Incest
Fant, Joseph, 244
Fantasy, 23, 108, 114, 115, 118, 154, 165, 173, 227, 228
Fasel, Ida, 253
"Father Abraham," 33, 213
Faulkner-Cowley File, 236, 240, 243
Faulkner in the University, 211, 213, 214, 215, 216, 219, 220, 226, 233, 237, 244